The Japanese Empire

The Japanese experience of war from the late nineteenth century to the mid-twentieth presents a stunning example of the meteoric rise and shattering fall of a great power. As Japan modernized and became the one non-European great power, its leaders concluded that an empire on the Asian mainland required the containment of Russia. Japan won the First Sino-Japanese War (1894–95) and the Russo-Japanese War (1904–5) but became overextended in the Second Sino-Japanese War (1931–45), which escalated, with profound consequences, into World War II. A combination of incomplete institution building, an increasingly lethal international environment, a skewed balance between civil and military authority, and a misunderstanding of geopolitics explain these divergent outcomes. This analytical survey examines themes including the development of Japanese institutions, diversity of opinion within the government, domestic politics, Japanese foreign policy, and China's anti-Japanese responses. It is an essential guide for those interested in history, politics and international relations.

S.C.M. PAINE, William S. Sims Professor, U.S. Naval War College, has spent eight of the last thirty years engaged in research and language study in Japan, Taiwan, China, Russia, and Australia. Funding has included two Fulbright Fellowships along with fellowships from Japan, Taiwan, and Australia. *The Wars for Asia* received the Leopold Prize and PROSE Award for European & World History and was longlisted for the Gelber Prize. *Imperial Rivals* received the Jelavich Prize.

/

The Japanese Empire

Grand Strategy from the Meiji Restoration to the Pacific War

S.C.M. Paine

United States Naval War College

CAMBRIDGE
UNIVERSITY PRESS

CAMBRIDGE
UNIVERSITY PRESS

University Printing House, Cambridge CB2 8BS, United Kingdom

One Liberty Plaza, 20th Floor, New York, NY 10006, USA

477 Williamstown Road, Port Melbourne, VIC 3207, Australia

314-321, 3rd Floor, Plot 3, Splendor Forum, Jasola District Centre, New Delhi - 110025, India

79 Anson Road, #06-04/06, Singapore 079906

Cambridge University Press is part of the University of Cambridge.

It furthers the University's mission by disseminating knowledge in the pursuit of education, learning and research at the highest international levels of excellence.

www.cambridge.org
Information on this title: www.cambridge.org/9781107676169
10.1017/ 9780511997662

First published 2017

A catalogue record for this publication is available from the British Library

Library of Congress Cataloging in Publication data
Names: Paine, S. C. M., 1957– author.
Title: The Japanese empire : grand strategy from the Meiji Restoration to the Pacific War / S.C.M. Paine (United States Naval War College).
Description: Cambridge, United Kingdom ; New York, NY : Cambridge University Press, 2016. | Includes bibliographical references and index.
Identifiers: LCCN 2016024973| ISBN 9781107011953 (hardback : alkaline paper) | ISBN 9781107676169 (paperback : alkaline paper)
Subjects: LCSH: Japan–History, Military–1868-1945. | Japan–Military policy. | Strategy–History. | Japan–Foreign relations–1868-1912. | Japan–Foreign relations–1912-1945. | Great powers–History. | Political culture–Japan–History. | Imperialism–History. | BISAC: HISTORY / Asia / General.
Classification: LCC DS838.7 .P35 2016 | DDC 952.03–dc23
LC record available at https://lccn.loc.gov/2016024973

ISBN 978-1-107-01195-3 Hardback
ISBN 978-1-107-67616-9 Paperback

To John P. LeDonne
scholar, mentor, teacher, and friend

Contents

List of Maps

Acknowledgments

This book relies on the research for my previous monographs, *Imperial Rivals: China, Russia, and Their Disputed Frontier 1858–1924*, *The First Sino-Japanese War of 1894–1895*, and *The Wars for Asia 1911 to 1949*, and book series coedited with Bruce A. Elleman on naval topics: blockades, naval coalitions, peripheral operations, and commerce raiding. The present volume turns my previous research inside out to focus on Japan, rather than on China or Russia, and, in so doing, to focus on the security problems faced by a maritime rather than a continental power. The lessons are relevant to the United States, which, like Japan back in the day, is prone to intervening abroad. Like Japan, its maritime location provides relative sanctuary, insulating it from problems elsewhere, so that intervention is often a matter of choice, not of necessity. Yet the choices matter. Some, as the Japanese discovered, are irrevocable.

I am particularly grateful to the superlative anonymous reviewer from Cambridge University Press, who patiently pointed out shortcomings and the necessary readings to resolve the deficiencies. I am also indebted to Robin A. Lima, William Corrente, Heidi Garcia, Jack Miranda, and Julie Zecher at the Naval War College Library for continuous help supplying books through inter-library loan and book purchases; to COL Paul Krajeski USA and CDR Ronald Oard USN (retired) for explaining developments in artillery and fleet tactics respectively; and, most important of all, to Bruce A. Elleman, who has written voluminously on China, Russia, Japan, and naval strategy.

Although the methodology employed in this work comes from senior colleagues at the Strategy & Policy Department at the Naval War College, which grants master's degrees in national security and strategic studies, and war and strategic studies, the thoughts and opinions expressed are those of the author and are not necessarily those of the U.S. Government, the U.S. Navy Department, or the U.S. Naval War College. Likewise, I claim credit for all errors in this work.

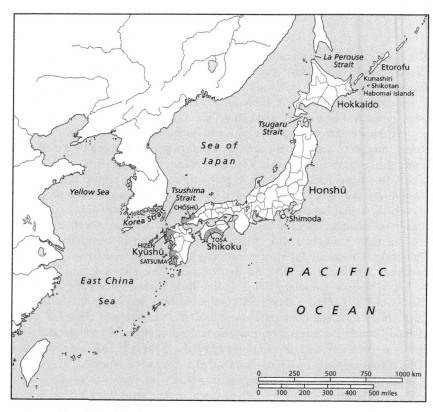

Map 1 Meiji Japan

1   The Meiji Generation

> The average Westerner ... was wont to regard Japan as barbarous while she indulged in the gentle arts of peace: he calls her civilised since she began to commit wholesale slaughter on Manchurian battlefield.[1]
>
> Okakura Kakuzō (1862–1913), philosopher, art critic, in reference to the Russo-Japanese War
>
> *The Book of Tea* (1906)

During two periods in the last century and a half, Japan has been governed by extraordinary generations of leaders, whose choices brought their citizens prosperity and their country the accolades of the world. They were the Meiji generation, which transformed Japan in the late nineteenth century into the first modern, non-Western great power, and the post-World War II generation, which transformed Japan after the disastrous Second Sino-Japanese War (1931–45) into an economic powerhouse soon emulated by all of its neighbors. These two generations bookend the narrative told here of a meteoric rise ending in a shattering fall encompassing all of Asia and destroying imperial Japan. It is a story beginning with brilliance and ending in tragedy.

Few nations have solved the conundrum of economic development. Yet the Japanese in the late nineteenth century became experts at economic development and their story has much to offer others concerning both the prerequisites and the pitfalls of transforming a traditional society into a modern country. Japanese leaders modernized and westernized their homeland in order to defend against the predations of increasingly intrusive Western powers. From 1894 to 1945, they fought a series of three wars to contain the march of Russian imperialism into Asia that became the march of Communist imperialism post-1917. While their strategy delivered rapid economic development and victory in the first two conflicts, the third war escalated into a global war that destroyed imperial Japan and produced mayhem on a scale unprecedented for

---

[1] Okakura Kakuzō, *The Book of Tea* (Rutland, VT: Charles E. Tuttle, 1958, reprint, first published 1906), 6. Paraphrase in Donald Keene, *Emperor of Japan: Meiji and His World, 1852–1912* (New York: Columbia University Press, 2002), 510.

humankind. Although the goal to become and remain a great power had not changed, the conflicts produced antithetical outcomes. The question is, why?

Traditionally, governments have wielded power through the creation of large armies to dominate citizens and neighbors, but since the Industrial Revolution, this approach has yielded low standards of living and often only fleeting military triumphs. In the twentieth century, some educated their young on a diet of xenophobic nationalism glorifying their own achievements and, if not demonizing others, then discounting the achievements of others. But this approach provided no basis for economic growth, which depends on expertise, not anger, for sustenance. Still others have used resource sales to underwrite political ambitions, but this leaves human resources to languish and generates insufficient wealth for more than a few to prosper.

Japan had no special resource endowment. Its archipelagic geography impeded national integration. Its mountainous topography limited agriculture. It had never been the richest part of Asia, nor the dominant regional power. In the nineteenth century, it was technologically backward when compared to the West. Yet in the twentieth century, Japan became the only non-Western great power by two defining measures: a high GNP and a high per capita GNP. In the late twentieth century, the only other non-Western countries to achieve that status were its former colonies, South Korea and Taiwan. Today, Japan remains the only non-Western member of the prestigious Group of Seven that requires economic achievements of the highest order. In other words, the Japanese made possible what others have found to be impossible.

The Industrial Revolution and the New World Order

In the mid-nineteenth century, Japan's world changed, not because of anything it had done, but because of exogenous events taking place on the other side of the globe in Western Europe. Suddenly, Japan faced an unprecedented national security threat in the form of the Industrial Revolution, which began in England in the late eighteenth century and bore down upon East Asia by the mid-nineteenth century. The Industrial Revolution, which initially produced 3 percent economic growth rates, was a catastrophic event for traditional societies – none of which emerged unscathed or unchanged. It transformed once comparatively static societies into juggernauts of economic growth and scientific innovation, with per capita standards of living doubling every generation. This opened a growing chasm between those who joined the forced march to industrialize and those who stood apart. After several generations of compounded growth, it upended the global balance of power, when traditional societies suddenly felt powerless to defend themselves. Over two centuries later, the Industrial Revolution continues to define the international balance of power, leaving the least industrialized countries, whatever their preindustrial cultural glories, to form the ranks of the poor and powerless.

Japan witnessed its immediate neighbor, China, defeated twice in war. During the Opium Wars (1839–42 and 1856–60), Britain and France imposed what became known as the treaty port system. It had four defining characteristics: First, a series of bilateral treaties designated certain ports "treaty ports" open to international trade. Second, the West, not China, set, collected, and paid to the Chinese government the tariffs on the trade. Third, expatriate Westerners were subject to the laws of their home countries, not Chinese law, whereas Chinese received no such extraterritorial privileges when in the West. Fourth, the treaties contained most-favored-nation clauses that meant that the benefits negotiated by one accrued to all the favored.

As China proved ever less capable of countering the industrializing powers, Russia stood poised to fill the developing power vacuum. It took advantage of the Opium Wars to negotiate treaties to set a very advantageous boundary. It gained land at Chinese expense exceeding U.S. territory east of the Mississippi river and acquired a 3,000-mile eastern coastline that eventually enabled it to become both a Pacific Ocean power and a force in Asia.

The Japanese looked at Western commercial and Russian territorial expansion to conclude that they would be next. In 1854 the United States imposed the treaty port system on Japan. That year, U.S. Commodore Matthew C. Perry, in command of modern naval vessels dwarfing local ships, coerced Japanese leaders into signing the Treaty of Kanagawa (the prefecture where Yokohama, the port city to Tokyo, is located). The agreement turned Hakodate on Hokkaido, and Shimoda at the outer entrance to Tokyo Bay, into treaty ports and established a U.S. consulate in the latter. In Japan the U.S. naval vessels became known to future generations as the "black ships." They symbolized the war-fighting capabilities of the industrial age and the West's many impositions on Japan. Just as China was losing the Second Opium, or Arrow, War, in 1858 the new American consul in Shimoda, Townsend Harris, negotiated a second treaty, bringing Japan's total number of treaty ports to five and establishing the principle of extraterritoriality for Americans residing in Japan, foreign control of Japan's tariffs, and most-favored-nation treatment. The other powers followed suit.

China soon became Japan's negative example of what not to do. The Chinese regarded Western civilization as barbaric. They intended to preserve theirs, which like all civilizations embodied an entire way of life and an international order encompassing the known world. China's leaders wanted no part of the Western trade or the accompanying "spiritual pollution" (a modern Chinese term), but the Western sampling of Chinese exports did not sate but whetted the foreign appetite for commerce. So China's leaders tried to compel the Westerners to leave, as did the leaders of so many other traditional societies when confronted with the intrusions of the Industrial Revolution. Like these other civilizations, China's leaders employed strategies of military coercion that had long proven effective against past enemies.

The strategy of military resistance did not address the unprecedented technological gap that left China poorly prepared to defend itself. Chinese elites' pervasive contempt for foreigners had discouraged the study of the West. They failed to appreciate the unprecedented nature of the threat, let alone the need to counter with an unprecedented strategy. Even the importation of military technology did not address the fundamental security problem, which was the rapid pace of change in the West. So coercion counterproductively inspired Western countermeasures backed by the military technology of the Industrial Revolution that China could not match.

As Japanese leaders observed these events with growing horror, some rapidly concluded that they needed to learn more about the nature of the threat. Serious study of the West began in 1857 with the Tokugawa shogunate's establishment of the Institute to Study Western Books – a think tank of its era. Government missions abroad soon followed. Not only the central government but also the large domains sent students abroad, initially to study law, navigation, and medicine, but the fields of inquiry rapidly expanded to encompass the full array of Western institutions, both military and civil.

The intrusions of the industrial West greatly contributed to the fall of the Tokugawa house. The West challenged, not by intent but in practice, the legitimacy of traditional governments worldwide. Those on the receiving end of westernization via foreign policy initially perceived the military underpinnings of Western power. The process of learning the mechanics of the weapons systems to counter the intrusions entailed the study of mathematics, engineering, and the natural sciences, all subjects based on logic. One of the fundamental principles of logic going back to the ancient Greeks is that of noncontradiction – what Westerners call logical consistency. Westerners applied this principle to traditional societies to devastating effect, highlighting revered practices that fell short when evaluated in terms of consistency, efficiency, or efficacy, and detailing the logical roots of these failings. Before long, those in traditional societies studying Western subjects applied the principles of Western logic to their own societies with tumultuous effects. Logic gives no quarter to tradition.

The reforms to redress the perceived failings of traditional societies have been highly destabilizing, generally entailing domestic unrest, revolution, and regional war. Reform undermined traditional societies from two directions: unprecedented change tended to alienate the traditional power base essential for regime continuity while simultaneously galvanizing the opposition in the expectation of even more radical reforms, so that competing new orders gathered strength just as the old order lost control. While a consensus might develop that the old order must go, there was rarely agreement on the optimal new order to follow; rather, as venerable old institutions teetered toward collapse, bitter disagreements arose over what should come next.

In Japan key deaths provided an opportunity for change. In 1866 the twenty-year-old shogun, Tokugawa Iemochi, who had been nominally in charge since the tender age of twelve, died only to be replaced by the same twenty-nine-year-old distant cousin, Tokugawa Yoshinobu, who had been runner-up during a preceding contentious leadership struggle back in 1858. Later in 1866, the virulently antiforeign Emperor Kōmei also died at a youthful thirty-six, leaving the throne to his fourteen-year-old son. At this juncture, mid-level samurai predominantly from the domains of Satsuma (Kagoshima), Chōshū (Yamaguchi), Tosa (Kōchi), and Hizen (Saga) organized to overthrow the government. These domains had been among the losers in the decisive Battle of Sekigahara in 1600 that had brought the Tokugawa clan to power. These "outside" domains had suffered discrimination thereafter.

In the 1860s, key samurai from these domains believed that Japan's response to the Western challenge required more radical changes than the shogunate would allow. As Satsuma and Chōshū prepared their armies, the last Tokugawa shogun initially resigned but reconsidered upon the outbreak of the Boshin War (January 1868–June 1869), only to reconsider again and step down for good when his forces lost the Battle of Toba-Fushimi (27–31 January 1868). Loyalists in the northeastern domains fought on until the surrender of the Tokugawa navy in Hakodate, the southernmost port on the northernmost main island of Hokkaido.

The war put the so-called Meiji generation in power. The coup leaders sought legitimacy through the now fifteen-year-old Emperor Meiji and used his name to designate an era, known as the Meiji Restoration, to suggest the restoration of imperial rule and the end of shogun usurpation. In fact, the Meiji generation promoted not the restoration of tradition but a program of rapid westernization.

The emperor, like his predecessors, reigned but did not rule. For thousands of years, the imperial house had legitimated the de facto rule of others, who until modern times were Japan's military leaders. The relationship eventually became formalized into shogunates. (*Shōgun* is the Japanese word for "general.") Each shogun clan ruled for generations until overthrown by a successor shogunate. Various shogunates ruled from 1192 to 1867 (the Kamakura period through the fall of the Tokugawa). Notably, the Meiji generation created not only new military but also new civil institutions in a land historically dominated by those in military, not civil, employ.

The government formalized its assumption of power with the Charter Oath of 1868 that promised to strengthen imperial rule by uniting society behind economic development, governing through a new public assembly, allowing all classes to pursue legitimate aspirations, discarding obsolete customs, and, most critically, seeking knowledge worldwide. The new government sent even more delegations of high-level civil servants and officers abroad on year-long fact-finding missions to study the full array of Western civil and military institutions.

The most famous was the Iwakura mission. Until his death in 1883 Iwakura Tomomi was among the most influential of the Meiji reformers. His delegation of fifty senior statesmen plus students and others spent nearly two years in Europe and America, visiting twelve countries, to study their military, political, economic, legal, social, and educational institutions. Included in his entourage was Itō Hirobumi, who would go on to draft the Meiji Constitution. Its members thought Japan should emulate American one-room schoolhouses and British industrial and naval development, but Prussia impressed them most. They arrived in Europe just as Otto von Bismarck was completing the unification of the numerous Germanic principalities under Prussian hegemony to create the modern state of Germany. The Japanese took note because until 1868 their country had also been divided into numerous competing semi-independent domains, so Prussia seemed to offer a highly relevant model to transform Japan into a unified state and regional power. They emulated its constitutional monarchy with a dual line of authority between the emperor and the legislature, which predisposed military power to trump civil authority.

Modernization and Westernization

The Iwakura mission concluded that the sources of Western power were not merely technological or military, but also institutional and civilian. That is, the problem was not simply modernization, meaning the acquisition of the most up-to-date technology and particularly military technology and armaments, but also westernization, meaning the introduction of westernized institutions – and not simply westernized military institutions, but a whole array of civil institutions as well.

The decision to modernize with versus without westernization has divided the responses of traditional societies to the Industrial Revolution ever since. Most, like the Qing dynasty of China, have embraced modernization, while reviling the westernized societies that created the coveted technologies. Most have correctly understood that to change domestic institutions is to change a way of life. Therefore they have correctly perceived westernization as a mortal threat to their way of life and have responded accordingly. China chose the first variant, modernization without westernization, while Japan chose the second. The ramifications of their choices have been both consequential and enduring.

The question remains: can one have modernization without westernization? Is it possible to have the fruit without the garden? Can a country become modern, meaning to have available the full array of modern technologies and to enjoy a high general standard of living, without a wide array of westernized civil and military institutions? The Japanese in the late nineteenth century concluded that the answer was no. They believed that some degree of westernization was necessary to become a producer and creator of these technologies, rather than a mere consumer of them. It is interesting that they reached this conclusion and that they did so early.

In contrast, the Chinese government set a course of modernization without westernization. Their overarching policy objective became the preservation of Confucian civilization untainted by the pollution of Western civilization. Japan's decision to westernize marked the parting of the ways for Japanese and Chinese economic and political development, and also for their friendship. Previously, the Japanese had patterned many of their institutions on Chinese models. Henceforth they would emulate Western models instead. This defied the Chinese conceptualization of civilization as a single one-way street, forever in their direction. Japan took a U-turn on the road to civilization when it traded in sinification for westernization and the Chinese have never gotten over it.

Prior to the prolonged trips abroad, Japan's most senior leaders, like those of China, had favored armed resistance, but after observing railways, telegraph systems, steam navigation, steam-powered manufacturing bases, and gaslit cities, they concluded, like it or not, that should Japan fight the Western powers, it would lose. Instead they set their country on a path to rapid westernization and modernization in order to deal with the West on an equal footing. They did not do so out of any cultural affinity with the West, but out of a hardheaded appraisal of the balance of power. The institutional changes entailed the sacrifice of many venerated traditions, such as the privileged position of the samurai, or warrior, a status that many of the reformers held. They replaced the virtuosity of the samurai with the massed power of the conscript army. Children received westernized instead of sinified educations. Old and young, privileged and unprivileged, all faced great changes in the way they lived. Only elements of traditional Japanese culture, most notably Shintō, survived the hybridized westernization promoted by the Meiji reformers. The reformers used Shintō beliefs to serve as the social glue, binding citizens to the state via loyalty to the divine emperor, who became the symbol and legitimator of the state. The decision to westernize upended tradition and angered the general population, who resented imposed changes in the way they had lived for generations.

On the basis of an assessment of the international situation made during the fact-finding missions, the Japanese government set a policy objective and a grand strategy to reach it. Grand strategy, in distinction to military (or operational-level) strategy, integrates all relevant elements of national power. It extends far beyond military power to encompass economic influence, co-ordination with allies, intelligence gathering and analysis, propaganda, institution building, international law, etc. In modern governments, cabinet positions tend to represent many of the elements of grand strategy.

The Meiji generation's overarching objective was the preservation of Japan's security and independence in the face of accelerating Western and Russian imperialism. Since empire was the hallmark of a great power at that time, Japan would follow the model. They devised a sequential grand strategy: first a domestic phase of institution building, followed by a foreign-policy phase of wars to win an empire. Domestic reforms would both lay the foundations for Japan to become a great power and also remove the restrictions of the treaty port system, impinging on its sovereignty. Wars would both stake a claim to an empire on the Asian mainland and also contain Russian expansion that would preclude empire. A key 1873 document makes this sequence clear: "The first thing is to revise the treaties [with the European powers], the Korean business [the conquest of Korea] comes after that."[2]

During the ensuing two decades, Japan westernized a whole array of institutions. The list of reforms is impressive: In 1869, a year after the new government formed, it overturned the internal distribution of power by eliminating the feudal domains that had long fragmented Japan. It then turned from the top of the social pyramid to the bottom, children. In 1872, it made elementary education compulsory in recognition that modernization depended on an educated citizenry. In 1882, it turned to financial and legal institutions: it founded the Bank of Japan and promulgated a westernized criminal code. In 1885 it began reforming political institutions by creating a Cabinet subordinate to a prime minister. In 1886, it founded Tokyo Imperial University to become the center of higher westernized learning. In 1887, it instituted a modern civil service examination system. In 1889, it promulgated a Constitution, and in 1890 it convened the first Diet, reorganized the judicial system, and introduced a westernized code of civil procedure. These collectively became known as the Meiji reforms.

The Meiji reforms included a major military buildup. In 1873, the year after elementary education became mandatory, universal conscription became law. In 1878 the Meiji reformers created an army General Staff based on the Prussian model in order to provide continuity in military leadership and to smooth the transition from peace to war. In 1881 General Yamagata Aritomo, the father of the modern Japanese army, described the imperative for Japan to become a "floating fortress" able to "exercise power in all directions."[3] In 1883 the General Staff established the Staff College to educate officers to lead the

---

[2] Ōkubo Toshimichi cited in Hilary Conroy, *The Japanese Seizure of Korea, 1868–1910: A Study of Realism and Idealism in International Relations* (Philadelphia: University of Pennsylvania Press, 1960), 48.

[3] Quoted in Meirion Harries and Susie Harries, *Soldiers of the Sun: The Rise and Fall of the Imperial Japanese Army* (New York: Random House, 1991), 43.

new westernized army and soon employed Prussian-trained faculty members. In 1888 the army jettisoned its organization based on static garrisons in favor of mobile divisions, capable of sustained operations abroad, and created the Army Service Corps for logistical support. In 1892, the army engaged in comprehensive war games. Japan also built an extensive railway grid linking its military bases to facilitate mobilization.

The same year that conscription became law, Japan also created a Navy Ministry separate from the War (Army) Ministry. In 1882 the Imperial Japanese Navy formed its first fleet, in 1889 it established the Standing Fleet of first-line non-reserve warships, in 1893 it created a second standing fleet known as the Western Seas Fleet, and in 1894 it unified the Standing and Western Seas Fleets into the Combined Fleet. The navy rapidly grew from just nineteen warships in 1882 to thirty-one by 1894, plus numerous torpedo boats. The largest four warships were completed between 1892 and 1894. The Meiji government modeled this fleet on the British Navy and its naval doctrine on the teachings of a U.S. admiral, Alfred Thayer Mahan, the world-renowned naval theorist of the 1890s. More of his writings were translated into Japanese than into any other language.

Once the domestic reforms were in place, the government turned to renegotiating its treaties on the basis of juridical equality. Japan played back the law of noncontradiction on the West: domestic westernization removed the Western rationale for the treaty port system because the Japanese judicial system now followed Western practices, obviating the need for special legal protections for expatriates. Therefore Japan should be treated like any European power. On 16 July 1894, it concluded a new treaty with Britain, the international precedent-setter and greatest of the great powers. The other powers soon followed suit and renegotiated their treaties. Treaty revision marked the end of extraterritoriality and fruition of the domestic phase of Japan's grand strategy.

Thus Japan eliminated the treaty port system a full half-century before China did in the 1940s with the West and in the 1950s with the Soviet Union, and arguably not fully until the 1990s with the return of Macau and Hong Kong. During this domestic phase, the government had carefully avoided foreign wars to avoid derailing the domestic reform program. In contrast, a strategy of resistance entangled China in one conflict after another so that it accomplished little reform of any kind and the industrializing powers imposed ever more onerous treaties after the Opium Wars, the Sino-French War (1883–85), and the Boxer Uprising (1899–1900).

During the domestic phase of Japan's grand strategy, the reforms remained unpopular. The political parties populating the Diet were mainly hostile to the unelected senior statesmen, also known as the oligarchs, or *genrō* (元老 original elders), who actually set policy. Prior to Japan's gambit for empire that began with the First Sino-Japanese War (1894–95), there was constant bickering over appropriations between the Diet members and the oligarchs. The latter demanded increasing military budgets. The Diet members resisted. So the oligarchs prorogued the Diet and spent as they pleased on the military, very much as Otto von Bismarck had done in Prussia when he had fought a series of wars in the 1860s and 1870s despite strong initial legislative opposition concerning the military budget.

Immediately upon completion of the domestic phase, the oligarchs embarked on the foreign-policy phase of their grand strategy. They observed that the great powers of the late nineteenth century possessed enormous wealth, strong militaries, and great territorial extent, usually in the form of empires. They saw no reason why their country should depart from the established model for economic development. Given Japan's geography, they believed that empire would lie across the Korea Strait on the Asian mainland from Korea westward into Manchuria, where China and particularly Korea suffered from increasingly debilitating internal instability. They also expected the empire to extend southward along the island chains from Japan to the Ryukyu Islands and on to Taiwan, and northward to the Kurils and Sakhalin Island. Because Russia also had designs on Manchuria, Korea, Sakhalin, and the Kurils, Japanese leaders perceived Russia as the greatest threat to their ambitions.

Japan's new leaders saw Korea as the essential starting point for these plans and saw its instability as a dire threat to Japan's national security. In the 1880s, Korea suffered a succession of coup attempts when royal relatives exchanged package bombs detonating royal palaces, and revolutionaries beheaded ministers at a particularly notorious official banquet. The instability brought intrusive foreign intervention by an array of powers. Britain had become increasingly active in Korea where, as in China, it managed the tariff collection for the treaty port system. China considered Korea to be its most important tributary, but internal rebellions and regional wars long hobbled Chinese foreign policy.

Russia also had plans for expanded empire. In 1891 the Russian government decided to build the Trans-Siberian Railway, enabling it to unleash its huge standing army on Asia. Contemporary analysts expected its completion to overturn the East Asian balance of power when Russia could deploy troops efficiently where none of the other regional powers could. Japanese leaders noted the magnitude of the railway investment in comparison with the unpopulated, inhospitable part of the Russian empire it would service, to conclude that its purpose was not internal development but external expansion. If Russia filled the developing power vacuum in Northeast Asia, this would foreclose Japan's prospects for empire. Worse still, Japanese leaders considered Korea to be not only the most desirable area to pursue empire and economic growth, but also the most likely potential invasion route into Japan.

Given this security environment, Japanese leaders saw a very rigid timetable for the execution of the foreign-policy phase of their grand strategy. The window of opportunity would not open until the completion of the domestic reform program, a military buildup sufficient to take military action, and treaty revision with Great Britain, all in place in 1894. This same window would slam shut as soon as Russia completed the Trans-Siberian Railway, anticipated soon after 1900.

On 25 July 1894, nine days after Japan had concluded the precedent-setting treaty revisions with Britain that completed the domestic phase of its grand strategy, it went to war with China over the control of Korea. This would be its first war in the series of three aimed at the containment of Russia in order to create and then preserve the Japanese empire. These wars were the First Sino-Japanese War, the Russo-Japanese War a decade later, and the Second Sino-Japanese War (1931–45), which then escalated into World War II (1941–5). The first two conflicts produced settlements exceeding Japan's original objectives, while the third escalated into a global war that brought down the empire.

Japan's tale reveals the risks, rewards, costs, and feasibility of grafting elements from an alien civilization onto domestic practices.[4] It is a story told in five parts: two wars, a transition period, and two more wars. The first pair of conflicts achieved their intended objectives, while the second pair precluded them. It is a tale about the difficulties of economic and political catch-up, about the dangers of a collapsing international order, and about the limitations of warfare to achieve national objectives.

---

[4] The framework of risk, reward, costs (including opportunity costs), and feasibility is a long-standing framework used in the Strategy & Policy Department at the U.S. Naval War College as one method to evaluate alternative strategies.

Map 2 First Sino-Japanese War

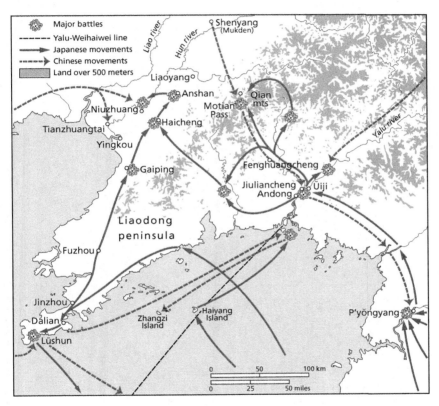

Map 2 (cont.)

Photo 1 Itō Hirobumi (1841–1909)
http://www.ndl.go.jp/portrait/e/datas/12_1.html (National Diet Library, Japan)

2   The First Sino-Japanese War (1894–1895)

> Most people are surprised ... while possessing as she does some of the finest
> types of modern warships, the Chinese army is still in many respects abso-
> lutely what it was three hundred years ago – merely an armed undisciplined
> horde.[1]
>
> Sir Robert Hart (1835–1911), inspector general, Imperial Maritime Customs for
China (1863–1908), interview in 1892
>
> With passionate effort the Japanese have ransacked the Western world for its
> treasures of knowledge, and have vigorously applied what they have learned.[2]
>
> *The Times*, London, 1894, on the eve of the First Sino-Japanese War

Japan westernized, China did not, and there were consequences.[3] Although
in the eighteenth century the ruling Manchus had created the richest empire
in human history and the second-largest in Chinese history, by the nineteenth century they were on the decline just as Japan began its ascent and the
West had reached its stride. An unprecedented wave of internal rebellions
wracked China followed by a succession of regional wars. In this period,
China's government had great difficulty setting feasible strategic goals and
then matching a grand strategy to secure them. In contrast, Japan's leaders
laid plans to use the window of opportunity between treaty revision and the
completion of the Trans-Siberian Railway to pre-empt Russia by seizing
Korea from a failing China. While Japanese leaders' stated goals emphasized the restoration of order and the protection of Japanese nationals in
Korea, their much more important unstated goals concerned the larger issue
of the regional balance of power, which they intended to overturn at Chinese
and Russian expense.

---

[1] "A Talk with Sir Robert Hart at Peking," *North China Herald* (Shanghai), 21 September 1894,
p. 500.
[2] "The War in the East," *The Times* (London), 26 December 1894, p. 4.
[3] This chapter is based on S.C.M. Paine, *The First Sino-Japanese War of 1894–1895: Perceptions,
Power, and Primacy* (Cambridge: Cambridge University Press, 2003).

Underlying and Proximate Causes

Wars arise from underlying and proximate causes. The underlying causes are the tinder composed of the belligerents' mutually exclusive objectives, while the proximate causes serve as the lit match of immediate grievances setting off the conflagration. Many people identify the last proximate cause as the reason for the outbreak of hostilities, when in fact it is just the last in a long succession that finally ignited the accumulation of underlying tensions. Although a specific event may trigger hostilities, it occurs against a backdrop of issues setting the belligerents at cross-purposes. These underlying causes constitute the real reasons for war, not the headline-grabbing provocations. The latter reveal the symptoms, not the underlying disease. The growing accumulation of underlying causes is no secret, and often builds over a period of years if not decades, and so is obvious to anyone who bothers to look. Yet the timing of the outbreak of hostilities is often a great surprise because the importance of the many intangible factors culminating in war cannot be measured with any accuracy.

The underlying causes of the First Sino-Japanese War concerned the changing Asian balance of power, the instability this created, and the underlying fear that Russia, not Japan, might become the beneficiary. First, Japan's generation-long rise positioned it to supplant China as the dominant power of Asia not only because of Japan's domestic reforms, but because of China's domestic implosion. Second, long-term Chinese decline undermined the ability of the original guarantor of the Asian order to uphold its end of its suzerain–tributary relationship with Korea. Third, given this situation, foreign policy gave the Meiji reformers the opportunity to legitimate their highly controversial domestic westernization program with vindicating foreign-policy successes. Fourth, Chinese actions then expanded the opportunity: their refusal to recognize the changing balance of power or to accord the Japanese even a modicum of respect caused deep resentment and fed a widespread, retaliatory Japanese nationalism, which battlefield success then gratified. But retaliation hardened Chinese intransigence, which fed Japanese resentment in an escalatory and pernicious cycle.

China's decline had become obvious by the 1850s. Since the early nineteenth century, a cascade of civil wars had nearly toppled the Qing dynasty. The most prominent were the Eight Trigrams Revolt (1813), the Taiping Rebellion (1851–66) and the Nian Rebellion (1851–68) that attempted to overthrow the dynasty, and three Muslim rebellions – the Panthay (1855–73), the Donggan (1862–73), and Xinjiang Rebellions (1862–78) – that attempted to secede from empire. These were simply the most famous of hundreds of uprisings that together killed tens of millions and devastated the core provinces as well as the periphery. China first felt the impact of the Industrial Revolution amidst this succession of civil wars. Thus the timing could not have been worse.

Then the very achievements of Chinese civilization blinded national leaders, who did not grasp the implications of changes on the far side of the globe. They assumed that China would remain what it always had been – the dominant civilization, military power, economic center, source of technological innovation, and benchmark for human achievement. They assumed that the world order that their ancestors had fashioned on the basis of these achievements would continue to organize international relations.

That world order was the tributary system, whereby China maintained bilateral relations with its many immediate neighbors. It sat at the center of this world – the Central Kingdom (*zhongguo* 中國) – surrounded by concentric rings of ever more barbarous neighbors. There was only one civilization: Chinese civilization, surrounded by a barbarian sea. An even more encompassing name was All under Heaven (*tianxia* 天下). Over time, the nearest neighbors adopted its practices and did not dispute its pretense to control their foreign policy. They could trade on the periphery of the empire and participate in annual tribute missions to Beijing, where they received luxury goods valued in excess of their offerings. This limited trade was intended to buy border security. Other neighbors, who lacked formal states, could become part of the empire by adopting Chinese ways. "Sinification" described this process. It was a one-way street, by which the empire expanded and the neighbors became ever more like China. The remaining unsinified barbarians, who desired more and invaded to take what they could not legally acquire, met armed resistance and, if their predations persisted, genocide became a permanent solution to the security problem. This was the fate of the Zunghar Mongol and Jinchuan Tibetans in the eighteenth century. The tributary system organized the known world for thousands of years. The Chinese assumed that what had functioned so well in the past would do so in the future. They were wrong. They saw history's continuities but not its equally important discontinuities.

Pride in the past produced an overconfidence in the present that translated into military defeat in a succession of conflicts against the industrializing world: the Opium Wars, the Ryukyu Islands conflict with Japan (1879), and the Sino-French War (1884–85). These conflicts precluded active intervention in Korea until the 1880s, when the Chinese thought the wave of civil and regional wars had subsided. This calculation overlooked Japan.

For Japan, China's decline created both a threat, in the form of a widening power vacuum in an immediate neighbor, and an opportunity for empire created by the vacuum. On the eve of the First Sino-Japanese War, Minister to the United States Tateno Gōzō told Secretary of State Walter Q. Gresham, "Our situation at home is critical, and war with China would improve it by arousing the patriotic sentiment of our people and more strongly attaching them to the Government."[4] At issue was not so much the balance of power between the political parties and government officials, but more fundamentally public

[4] Cited in Jeffrey M. Dorwart, *The Pigtail War: American Involvement in the Sino-Japanese War of 1894–1895* (Amherst: University of Massachusetts Press, 1975), 23.

support for the new westernized governmental institutions themselves, which had yet to yield tangible benefits to the general population. Thus the war was connected with the larger problem of state building and governmental legitimacy. Meiji institutions were new and unpopular among many. This was the period when prisons swelled with those hostile to westernization.

The rise of Japan, the decline of China, and the domestic legitimacy problem exacerbated another underlying cause of the war. The Chinese insisted upon treating the Japanese as inferiors. Their declaration of war repeatedly referred to the Japanese as dwarfs or midget pirates (*woren* 倭人, or *wokou* 倭寇), the ancient and highly derogatory terms for the Japanese commonly used in official Chinese documents through the 1940s. During the millennia of China's ascendancy, the Japanese had acquiesced to such pretenses of superiority. The long years of hard work bringing the Meiji reforms to fruition, however, raised expectations that at long last China would treat them with the respect they believed they had earned. Westerners, who came from less hierarchical societies, extended juridical equality to the other "powers." The Chinese, however, did not have this tradition, since their country had been the single great power in East Asia prior to the arrival of Western representatives. Like most dominant powers, the Chinese had no intention of changing an international system created according to their specifications.

These underlying causes of the war all concerned a changing balance of power in East Asia that China refused to recognize. The underlying causes – the rise of Japan, the decline of China, institutional legitimacy in Japan, and Japan's quest for international respect – were all variables in the East Asian balance-of-power equation. Historically, this equation had always yielded an answer of China on top, but the values of the variables had changed. China refused to do the math. Japan used the First Sino-Japanese War to force a retabulation before Russia could intervene.

Journalists at the time focused – as they do now – on the proximate causes of the war, the incidents igniting the conflict, not on the accumulating and highly flammable tinder that had transformed war from a possibility into a probability. The underlying causes then tied the hands of policymakers by eliminating choices that people at the time and especially later generations believed should have existed. Underlying causes often constitute the constraints bounding policymakers.

The proximate cause of the First Sino-Japanese War appeared to be the sinking of the British transport *Kowshing* on 25 July 1894 but actually this incident was the fifth in a series of cascading proximate causes that together added up to war: first, the escalating infighting in the Korean royal household over the appropriate choice of a great-power ally; second the assassination of the revolutionary Kim Ok-kyun on 28 March 1894; third, the Korean response to the Tonghak Rebellion to request Chinese deployments on 3 June; fourth, the

Chinese and Japanese troop buildups in Korea in early June; and finally the sinking of *Kowshing*. All were interconnected: the transport ship was attempting to deliver Chinese troops both to counter Japanese deployments and to suppress the Tonghak Rebellion that broke out when the Korean royal family focused on imperial infighting and the elimination of elite reformers.

During the nineteenth century, the in-law clans of Korean kings, all of whom ascended to the throne as children, attempted to dominate the throne, particularly during the regency periods. Late Yi dynasty (1392–1910) politics had a tabloid quality. The Grand Prince, who served as regent during his son's minority, was fond of power and did not want to relinquish it to his son. To the Grand Prince's credit, he initiated a variety of reforms that reduced corruption and improved government finances, but he did so to the horror of the aristocrats whose slush funds he curtailed. The horrified included his son's wife, Queen Min, and her numerous grasping relatives, who equated governance with personal enrichment. The queen believed that the Grand Prince had poisoned her firstborn son in 1871. Allegedly, the Grand Prince was also the source of the package bomb that blew up the queen's brother and incinerated the latter's mother and nephew in the resulting conflagration. In 1875 the Grand Prince allegedly detonated the queen's bedchamber, reducing the palace to ashes, but the queen had been elsewhere.

To tip the balance in this fight, feuding imperial factions encouraged the intervention of a kaleidoscopic array of foreign powers. The intervention of any one foreign power, however, tended to precipitate the intervention of its rivals so that the imperial household, instead of exercising leadership to settle differences internally, outsourced this vital responsibility and, in so doing, became hostage to the foreign powers. The queen's clan sought out China. The king initially approached Japan and, after that soured, turned to Russia. The Grand Prince vacillated between working with Japan and China, until the Japanese finished his career. Various aristocratic Korean reformers usually tried to work with either Japan or Britain. One of these was Kim Ok-kyun, whose assassination constituted the second proximate cause of the war.

The Japanese had cultivated the aristocratic Andong Kim clan and one of its members, Kim Ok-kyun, in particular. The clan was extremely well connected, having provided four queens to successive kings since the late eighteenth century. Kim believed that Korea should sever traditional connections with China to follow Japan's lead to modernization. Although Kim's goals may have appeared modern, his means were anything but. He proposed political transformation through murder. The venue was a postal banquet in 1884, where his accomplices decapitated six ministers and sundry others. The rebels failed to make a pre-coup tally of Chinese and Japanese troops in Seoul, where the former outnumbered the latter by a ratio of seven to one. China intervened to restore the status quo. The coup produced the opposite of its intended outcome: execution or exile for its perpetrators, expanded Chinese influence, the suffocation of reform, and a growing Min clan dependence on the Chinese for survival. In other words, Kim was no strategist.

Kim Ok-kyun and his co-conspirators sought refuge in Japan. Failure transformed Kim from a potential political asset into a political liability and constant source of friction in Japanese–Korean relations. The Min clan and King Kojong repeatedly tried to extradite him and, failing this, to assassinate him. A fellow Korean, Hong Chong-u (also from a distinguished scholar–aristocratic family and then in the employ of King Kojong), befriended Kim, lured him to Shanghai, and murdered him there on 28 March 1894. Although Japanese interest in the Korean reformers had been on the decline, the murder instantly reversed the situation.

British authorities in Shanghai arrested the accused assassin and, in accordance with their treaty obligations, surrendered him to the Chinese authorities for trial. Instead the Chinese immediately freed the assassin, who became a celebrity, and declined to give custody of the corpse to Kim's Japanese friends. On 12 April, the Chinese then delivered to Korea both the corpse and the assassin aboard the same Chinese warship. For many Japanese, this behavior implicated the Chinese government in the crime. Japanese public outrage grew when the assassin received a hero's welcome, while the Korean government had the victim's corpse decapitated, and delivered body parts throughout the country for public exhibition. Before long, the Korean authorities had Kim's father hanged and his brother, wife, and only daughter imprisoned. For weeks, Kim's postmortem made headlines in the Japanese press. From the Chinese and Korean point of view, Kim had committed high treason in the postal massacre a decade prior and so deserved his fate. From the Japanese point of view, China and Korea had insulted Japan in every possible way.

These headlines occurred against a backdrop of gathering unrest across the Korean countryside. In January 1894, the greatest peasant rebellion in Korean history had broken out in protest against oppressive taxation and incompetent financial administration, two hallmarks of the late Yi dynasty. This was the Tonghak Rebellion. Its followers called for the punishment of corrupt officials and the expulsion of foreigners. The latter became a convenient scapegoat for Korea's ills – easy to pick out, pick on, and pick off. The endemic poverty and government malfeasance, however, had a far more complicated pedigree than the presence and pretenses of foreigners. Yi dynasty decline preceded both the arrival of Westerners and the Meiji Restoration, and was domestic in origin.

When rumors reached the Tonghaks that China and Japan were verging on sending troops, the rebels agreed to a cease-fire on 1 June 1894, thus removing the grounds for foreign intervention. Nevertheless, on 2 June, the Japanese

Cabinet decided to send troops, should China do so. On 3 June, the Korean king, who apparently had less insight into the dangers of escalation than did the rebels seeking his overthrow, requested that China send troops to help suppress the rebellion. In doing so, King Kojong unwittingly handed Japanese military leaders the pretext to intervene massively that they had long sought. Both countries soon deployed troops, China with Korea's blessing and Japan despite Korean protests. War preparations continued apace.

Japan began the First Sino-Japanese War without a prior declaration of war but with a surprise attack, establishing a pattern for its three major twentieth-century wars: the Russo-Japanese War, the Second Sino-Japanese War, and World War II. In all but the Second Sino-Japanese War, the surprise attacks were naval. On 25 July 1894, in the Battle of Feng Island, three Japanese cruisers attacked two Chinese warships on the homeward voyage from Asan, Korea. They clashed in the vicinity of Feng Island, which lies on the sea approaches to both Asan and Chemulp'o, the port city for the capital, Seoul. The attack, disabling one Chinese vessel and damaging the other, marked the de facto beginning of the First Sino-Japanese War.

While pursuing the damaged vessel, the Japanese sighted the Chinese-leased but British-owned steamship *Kowshing*, which was transferring to Korea 1,100 Chinese troops and officers. The Chinese generals on board refused to heed the Japanese order to follow them to port, whereupon the crew mutinied and demanded to return to Dagu, the military base protecting Tianjin and, by extension, Beijing. During the several hours of fruitless negotiations, the British-trained Japanese commander, Captain Tōgō Heihachirō, carefully examined the relevant provisions of international law. Upon finding the law to be on his side, he sank *Kowshing* and virtually all Chinese aboard drowned. British courts later upheld his interpretation of the law. The Japanese made an effort to pick up only the European military advisers stranded in the water. They damaged a cruiser, captured one gunboat, and sank another, while two other ships escaped. By the end of the war, Tōgō had been promoted to rear admiral and, a decade later, he went on to command the Japanese fleet in the Russo-Japanese War and the surprise attack that began that war. The Battle of Feng Island and the sinking of *Kowshing* precipitated formal declarations of war on 1 August 1894.

The Chinese war plan called for a pincer movement against Seoul from P'yŏngyang, 125 miles to the north, and from Asan, eighty miles to the south. On 20 July 1894, China had begun massing troops in Korea. General Ye Zhichao had requested reinforcements for Asan that *Kowshing* had supplied. Once the war broke out, General Ye, an aging veteran of the suppression of the Nian Rebellion, became the theater commander for Korea.

These spiraling events – royal infighting, Kim's assassination, the Tonghak Rebellion, the Sino-Japanese troop buildups, and the sinking of

Kowshing – provided the proximate causes of the war: the match. Stories of the sinking of *Kowshing* filled the Western press. Stories of the Tonghak Rebellion and especially the assassination of Kim Ok-kyun filled the Japanese press. Journalists saw the fuse but failed to identify the highly flammable underlying causes that the fuse ignited. Wars do not erupt without the tinder for a bonfire.

Policy Objectives and the Elements of Grand Strategy

Just as people at the time and later historians have had more difficulty isolating the underlying than the proximate causes of a war, for obvious reasons they also have more difficulty discerning unstated from stated war objectives. The Japanese government made clear its intent to expel China from the Korean peninsula on the justification that Chinese intrusions violated Korean sovereignty (as did Japan's). The Japanese government also made clear its intent to force upon a reluctant Korea a Meiji reform package in the belief that only such comprehensive reforms would lift Korea out of endemic poverty, eliminate governmental dysfunction, and bring prosperity to Japan in the process through expanded trade. Japan planned to assume the role in Korea played by Britain in China and the United States in Japan: Japan would open Korea to the global economy, a win–win solution for both countries. The Koreans, of course, did not see things this way. The Japanese overlooked their own aversion to the unequal treaty system whose elimination had been a cornerstone of their grand strategy.

Japanese leaders also had important unstated goals. They intended to preempt and contain Russia by dominating Korea before the Russians could arrive in force upon the completion of the Trans-Siberian Railway. Russia, not China and Korea, was the main national-security concern for Japan. Korea became a problem because it was a failing state led by a disintegrating dynasty exposed to the intrusions of others. Likewise China became a problem as it disintegrated into a failing state, no longer capable of upholding the traditional international order of its creation. The decline of China potentially put all of its tributaries up for grabs at a time when Russia was the most likely intruder in northeastern Asia, the primary area of interest to Japan.

The prevention of Russian expansion – "containment," in Cold War parlance – was Japan's primary negative objective. Negative objectives focus on preventing an outcome, while positive objectives focus on forcing an outcome. Positive objectives are tangible – a piece of territory changes hands, a government is overthrown, an indemnity is paid. Negative objectives are invisible. Who is to say that anything was prevented? Those who prevent disaster can never prove that they have done so. Therefore negative objectives are difficult to market to citizens at home or to allies abroad. Yet both types of objective can be equally important.

Japan's primary positive objective was to overturn the East Asian balance of power by replacing China as the dominant regional power. No one but the Japanese saw this coming. They deliberately emulated the shrewd strategy of Prussia's Otto von Bismarck, whose succession of short, regional wars – the Danish War (1864), the Austro-Prussian War (1866), and the Franco-Prussian War (1870–71) – together had overturned the European balance of power under the noses of the other European powers, which had so much to lose from the rise of Germany, as they later discovered in two world wars. Prussia's neighbors failed to intervene when they still could because they did not perceive Prussia's grand strategy. They focused on the details, missing the larger purpose. Prussia incrementally elevated its position from the weakest of the five European great powers (Britain, Russia, France, Austria, and Prussia) to the number two spot. The Iwakura mission had arrived in Germany immediately after the third war. Its members were particularly impressed by the Battle of Sedan that had destroyed much of the French Army in a double envelopment. They found much to emulate.

As in many wars, Japan's unstated goals were more important than its stated goals. Expelling China from Korea and reforming Korea were elements of an overarching agenda to overturn the East Asian balance of power, taking over parts of the disintegrating Qing empire before Russia could and containing Russia thereafter. Like Prussia, Japan was a rising power on the march – a nightmare for dominant powers like China, which cleave to a status quo of their own creation. Japan, like Prussia, intended to overturn the regional balance and make itself pre-eminent. Moreover, Japan envisioned a new regional order, based not on the tributary system but on imperialism.

Japan formulated a comprehensive grand strategy to achieve its goals. Elements of this strategy included extensive prewar state building, diplomacy, finance, industrialization, logistical preparations, intelligence gathering, and the buildup of both land and naval forces. Japan had engaged in years of patient state building not only to secure treaty revision with Britain but also to prepare for war. The westernization of domestic institutions provided the organizational structures to marshal its resources to prosper at home and to project power abroad, while economic development produced the resources to marshal. Treaty revision marked the end of diplomatic preparations.

Japan prepared to fund the war in the manner of wealthy Western nations, by issuing domestic loans to create a national war fund to be repaid with an indemnity from a defeated China. This depended on the establishment of the necessary financial institutions, in particular the Bank of Japan. China had not westernized its financial institutions and, despite its far greater wealth, could not access it efficiently.

Japan also had a much more extensive industrial base and produced a wider array of the industrial goods necessary to fight a modern war. It had developed an indigenous arms industry, which manufactured state-of-the-art weapons for land warfare as well as many modern naval vessels. Although neither country could build the largest capital ships, Japan produced excellent artillery and its domestically manufactured Murata magazine rifles equaled the best of Europe's. Its artillery would undermine China's preferred tactic of firing from behind old city walls, which would crumble under the impact of modern shells. China, by contrast, had extreme difficulty matching ammunition to armaments and appropriate gunpowder to guns. Many of its soldiers still used the gingal, an obsolete firearm, so heavy that it required one soldier to shoulder it, while the other aimed and fired. The Japanese General Staff estimated that only three-fifths of the Chinese army had some kind of rifle. The rest relied on pikes, spears, and swords, and far too many packed opium in their kit.

The Japanese government had long recognized the importance of mobility. It had crisscrossed Japan with railways. Despite intensive lobbying by Viceroy Li Hongzhang, the most famous representative of the self-strengthening generation that attempted to modernize China's military after defeats in the Opium Wars, the Chinese government rejected railway building as an affront to nature and civilization. Railways disrupted *fengshui*, the rules of geomancy requiring the placing of new structures in auspicious locations. At the outbreak of hostilities, China had only one railway, a short section between Tianjin, the port city for Beijing, and Shanhaiguan, located where the Great Wall meets the sea. Given China's poorly maintained road system, troops could not be rapidly deployed or consistently supplied even in China. The Korean road system was even worse. Japan also subsidized its large steamship companies so that their vessels would be available in time of war and its merchant marine was three times the size of China's. Japan's integrated land and sea transportation grid allowed the delivery of men and materiel where needed, while China could not easily do either.

Japan had also invested resources in breaking China's code for encrypting messages. By June 1894, prior to the opening of hostilities, the Japanese were reading Viceroy Li Hongzhang's many telegrams to his military subordinates and to his imperial superiors. Li combined in his person three positions: theater commander, de facto foreign minister, and grand strategist for the war. Because of China's deficient communications and transportation system and because of Li's advanced age – he was seventy-one at the opening of hostilities – he mostly stayed put, in communication with the capital and his commanders via telegram, undoubtedly facilitating Japanese intelligence gathering.

There is little information concerning the consequences of this intelligence coup, but one can surmise that the advantage must have been considerable, particularly in the diplomatic endgame terminating the war. During the hostilities, foreknowledge must have simplified Japanese military deployments since they probably understood the general outlines, if not all the details, of Chinese war plans and deployments.

Unlike China, Japan had fully modernized both its army and its navy. The Japanese army was national and based on universal conscription with a standard term for service. Their standardized kit included the Japanese-made, single-shot, Murata breech-loader rifle. Thorough officer training meant that commanders were given precise objectives during the war but the flexibility to decide how to reach them. The Japanese army was composed of six divisions under unified command and included a well-developed medical corps, engineering corps, and commissariat.

The Chinese army had none of the above, but remained a hodgepodge of regional units including banner forces segregated by race (Manchu, Mongol, Muslim, and Han Chinese), a huge Han Green Standard Army barely capable of constabulary functions, small numbers of hired mercenaries, and a small foreign-drilled army. While the Qing dynasty segregated the Manchus into elite banner units to serve as the Praetorian guard for Manchu minority rule, the dynasty deliberately fractured the vast Han military by province, by type of unit, and by army in order to prevent the emergence of a unified Han army that might be tempted to restore Han majority rule. This meant that there was no unified national defense, only provincial defense, with each governor left essentially on his own. Their most competent units – their hired mercenaries and Western-drilled recruits – together represented perhaps 10 percent of the total.

These modern troops included the personal army of Viceroy Li Hongzhang, the founder of the Huai Army. All told, Li controlled perhaps three-fifths of the forces deployed. As governor-general of Zhili, the location of the capital, Li commanded his provincial forces, but not the imperial bannermen in Beijing, responsible for guarding the capital and the imperial clan segregated in the walled Manchu city within. He commanded all troops engaged in the Korean and Manchurian theaters, but not the provincial armies from Heilongjiang, Jilin, and Fengtian, the three provinces comprising Manchuria, the homeland of the ruling dynasty. Although as commissioner for the Northern Seas, he controlled China's most modern fleet, the three other regional fleets further south remained under the command and control of the province containing their respective home base.

Chinese inattention to the needs of their soldiers undermined morale. Few could count on regular pay. China provided no medical services, so most serious wounds were terminal. In the absence of a commissariat and transport services, Chinese forces pillaged in order to survive, making the Chinese peasantry dread the arrival of their own troops. The Japanese contributed to this Chinese public-relations disaster by paying for goods and services as they went. In China, unlike in Korea, the Japanese made no attempt to alter local institutions. The Japanese faced no Chinese peasant insurgency in occupied areas because the peasants felt safer under Japanese than under Manchu occupation. This situation ate away at loyalties to the dynasty. In Korea, where Japan tried to impose a Meiji reform package, the Tonghak Rebellion resurged upon the opening of hostilities and an insurgency festered for the duration of Japanese colonial rule.

Initial War Plans: The Korean Campaign and the Battle of the Yalu

Minister of War Yamagata Aritomo's war plan envisioned a rapid Japanese occupation of Korea followed by an invasion of the Manchurian homeland of the ruling Qing dynasty in the direction of the historic Qing capital in Shenyang (Mukden), and also in the direction of the actual capital in Beijing. Japan planned to eliminate China's two key naval bases in order to cut off Beijing by sea and then to make a pincer movement on the capital. The plan assumed that the Qing dynasty would not risk either capital for Korea, so rapid capitulation would follow. If this operational plan proved infeasible, Japan would settle for the occupation of Korea. However, if disaster struck and China, not Japan, took command of the sea, then Japan would focus on its own coastal defenses to prevent a Chinese invasion.

The Japanese took great risks. Their plans required early and sustained command of the sea because they could not reach the theater by any other route. Yet before they had neutralized the Northern Seas Squadron, they mobilized well over 100,000 men and after the declarations of war poured soldiers into Korea. Disposing of these armies at sea would have been China's most efficient and effective means of undermining Japan's military strategy.

The Japanese campaign plan entailed the division of its forces into two armies. The First Army under General Yamagata Aritomo would invade Korea and enter Manchuria from the north, while the Second Army under Minister of War General Ōyama Iwao would invade Manchuria from the south to take Lüshun, the naval base on the Liaodong peninsula, known in the West as Port Arthur. General Ōyama had participated in the civil war overthrowing the Tokugawa shogunate and played a crucial role in creating the modern Japanese army. In the Russo-Japanese War he would become the theater commander for Manchuria.

Viceroy Li's strategy remained conflict avoidance. Thirty years prior, when in his prime, he had been a key commander in charge of suppressing the Taiping Rebellion and thereafter had led the self-strengthening movement to modernize China's military. He had built China's only railway line, and opened some of its first modern mines, its first cotton spinning mill, the Tianjin Military Academy, and the Chinese Educational Mission to send students to study in the

United States. His adopted son, Li Jingfang, had just returned from serving as minister to Japan from 1890 to 1892.

The viceroy, in contrast to virtually all other Chinese leaders, was well aware of Japan's many modernization efforts. He hoped to keep up the pretense of Chinese suzerainty without triggering hostilities. After the initial troop deployments, he made no further preparations, nor did he attempt to match Japan's. When Japan continued to escalate, he tried to enlist great-power intervention, but found his extensive international contacts surprisingly reluctant to intervene and dangerously supportive of Japan's westernization agenda for China and Korea.

Apparently Li also misread the domestic political situation in Japan. Chinese officials, aware of the constant feuding between the Diet and the Cabinet, particularly over military budgets, seemed to have concluded that these political divisions would prevent Japan from prosecuting an effective military campaign. Perhaps they projected their own political problems onto Japan. Whereas the Manchu–Han division hamstrung China's military modernization and precluded a unified military effort, the Japanese shared a national identity, and their leadership a foreign-policy consensus, which fused Japanese domestic political divisions once the war began. The Chinese were not alone in making this sort of mistake. Wars often have a difficult-to-predict galvanizing effect on one side but not on the other.

In late July 1894, Li Hongzhang did send large reinforcements to Korea. By this time, his original policy of conflict avoidance succumbed to a crosscutting imperative to keep up the pretenses of Chinese suzerainty over Korea in order to shore up the domestic legitimacy of the Qing dynasty. When Japan brought war upon China, this left Viceroy Li with only his operational strategy intact. He intended to fight the Japanese on land, first in the vicinity of Seoul and, failing that, at P'yŏngyang. If this too failed, he presumably envisioned a war of attrition in which China's superior manpower and resource endowment would prevail. Even though he had a state-of-the-art fleet equal to that of Japan while his land forces were mostly antiquated, he still envisioned a land war. Given his distinguished career in the army, undoubtedly he understood land warfare far better than naval warfare. Similarly, his operational naval commander, fifty-eight-year-old Admiral Ding Ruchang, was another army man, who had begun his military career fighting Taiping and Nian rebels. Only recently had he become commander of the Northern Seas Squadron.

On the same day as the Battle of Feng Island, Japanese forces sought out Chinese forces south of Seoul to do battle. In the ensuing Battle of Sŏnghwan that erupted on the night of 28 July 1894, the Chinese fought hard, but could not hold Sŏnghwan. The troop delay meant that reinforcements did not arrive in time for the battle. This produced an easy and morale-generating victory for Japan. Chinese troops fled all the way north to P'yŏngyang, a former capital of Korea and future capital of North Korea, located just 100 miles south of the Chinese border. Thus, within one week of the opening of hostilities, the Chinese had abandoned the king of Korea to his fate, given up Seoul without a fight, and effectively ceded the southern three-quarters of the Korean peninsula to Japan.

Apparently, Viceroy Li intended to preserve his modern navy intact to defend the capital and, after the war, to fight Japan another day. In doing so, he unwittingly played into Japanese strategy. He ordered his fleet not to sortie east of the Yalu river–Weihaiwei line; that is, anywhere off the Korean peninsula. His order ceded to the Japanese the command of the sea that their war plans required, allowing them to land troops and supplies unmolested. His order also ceded the initiative to the Japanese, who then chose the time and location of hostilities so that China fought on Japan's, not China's, terms. In doing so, China became a co-operative adversary, in the sense that its actions played into its adversary's plays. So-called co-operative adversaries fail to leverage their strengths or target enemy vulnerabilities.

The engagements at Feng Island and Sŏnghwan were but preliminary skirmishes. The major battles in the Korean theater concentrated in a three-day period in mid-September at P'yŏngyang, and in the coastal waters off the Yalu, the boundary river between Korea and China. P'yŏngyang lay on the right bank of the Taedong river, which was deep enough to allow shipping from the Yellow Sea for efficient troop and supply transport. For almost two months, while the Japanese made the exhausting march to the battlefield in search of a Chinese army willing to stand and fight, the Chinese had prepared, reinforced, supplied, and massed. They had sent 13,000 men and their most modern equipment, and had accumulated the provisions to withstand a prolonged siege and to retake the peninsula.

While all the advantages seemed to belong to the Chinese, the real situation became less favorable once the battle began. The four Chinese armies at P'yŏngyang failed to co-ordinate. Apparently, they had no plans for a worst-case scenario – in the event that they could not hold in Korea at all. Comprehensive war plans contain branches and sequels anticipating different levels of operational success or failure. Chinese strategy seemed to mistake hope for strategy – they hoped that the worst case could not materialize. The Japanese war plan contained the branch to operational disaster with the sequel of homeland defense.

For the Japanese, the city of P'yŏngyang had tremendous symbolic importance, since it had been the northernmost point of advance by Toyotomi Hideyoshi's invading army in the sixteenth century. He was a national hero in Japan for ending a period of terrible civil wars and making possible the long peace under the Tokugawa shoguns, but in Korea his invasions laid waste to the peninsula and he remains among the most hated figures in that country's pantheon of foreign desecrators. The geography of P'yŏngyang made the city difficult to approach from the south or the east because of the Taedong river and the cliffs above it, but easier from the north, provided that the attacking army had successfully crossed the river, when it would risk annihilation. Focusing the attack on the north was a high-reward, high-risk strategy.

From 15 to 16 September, approximately 16,000 Japanese troops launched a three-pronged attack. The Japanese began in the pre-dawn hours of 15 September with an artillery barrage from the east aimed at the forts on the west bank of the Taedong in order to divert Chinese attention from the main attack, which would come from the north and the northwest. The Japanese also made a feint from the south. The Chinese put up one of their stiffest resistances of the war, but they committed a key error when they did not take advantage of the natural barrier created by the river. They did not attack the Japanese columns when most vulnerable during the river crossing, but waited behind static fortifications. These proved no match for modern artillery, which had greatly improved in the years since the Taiping and Nian Rebellions, the formative years for Li Hongzhang and his commanders. The Japanese got by despite remarkably poor logistics. Since they had no pontoon bridges, they had to scrounge up enough Korean riverboats to cross the river in secret. The night after the battle, Chinese forces fled.

The day after P'yŏngyang, the second major battle of the war took place. The Japanese fleet had been trying to engage a very reluctant Chinese fleet. It discovered the Northern Seas Squadron on the home voyage from convoy duty, headed to Lüshun, midway from the mouth of the Yalu river in the vicinity of Haiyang and Zhangzi Islands. There on 17 September, one of the two great naval battles of the war erupted.

Both Japan and China had modern navies ranking among the world's top ten. Chinese naval bases were nearer to the war theater, where China, not Japan, enjoyed interior lines of communication. The Chinese navy also possessed twice as many warships, the best two of which were superior in armaments and armor to any Japanese ship. Most of China's vessels, however, were out of date, built before 1887, while most of the Japanese ships had been built since 1890. Although the Chinese ships had better armor and heavy guns, the Japanese vessels had superior speed and quick-firing guns. The Northern Seas Squadron had neither standardized nor matched guns and ammunition.

China's four naval squadrons, naval academies, and arsenals remained the property of their province of origin and could not be counted on to supply other provinces in the event of hostilities. During the Sino-French War, Viceroy Li had ignored the call for aid from the Southern Seas Squadron, allowing France to take possession of Vietnam (Annam). The Southern Seas Squadron would return the favor during the First Sino-Japanese War by ignoring Viceroy Li's pleas for help.

The fighting was brutal. About ten major ships from each side participated. The Northern Seas Squadron tried to form a line abreast with the weakest vessels on the wings. Because of mixed signals and different speeds, the formation soon degenerated into an asymmetrical wedge shape, with the weaker vessels unable to keep up. The Japanese fleet assumed a column formation with the flying squadron out in front of the main squadron. The flying squadron had instructions to attack the right flank of the Chinese to annihilate the weak boats on the end of their formation. Upon seeing this, Admiral Ding Ruchang ordered his ships to change course from the line-abreast formation to a line-ahead-by-sections formation. This would have exposed his ship, the flagship, but put the rest of the squadron in a good position to fire on the Japanese fleet. Admiral Ding's immediate subordinate on the flagship, Commodore Liu Buchan, ignored the order to change formations. Before the Japanese fleet came in range, he had the main guns fire, demolishing the temporary flying bridge on which Admiral Ding was standing. The collapse of the flying bridge was a well-known consequence of firing straight ahead. Ding's leg was crushed, putting him out of action for the rest of the battle and leaving Liu in command.

According to Vice Admiral George A. Ballard of the British navy, China's battle formation was flawed from conception, since line abreast required the strongest, not the weakest, vessels on the wings in order to prevent the weakest from being picked off one at a time.[5] The Chinese then failed to change course to prevent the Japanese from going around their wing with each Japanese vessel delivering a full broadside at close range on the wing ships. This destroyed China's right wing while two boats on the left wing seized the opportunity to flee. The Japanese also destroyed the flagship's foremast, which ended communications among the Chinese fleet – the vital signals could not be hung from the missing foremast. In addition to defective tactics, the Chinese also had defective ordnance. The Japanese discovered, to their relief, that some of the Chinese shells were filled with cement and other non-explosive materials. At most such shells pierced. Catastrophic damage required exploding ordnance. Even worse, much ordnance was of the wrong caliber, making it impossible to fire.

Yet China still had some good cards to play. According to the U.S. Secretary of the Navy, Hilary A. Herbert, the Battle of the Yalu "was nearly a drawn battle." Although China lost four boats with an aggregate displacement of 7,580 tons while Japan lost none, "Most of the Japanese fleet had suffered severely." Had Chinese vessels been supplied with the proper ammunition – more exploding shells instead of armor-piercing shells – China might

---

[5] G.A. Ballard, *The Influence of the Sea on the Political History of Japan* (New York: E.P. Dutton, 1921), 147–51.

have carried the day.[6] Afterward, the Northern Seas Squadron still could have taken on the Japanese navy to interfere with its ongoing troop buildup on the Asian mainland. As Vice Admiral Ballard later pointed out, China's two main battleships, for which Japan had no counterparts, "should have been more than a match for the six best ships of the Japanese Navy."[7] The Japanese victory at the Battle of the Yalu shattered the morale of the Northern Seas Squadron, which never fought again on the open seas. Thus Japan gained the command of the sea so vital to its military operations.

Japan leveraged the Battle of P'yŏngyang and the Battle of the Yalu to emerge victorious in the media campaign to win friends abroad and at home. The Japanese government considered the battle for international elite public opinion to be a key theater in the war because Japan required foreign sympathies both to preclude foreign intervention on the side of China and to achieve the international recognition necessary to become a great power. Therefore it conveniently packaged war bulletins in Western languages so that foreign correspondents soon based their articles on Japan's crib sheets. As a result, the foreign press unintentionally highlighted the Japanese point of view. There were also difficult-to-verify allegations of Japanese bribery of Western journalists.

While the Japanese had little cause to lie because they were winning, Chinese commanders faced capital punishment for failure in the field. So they issued one falsehood after another detailing fictitious victories. It took the Chinese government months to understand the extent of the cover-up. Such blatant lying transformed the tenor of the international coverage, which originally had favored China. By war's end the Chinese government had won the derision of both the home and the international audiences.

Meanwhile, Japan earned respect at home and abroad. For the home audience, the Japanese military provided the details of the deaths of ordinary soldiers, who had performed extraordinary deeds. Each day the domestic press highlighted these war heroes, whose devoted service inspired a growing nationalism. Newspaper readership rapidly grew. Japanese from all backgrounds shared a growing common pride in the achievements of their country, which translated into support for the government and its new westernized institutions. The rapidity of the military's conquests and the success of the government's media campaign so far exceeded expectations that Japan's civil leaders could not easily limit the territorial objectives of its military commanders. The goals set by the military and demanded by the public grew in tandem with battlefield victories. Nationalism took on a life of its own.

---

[6] Hilary A. Herbert, "Military Lessons of the Chino-Japanese War," *The North American Review* 160, no. 463 (June 1895), 693–94.
[7] Ballard, *The Influence of the Sea on the Political History of Japan*, 134.

Without adequately considering the likely consequences, the Japanese military demanded and public expected expanded war goals from the limited objective of expelling China from a tributary state to invading China proper to unseat a dynasty. This would have left Japan in nominal control not only of Korea, but potentially of all China. Unseating the Qing dynasty would have affected the interests of virtually all the great powers. Diplomats in the Japanese Foreign Ministry saw that expanded objectives risked great-power intervention and argued for much more limited war aims. Their turn would come during the peace negotiations.

The Naval Balance: The Manchurian, Shandong, and Taiwan Campaigns

After the Korean campaign, Japan launched a succession of three others. The first two, the Manchuria and Shandong campaigns, focused on the land and sea approaches to Beijing, threatened a pincer movement on the capital, and eliminated Chinese naval power for over a century. The third, the Taiwan campaign, secured empire and coincided with the peace negotiations terminating the war.

After the Battle of P'yŏngyang, the Chinese did not make another stand until they crossed the Yalu back into China at Jiuliancheng. In doing so, they ceded all of north Korea without a fight, delivering to Japan its original operational objective within two months of the outbreak of hostilities. In the Manchurian campaign, plans called for clearing the way from the Korean border to the Liaodong peninsula to take the vital fortress and naval refitting station at China's main naval base at Lüshun, located at the end of the Liaodong peninsula on the northern shore of the Gulf of Bo Hai. Guarding the southern shores of the Bo Hai was China's second-most-important naval base at Weihaiwei on the northern coast of the Shandong peninsula. The latter would be the focus of the Shandong campaign. To deliver the *coup de grâce* to the Qing dynasty, the Japanese were organizing a Third Army at Hiroshima in anticipation of an amphibious landing at Dagu on the river approach to the capital. These were the evolving war plans of the Imperial Japanese Army, which prepared for the unlimited objective of overthrowing the Qing dynasty.

After the defeat at P'yŏngyang, Viceroy Li reorganized the army and put it under the command of seventy-four-year-old Song Qing, another veteran of the Taiping and Nian Rebellions. The Yalu river was deep and wide and so presented a formidable obstacle for the advancing Japanese army. Two fortified outposts faced each other from opposite banks of the river, Jiuliancheng on the Chinese side and Ŭiji on the Korean side. These became the headquarters for the opposing armies. General Song fortified the northern bank of the Yalu for seven miles to the south as far as Andong and for ten miles to the north to Hushan and beyond. Apparently he envisioned another static defense behind fortified positions. Twenty-eight thousand Chinese defended Jiuliancheng.

The Japanese had learned their lesson at P'yŏngyang and this time had made careful preparations to ford the river. On the night of 24 October, they erected a pontoon bridge at Ŭiji for their primary troops. Again the Chinese failed to perceive the river crossing as an opportunity to attack the Japanese at their most vulnerable. On 25 October the main assault began. Had the Chinese chosen to defend, they might have inflicted heavy casualties, but they fled the city during the night of 25–26 October. As usual, they left behind quantities of weapons and rice and, in doing so, provided commissariat and logistical services for the invading army.

One line of attack proceeded from Jiuliancheng to Fenghuangcheng, located thirty miles to the northwest, and from there pursued Chinese forces toward the vital Motian Pass (literally "Scrape-the-Skies Pass") in the direction of Liaoyang and Shenyang. The territory from Fenghuangcheng westward to Liaoyang was hilly and accessed by difficult roads, affording the Chinese an excellent opportunity to defend.

The other line of attack followed a northwestern arc in pursuit of fleeing Chinese forces. These two offensives combined at Lianshanguan, which fell on 12 November. Lianshanguan lay just to the east of the Motian Pass. This feint toward Shenyang pinned two Chinese armies, making them unavailable for the defense of Lüshun. A third First Army offensive proceeded from Jiuliancheng down the Yalu river, along the southern coast of the Liaodong peninsula as far as Dagushan, and then inland, recombining with the rest of the First Army for an attack on Haicheng, the gateway to the Manchurian plain.

While the Japanese First Army moved from the Yalu river westward across Manchuria in a feint toward Shenyang, the Second Army had responsibility for taking Lüshun, the crucial naval base on the Liaodong peninsula, which alone had the refitting facilities capable of repairing China's state-of-the-art navy. Without repairs, over time the Northern Seas Squadron would succumb to a Japanese naval strategy of attrition, if not sooner from a catastrophic naval defeat. Admiral Ding's instructions throughout the war remained to defend the Bo Hai coast from Weihaiwei to the Yalu river – in other words, to protect the Qing dynasty ensconced in Beijing. The Chinese never perceived Japan's navy or merchant marine as a critical vulnerability to be attacked.

The Chinese, including Li Hongzhang, did not understand the naval dimension of the war. They had bought the most capable ships money could buy, but they lacked the organizational structures and education to use them effectively. They had invested in things, not people. They had construed modernization narrowly in terms of technology and particularly military technology, failing to appreciate the extensive institutional, civilian, and human foundation required for modernization and laid by Japan through its westernizing reforms.

The Imperial Japanese Navy covered the landing of the Second Army, midway along the eastern coastline of the Liaodong peninsula. From there the army marched southward, traversing the peninsula along two routes. Jinzhou fell on 6 November and Dalian on 7 November, severing the peninsula at its narrow neck and cutting off Lüshun by land. The Chinese, in their haste to flee Dalian, left behind the plans for the minefields in the harbor as well as the plans for the defenses of Lüshun. This blunder greatly simplified the task of opening the harbor for Japanese vessels so that Dalian soon became a base to attack Lüshun.

General Nogi Maresuke, another veteran of the civil war bringing the Meiji generation to power, would take Lüshun twice in his career, once in the First Sino-Japanese War and again, at far greater cost, in the Russo-Japanese War a decade later. On 21 November, the main attack began. The Japanese lacked the proper grade and range of ammunition for their siege guns, so that the Chinese should have had a real advantage. The modern fortifications should have been very difficult to reduce since they were well situated, up to date, and amply supplied with modern equipment. Defense by land required co-ordination among the forts on the semicircle of hills surrounding the fortress. In the absence of this co-ordination, the Japanese picked off the forts one by one and turned the captured forts' artillery on the arsenal and dockyard. Chinese officials fled, their troops fought poorly, and once again they failed to destroy the fortifications or munitions before decamping. On 22 November, Lüshun fell to the Japanese with all the forts and abandoned dockyard in working order. The coal supplies left behind soon powered Japanese naval vessels for their attack on Weihaiwei.

One event marred the Japanese victory at Lüshun. On 18 November, the decapitated heads of fallen comrades, surmounting the arch over the main street, greeted the Japanese forces entering Lüshun. Throughout the war, the Japanese had encountered many equally mutilated bodies, but until Lüshun they had not taken revenge in front of Western correspondents, who soon reported a five-day orgy of killing by uniformed Japanese soldiers taking the lives of unarmed men, women, and children, many of whom begged in vain for mercy. The Japanese Foreign Ministry deftly responded by announcing an immediate official investigation. The Japanese military soon promised an inquiry, which, after much ado, punished no one. By then Western attention had shifted to the peace terms.

With the conquest of Lüshun, unity between the Japanese diplomats and military leaders fractured. Eight days later, on 29 November, Prime Minister Itō Hirobumi arranged to have the emperor relieve General Yamagata Aritomo of his command, allegedly for medical reasons. In reality, General Yamagata favored a march on Beijing, which Prime Minister Itō predicted would backfire by triggering the collapse of the Qing dynasty and possible civil war. This would lead rapidly to Western intervention; "Should that happen," Itō warned, "Japan would be negotiating peace not with China but with the Western powers."[8] The civil leadership feared that if Yamagata remained in the field, he would defy orders and march on Beijing regardless (as future officers would do in the 1930s).

Prime Minister Itō's victory over General Yamagata ushered in a complete change in strategy, with emphasis on naval strategy. The ongoing Japanese military successes demonstrated the importance of sea power. Without command of the sea, Japan could not have deployed its troops at will or supplied its armies. Therefore a critical war objective became the long-term neutralization of Chinese sea power so that China could never interfere with Japan's vital sea lines of communication – vital in wartime to project military power and vital in peacetime to engage in international commerce. Beijing would no longer be the objective. Instead, the Second Army would take the Northern Seas Squadron's remaining naval base, Weihaiwei. This would not threaten Beijing directly, but it would allow Japan to destroy the fleet. Without a navy to project power, China would become a bit player in regional politics while Japan became the dominant regional naval power.

After taking Lüshun, the Japanese Second Army started to double back along the western coast of the Liaodong peninsula to take Fuzhou on 19 December 1894 and Gaiping on 10 January 1895. The Japanese victory resulted in a continuous line of their troops stretching from Gaiping on the western coast of the Liaodong peninsula northeast toward Haicheng and then eastward back to the Korean border at Jiuliancheng. The Japanese refused the Chinese request for a cease-fire.

Haicheng was the most bitterly contested city of the war. After it fell on 13 December 1894, the Chinese launched a succession of five unsuccessful counterattacks to regain it between 17 January and 27 February 1895. The city sat at a very strategic crossroads connecting the capital, the important treaty port of Niuzhuang (also known as Newchwang), and the cities of Shenyang and Liaoyang, located in the valley formed by the Hun and Liao rivers. Haicheng gave Japan access to the Manchurian plain via a pass through the Qian mountains that ran northeast from the top of the Liaodong peninsula into the mountain chains all along the Korean border. Taking Haicheng enabled the Japanese to link land communications between their First Army in eastern Manchuria and the Second Army in southern Manchuria, while simultaneously cutting off the Chinese in three directions and leaving them only a westward line of retreat toward the sea, where the Japanese could easily deploy in force.

---

[8] Edward I-te Chen, "Japan's Decision to Annex Taiwan: A Study of Itō-Mutsu Diplomacy, 1894–95," *Journal of Asian Studies* 37, no. 1 (Nov. 1977), 68.

Back in early November, Li Hongzhang had ordered the Northern Seas Squadron to depart for Weihaiwei, rather than to defend the naval base at Lüshun. Whereas at Lüshun Japan's operational goal had been the capture and retention of the naval facilities for their present and future use, at Weihaiwei the goal would be the destruction of the Northern Seas Squadron.

In January 1895, as the Japanese continued their march from the Korean border through Manchuria toward Beijing, they prepared for a joint (army–navy) attack on Weihaiwei, where the Northern Seas Squadron sat in port. The Second Army divided its forces to make a feint to the west of Weihaiwei at Dengzhou, while the main force landed to the east at Rongcheng, a hamlet on the tip of the Shandong peninsula. The disposition of Chinese forces defending Weihaiwei anticipated an attack from the direction of Dengzhou. While Admiral Ding had closed the harbor with booms to prevent any unwelcome visitors, the Japanese then laid contact torpedoes and patrolled the entrance to prevent any unwelcome escapes. This left the Northern Seas Squadron bottled up in port, incapable of making either an effective offense or defense. The Chinese defensive strategy assumed a futile Japanese naval attack on the heavily defended harbor. General Ōyama Iwao, commander of the Japanese land forces, and Admiral Itō Yūkō, commander of the Combined Fleet, had other plans. They intended to take the naval base by land, as they had done at Lüshun.

After the successful landing at Rongcheng between 20 and 23 January, Japanese forces converged on Weihaiwei. Despite the bitterly cold weather and snow-covered ground, they launched a three-pronged attack on 30 January 1895, and soon took the main forts to the south and east of Weihaiwei. The next day they attacked the forts in the immediate vicinity of the city, shattering Chinese morale. When the Japanese entered the city on 2 February, they found the garrisons abandoned. Although Admiral Ding succeeded in destroying some of the forts surrounding the harbor, the Japanese took the majority and soon trained the repairable guns on the remaining Chinese positions and on the fleet trapped in the harbor. Beginning on the night of 3 February, the Japanese navy began infiltrating torpedo boats into the harbor to pick off ships. When the army and navy launched their joint attack on 7 February, the fifteen seaworthy Chinese torpedo boats mutinied and unsuccessfully tried to run the blockade. Only one escaped. On 12 February Weihaiwei fell and Admiral Ding committed suicide. Soon after the battle, the Chinese government closed the Admiralty Board since it no longer possessed a navy.

Following the fall of Weihaiwei, in the latter half of February, the Chinese launched their fourth and fifth fruitless counterattacks to retake Haicheng. In early March, three Chinese armies massed to the north of Niuzhuang. Facing them were two Japanese armies: the First Army near Haicheng and the Second Army near Gaiping. Japan's First Army began by attacking Anshan not far southwest of Liaoyang on 2 March, before turning southward to the Liao river treaty port of Niuzhuang. The fighting at Anshan was reported to be some of the stiffest of the war and the number of troops engaged was large. The Chinese succumbed only when the Japanese used mountain guns to hit a powder magazine, creating an enormous explosion in the city. The foreign settlement at Niuzhuang fell to the Japanese on 5 March. The First Army then continued southward downriver taking Tianzhuangtai on 9 March. Meanwhile, on 7 March the Japanese Second Army took Yingkou, where the Liao river meets the sea. Soon the two Japanese armies converged. The fighting in Manchuria ended when the defeated Chinese forces under General Song retreated across the Liao river.

War Termination

Immediately after the fall of Lüshun, Li Hongzhang had approached the Japanese in the hopes of ending the war, but he did so without official authorization from the central government and the Japanese soon rejected the mission. After the fall of Haicheng, the Chinese government began organizing a second mission. It arrived in Hiroshima on 31 January 1895; that is, after the fall of Gaiping, after the first two failed counterattacks to retake Haicheng, and after the Japanese had launched the Shandong campaign to take Weihaiwei. When the Japanese discovered that the delegates lacked full authority to negotiate, they sent the Chinese envoys home two days after their arrival. The following day, Japanese troops entered Weihaiwei and closed in on the Northern Seas Squadron trapped in the harbor.

With the fall of Weihaiwei and the destruction of the Northern Seas Squadron, the Japanese threatened to continue toward the capital in order to force the Qing court to settle the war on Japanese terms. The Manchus appointed Viceroy Li Hongzhang, complete with the proper credentials. On 19 March 1895 China's great modernizer arrived in the southern port of Shimonoseki. His counterpart, Prime Minister Itō Hirobumi, later described these negotiations as the most difficult of his life, a testament to Viceroy Li's enormous diplomatic skill. China requested an immediate armistice. Japan refused, preferring to keep up the military pressure to ensure a favorable peace settlement. In the expanding list of Japanese objectives, Taiwan had attracted attention, particularly that of the Imperial Japanese Navy, which had a maritime vision for the future empire.

On 15 March, the Imperial Japanese Navy had sortied from its base at Sasebo. Admiral Itō Yūkō commanded seven ships and five transports with three battalions totaling approximately 2,800 soldiers. On 20 March, the day after Viceroy Li had landed at Shimonoseki, the fleet anchored at Bazhao, one of the southernmost islands of the Pescadore (Penghu) archipelago. The Pescadores lie at the southern end of the Taiwan Strait, which separates Fujian province on the Chinese mainland from the island of Taiwan. On 23 March, the Japanese fleet bombarded the coastal fortifications on the central island group and landed troops on the main island of Penghu, taking the primary fortress the following day.

On 24 March, when Viceroy Li left the negotiations to return to his lodgings, a Japanese youth, Koyama Toyotarō, approached his palanquin and shot him in the face, just below his left eye, appalling Japanese leaders with the security breach. The Meiji Emperor made a previously unthinkable offer. He granted a three-week armistice. The assassination attempt muted the cries for a march on Beijing. The fine print of the agreement made the armistice partial, not general: It would apply to mainland China but not to the Pescadores or Taiwan. On 30 March, just six days after the assassination attempt, the Pescadores fell. The archipelago had little to offer economically, but its possession provided the base from which to neutralize any attempts by China's remaining fleets to interfere with Japanese plans for Taiwan.

Despite the severity of the wound, within two and a half weeks Li Hongzhang returned to the negotiating table on 10 April. One week later, on 17 April 1895, and after much haggling, he and Prime Minister Itō signed a peace agreement, the Treaty of Shimonoseki. Its central provisions were: (1) Chinese abandonment of claims to suzerainty over Korea; (2) Chinese cession to Japan of Taiwan, the Pescadore islands, and the Liaodong peninsula; (3) Chinese payment to Japan of an indemnity of 200 million Kuping taels; (4) a temporary Japanese occupation of Weihaiwei and a temporary Japanese lien on Chinese customs revenues to insure payment of the indemnity; and (5) various ameliorations of Japanese trading conditions in China. The Chinese and Japanese exchanged treaties on schedule at Yantai on 8 May.

On 21 July 1896, signature of the new commercial treaty demanded by Japan formally ended the era of reciprocal relations between China and Japan. The treaty accorded Japan most-favored-nation treatment in China and consular jurisdiction. China did not receive similar privileges in Japan. Japan had transformed itself from the object of imperialism into one of the perpetrators by imposing its own unequal treaty.

The war produced both intended and unintended outcomes. Japan achieved its primary objectives. Operationally, it defeated the Chinese in every battle, occupied Korea, and eliminated China's modern navy. The destruction of the Northern Seas Squadron and the high indemnity precluded China's reconstitution of the fleet. Japanese leaders intended to eliminate Chinese naval power and succeeded beyond their wildest dreams. Few powers have great navies, because of their enormous cost. Postwar China could no longer afford to buy a new one. Only in the 1990s did China start rebuilding the blue-water fleet that it lost in the First Sino-Japanese War.

Strategically, the war overturned the long-standing East Asian balance of power, toppling China from its position of primacy and leaving Japan dominant – another intended outcome. In doing so, Japan became the only non-Western great power. While others have aspired, even today over a century later, the Japanese alone among non-Western countries have the aggregate gross national product and per-capita standard of living of a great power. For Japan, these were intended and expected outcomes.

Other outcomes were unintended, although an average imagination might have anticipated some of them, most notably the Triple Intervention, Sino-Japanese animosity, and a Russo-Japanese arms race. Carl von Clausewitz developed the term "culminating point of victory," meaning the point of maximal winnings, the point which, if exceeded, weakens, not strengthens; the point where, if it is not reached, some of the attainable is not attained.[9] If China exceeded its culminating point of defeat by failing to settle before it lost its fleet, Japan exceeded its own culminating point of victory by demanding the cession of the Liaodong peninsula. Although the Japanese military correctly predicted that China could not dispute this demand militarily, Japanese diplomats correctly predicted that Russia would weigh in on the side of China both politically and militarily. Russia had repeatedly warned that it would not tolerate a Japanese concession area in Manchuria.

While Japan could fight China to a standstill, it could not necessarily take on a major European power, let alone a combination of several. Therefore the Japanese Foreign Ministry made every effort to forestall foreign intervention. Days before the outbreak of war, Japan notified Britain that Shanghai would be outside the sphere of hostilities. This was a costly decision because the city had China's main arsenal and supplied munitions for the duration of the war. But Shanghai was also a key center of British commerce, which the Japanese did not want to disrupt. Lawyers with expertise in international law accompanied each Japanese army and fleet to prevent any international missteps. As Foreign Minister Mutsu Munemitsu wrote afterward, "As both we and the Chinese were seeking the sympathy of the Western powers for our respective positions, we deemed it prudent to avoid any Japanese action which might alienate foreigners and cause them to align themselves against us."[10] The Japanese Foreign Ministry understood that the public perceptions of the great powers constituted a key battlefield.

---

[9] Carl von Clausewitz, *On War*, ed. and trans. Michael Howard and Peter Paret (Princeton: Princeton University Press, 1984), Book 7, chapter 22, "The Culminating Point of Victory."

[10] Mutsu Munemitsu, *Kenkenryoku: A Diplomatic Record of the Sino-Japanese War, 1894–95*, trans. Gordon Mark Berger (Princeton: Princeton University Press, 1982), 66.

The Japanese military became intoxicated by its operational success and oblivious to the possibility, let alone the likely consequences, of a third-party intervention on the Chinese side. On 23 April 1895, six days after the treaty signing, the ministers of Russia, Germany, and France called on the Japanese Foreign Ministry to offer some "friendly advice." They recommended that Japan return the Liaodong peninsula to China on the grounds that its possession by Japan "would be a constant menace to the capital of China, would at the same time render illusory the independence of Korea, and would henceforth be a perpetual obstacle to the peace in the Far East."[11]

Although Russia had concrete economic and security interests in Northeast Asia, Germany and France did not. Wilhelm II of Germany had great-power ambitions in Europe that later landed him in World War I. In the meantime, he hoped to embroil Russia in East Asia to keep it out of Germany's way in Europe. A prior alliance with Russia pulled France into the intervention. French weakness relative to Germany and French revanchism concerning Alsace–Lorraine, the territory lost to Germany during the Franco-Prussian War, made the Russo-French alliance the cornerstone of French security. France felt compelled to follow Russia's lead in East Asia or jeopardize the alliance.

Should the powers intervene militarily, Japanese diplomats understood that the Treaty of Shimonoseki would become a dead letter, forfeiting not only the Liaodong peninsula but also all of its other provisions. Therefore, on 10 May the Meiji Emperor made a public-relations appearance to portray the retrocession of the Liaodong peninsula as an act of magnanimity.

For the returned territory, China agreed to pay Japan an additional indemnity of 30 million Kuping taels. The Russians pressured China into demanding the removal of a clause pledging that China would not cede the Liaodong peninsula to any other power, correctly interpreting the clause as aimed at them. The Japanese conceded the point, much to their regret three years later when Russia took the territory for itself. Chinese and Japanese representatives signed the retrocession agreement in Beijing on 8 November 1895, and the Japanese completed their evacuation on 25 December 1895.

In addition to the Triple Intervention, the Japanese might have foreseen a legacy of Chinese bitterness. Negotiations for the return of the Liaodong peninsula coincided with the Japanese campaign to subdue Taiwan. Although the Chinese government had agreed to cede Taiwan, the Taiwanese had not agreed to be ceded. On 23 May 1895, two weeks after the ratification of the Treaty of Shimonoseki, Taiwanese leaders proclaimed the independent Republic of Taiwan under the presidency of General Tang Jingsong, then acting provincial governor. In a prior posting, Tang had been deeply involved in China's unsuccessful strategy in the Sino-French War.

---

[11] Mutsu, *Kenkenryoku*, 203.

Japan responded to the declaration of independence by landing troops east of Jilong (Keelung) on the northern coast of Taiwan on 29 May. These forces were under the command of Imperial Prince Kitashirakawa-no-miya Yoshihisa and his subordinate, General Takashima Tomonosuke. Prince Kitashirakawa had been a contender for the Japanese throne during the civil war overthrowing the Tokugawa shogunate. His death from malaria near Tainan made him the first imperial-family wartime fatality in modern times.

Within a fortnight of the Japanese deployments, President Tang fled Taiwan, leaving the government in the control of his most senior general, Liu Yongfu, another veteran of the failed Sino-French War and a former bandit from the Guangdong border with Tonkin (North Vietnam), later an immigrant of necessity to Taiwan, and a close friend of the fleeing president. Liu's forces came mainly from the south China provinces of Fujian, Guangxi, and Guangdong, whence they had fled a decade prior after their defeat by France. Taiwan's indigenous non-Han population, who lived in the mountains, however, despised these recent immigrants and many aided the Japanese conquest.

On 3 June, the day after China officially turned over Taiwan to Japan, Japanese troops occupied Jilong, and then Taipei on 7 June. Control over the ports of Jilong and Danshui (the port city to Taipei) gave the Japanese bases for operations. It took five months for Japan to subdue formal resistance in Taiwan. After the initial disembarkations in the north in late May, the Japanese deployed troops several months later in the south at Anping. This allowed an occupation of the broad western coastal plain from two directions. With the occupation of Tainan on 21 October 1895, Japan eliminated organized resistance, took 7,000 prisoners, and overthrew the short-lived Republic of Taiwan. General Liu fled to China. Afterward an insurgency continued. During December 1895 and January 1896, uprisings in many areas required the deployment of Japanese reinforcements.

Before too long the local population in Taiwan appreciated the stability and economic development brought by Japanese rule in contrast to the half-century of civil war soon to begin in China. The Chinese, however, became increasingly embittered by the loss of their island. During the negotiations for the Treaty of Shimonoseki, Viceroy Li prophetically warned,

it is part of wise statesmanship, to negotiate such a peace as will make true friends and allies of these two great nations of the Orient, who are and must remain neighbours, and who have in common so many things in their history, literature, art and commerce ... Nothing will so arouse the indignation of the people of China and create in them a spirit of undying hostility and hatred, as to wrest from their country important portions of their territory.[12]

---

[12] Morinosuke Kajima, *The Diplomacy of Japan 1894–1922*, vol. 1 (Tokyo: Kajima Institute of International Peace, 1976), 223–31.

Prior to the Meiji Restoration and the First Sino-Japanese War, Sino-Japanese relations had been comparatively harmonious. The Japanese had emulated many Chinese institutions and admired Chinese cultural achievements. The war replaced old sentiments of respect and friendship with new feelings of anger and contempt. Japan's rejection of sinification for westernization shattered bedrock Chinese assumptions concerning the unwavering direction of history toward Confucianism. A century on, they still have not recovered from the humiliation of defeat and destruction of the Confucian world order they had promoted so successfully for so long. The Japanese reciprocated with contempt for a people who declined to join the modern world or to defend their homeland competently. Sino-Japanese relations began a long downward spiral from which, over a century later, neither country has emerged.

Not only were the Triple Intervention and Sino-Japanese animosity predictable, even if unintended, outcomes of the war, so was a postwar Russo-Japanese arms race. Japan had fought the war to contain Russian expansion, but the war's outcome had alerted the Russians to the need to contain Japanese expansion. Leaders in each country concluded that the containment of the other required a military buildup. The imperative for military strength to defend Japan's independence and future prosperity became the overwhelming lesson from the war drawn by civil and military leaders alike. A major rearmament program began with the integration of twelve captured Chinese warships into the Imperial Japanese Navy, increasing its tonnage by about one-quarter. The Japanese government then used China's indemnity to bankroll a huge rearmament program. In 1920, the Japanese Ministry of Finance estimated that the war had cost Japan less than two-thirds the final value of the indemnity, leaving funds for rearmament.[13] In November 1895, the Cabinet submitted a budget request to the Diet, raising the army's budget from 10 million to over 53 million yen and increasing its share of the national budget from 10.5 to over 30 percent. The Diet approved the measure, in marked contrast to its prewar obstructionist attitude toward military appropriations.[14]

The Japanese government planned to double the strength of the army from six to twelve divisions by 1903, increasing the peacetime army from 70,000 to 150,000 men and wartime numbers from 275,000 to 550,000 men. It also planned to quadruple the fleet to equal that of Italy or Germany and superior to that of any other navy in East Asia, including Russia's Far Eastern Fleet. The entire army and naval expansion and military-related infrastructure were to be funded over a ten-year period ending in 1906.[15]

---

[13] Giichi Ono, *Expenditures of the Sino-Japanese War* (New York: Oxford University Press, 1922), 36, 119.
[14] Paine, *The First Sino-Japanese War*, 327.
[15] Paine, *The First Sino-Japanese War*, 327.

In foreign relations, as in human relations generally, the actions of one side do not usually go unanswered. Appropriations for the Russian army, which from 1890 to 1894 had averaged 261 million rubles, would increase to an average of 302 million for the 1895–97 period. Between 1895 and 1899, Tsar Nicholas II began building up his fleet. In 1900, he authorized the construction of a Pacific fleet 30 percent stronger than that of Japan. The 1894 Russian fleet of 225,000 tons was to be tripled to 680,000 tons by 1907. An East Asian arms race was on.[16]

The Implications

Few would question that operational defeat has strategic implications, but pivotal wars – the wars that historians retrospectively say divide eras – have social, political, and economic consequences that no one ever imagined even in their most delirious moments. In addition to intended and unintended but predictable outcomes, the war had implications that no one intended or could possibly have foreseen, and these outcomes were by far the most consequential. The First Sino-Japanese War profoundly altered the domestic orders in both Japan and China, and left problems of regional instability that are with us over a century later.

The civil and naval leaders of the Meiji generation, unlike army leaders then and especially those of the next generation, understood the strategic ramifications of sea power. China's loss of its navy at Weihaiwei had strategic repercussions that affected the Chinese for generations. Navies are mostly invisible – either concentrated in naval bases or far out to sea. They often focus on preventing undesirable outcomes: deterring another power from disrupting trade or landing troops on home shores. Such functions generally go unnoticed when deterrence succeeds. Once the fleet is gone, troubles multiply. After the loss of the First Sino-Japanese War, the naval powers pounced on China in the scramble for concessions, which China could do little to stop.

Viceroy Li had secured foreign assistance in the Triple Intervention but at the unintended price of a postwar scramble for concessions. The uninterrupted battlefield losses eroded the legitimacy of the government internationally. The conduct and outcome of the war drove the foreign powers to conclude that the Manchu government was incapable of reform and, therefore, that protection of their financial interests required their assumption of the administrative

---

[16] Peter Gatrell, *Government, Industry and Rearmament in Russia, 1900–1914: The Last Argument of Tsarism* (Cambridge: Cambridge University Press, 1994), 21–24; Harold Perry Ford, "Russian Far Eastern Diplomacy, Count Witte, and the Penetration of China, 1895–1904" (Ph.D. diss., University of Chicago, 1950), 232.

responsibilities that the Qing had proven to be incapable of performing. Between 1895 and 1899, the great powers carved up China into a welter of spheres of influence. In June 1895 France established its sphere in Yunnan, Guangxi, and Guangdong, the provinces bordering on its colony in Tonkin (Vietnam). In 1897 Germany appropriated a section of Shandong province. In 1898 Britain put in its dibs for the Yangzi river valley.

Russia collected the most of all on 3 June 1896. After numerous threats and ultimatums, the Qing government signed a secret treaty of alliance whereby Russia agreed to protect China from Japan in return for a huge railway concession through Manchuria to complete the Trans-Siberian Railway. It comprised over 1,000 miles of track, built not in the narrow gauge used in China but in the wide gauge used in Russia, and made Russia the largest concession holder in China. Thus the long eastern section of the Trans-Siberian Railway was not Siberian at all, but Manchurian. Russia would not build the Siberian section until after it lost the Russo-Japanese War.

On 27 March 1898, Russia acquired a twenty-five-year lease for the Liaodong peninsula, the very lease that China had secured its alliance with Russia to protect. Russia also added a railway concession to connect the Liaodong peninsula's warm-water ports of Dalian and Lüshun to its trans-Manchurian railway system at Harbin, adding another 709 miles of track. After Russia took Lüshun on the northern shores of the Bo Hai, Britain responded on 5 October 1898 by taking Weihaiwei on the southern shores. Thus Russia and Great Britain became the sentinels on the sea approaches to Beijing. Most concessions remained in foreign hands until the 1940s, and Russia's until the 1950s.

Japan, whose military victory had made this postwar feeding frenzy possible, was the last to demand a slice of China proper. In 1898 it acquired a non-alienation agreement for Fujian, the mainland province opposite Taiwan, and a concession in Shashi, Hubei on the Yangzi river. This had been one of the cities that Japan had included in its original demands during the negotiations at Shimonoseki but had subsequently deleted.

The concession areas hamstrung Chinese foreign policy for the next two generations and undermined the power, authority, and legitimacy of the Qing dynasty. The large indemnity to Japan precluded the breathing space and financial wherewithal to fund the military programs necessary to protect China from either Russia or Japan, let alone both. The indemnity exceeded half of China's first government budget of 1911. The missed window of opportunity to use its navy when it had one during the First Sino-Japanese War never reopened. In 1911, the dynasty lost its struggle to remain on the throne in the Xinhai Revolution. It took China over a century to put its house back in order and the process remains incomplete.

The two-China problem of the early twenty-first century was born with Taiwan's transfer from the Qing to the Japanese empire. From 1895 onward

Taiwanese political, economic, and social development diverged from the rest of China's but mainlanders never accepted the island's loss. A century later, a Chinese war to retake Taiwan remained a possibility. Likewise, Korea remained a center of discontent and regional instability. For Koreans, the First Sino-Japanese War marked the beginning of a highly traumatic period of imperial Japanese rule followed by a vicious civil war, the Korean War (1950–53), which left a divided peninsula. A century after the First Sino-Japanese War, a North Korean attack on South Korea or Japan remained a possibility.

The war also profoundly altered the domestic politics of Japan. The war legitimized the controversial westernizing reforms because the Meiji government had delivered in two crucial areas – treaty revision and military victory – and together these transformed Japan into an internationally recognized power. The Japanese people rejoiced in their victory over China and derived a strong sense of national unity from their foreign successes. Nationalism would become the cement holding together Japan's factionalized politics. The war strengthened Shintoism, which accorded the emperor divine status, and which, when fused with nationalism and militarism, soon became Japan's martial ideology.

The intense nationalism eased two fissures – those between the Cabinet and the Diet, and public and government, which now agreed on a nationalistic foreign-policy agenda – but it created a new one in their stead within the government between civil and military authority. The war shifted the internal balance of power from civil to military institutions. Japanese public hostility over the return of the Liaodong peninsula soon turned from the three intervening foreign powers to the Japanese government for its acquiescence. A general feeling grew that the military had won the war but the diplomats had lost the peace. The Japanese press drew unfavorable comparisons between the heroism of the military and the backpedaling of the diplomats. According to Foreign Minister Mutsu, "Soon the air was filled with charges that the fruits of victory gained on the battlefield had now been lost at the negotiating table."[17] Political parties agitated to bring down the Itō Cabinet and succeeded on 18 September 1896.

Victory in the field greatly increased the prestige of the armed forces at the expense of the diplomats. Immediately after the war, Japanese military officers were already freelancing in Korea without the benefit of civilian input. The Koreans realized that the Triple Intervention signaled the end of undisputed Japanese ascendancy in their country and their political allegiances shifted accordingly. The war, ostensibly fought to save Koreans from outsiders, rekindled their historical hatred of the Japanese. The Korean monarchy sought out great powers to counterbalance Japan's growing influence. The powerful

[17] Mutsu, *Kenkenryoku*, 249.

consort, Queen Min, chose Russia and rapidly purged Japanese sympathizers from the government.

The Japanese government responded by replacing its minister to Korea with Lieutenant General Miura Gorō, who promptly began planning Queen Min's demise. Apparently, he and members of the military believed that they could succeed in Korea where the diplomats had failed. He had her murdered on 8 October 1895 – to the enduring outrage of the Korean people. Her consort, King Kojong, soon fled to the safety of the Russian Legation and fired his pro-Japanese ministers shortly thereafter, and the Japanese reform movement in Korea came to an end – not the outcome anticipated by General Miura. His afternoon of dabbling in Korean dynastic politics undermined Japanese interests in the near term and contributed to the poisoning of Korean–Japanese relations in the long term. He saw the ease of assassination, not the far-reaching strategic consequences of murdering the consort of a foreign monarch. Two weeks to the day after the assassination, foreign outrage compelled Japan to recall Miura for trial, where, after much ado, he was acquitted.

The First Sino-Japanese War overturned the East Asian balance of power. When Japan rapidly defeated China militarily, this not only proved that China no longer dominated but also shattered the Confucian world order. Japan's victory disproved the underlying assumptions of Confucianism, that sinification was a one-way street, that the world accommodated only one civilization, and that Chinese civilization was superior to all others. The Japanese had rejected sinification for westernization and had applied the newly acquired concepts to defeat China on the field of battle. Whereas the Western victories over China could be written off as weird barbarian aberrations, Japan's victory could not. Japan's victory shattered the Confucian bedrock of Chinese civilization and the Chinese have yet to find a replacement. When the Chinese entered the First Sino-Japanese War, they could not have imagined that their ancient framework for ordering domestic and foreign relations would collapse as a result. Thus pivotal wars can have unanticipated – and indeed unimaginable – consequences on the domestic orders of the defeated and the victor alike. Afterward, there is no going back to how things were.

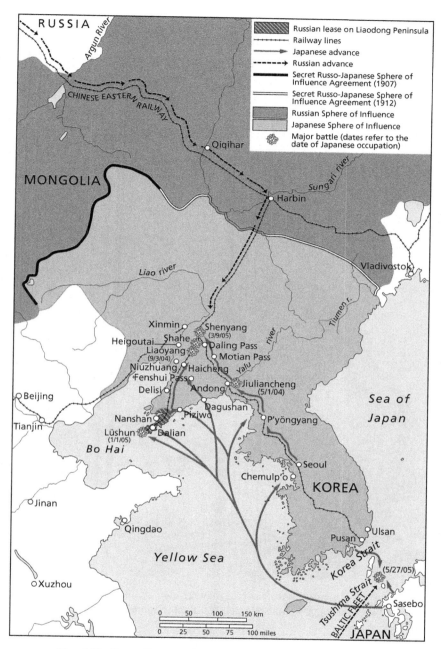

Map 3 The Russo-Japanese War

Photo 2 Yamagata Aritomo (1838–1922)
www.ndl.go.jp/portrait/e/datas/208_1.html (National Diet Library, Japan)

3   The Russo-Japanese War (1904–1905)

> It is certain that the situation in Asia will grow steadily worse in the future ... and we must make preparations for another war within the next ten years.[1]
>
> General Yamagata Aritomo, April 1895, at the end
of the First Sino-Japanese War
>
> In less than twenty years Japan has acquired the knowledge it has taken us centuries to learn.[2]
>
> George H. Rittner, *Impressions of Japan*, 1904, on the
eve of the Russo-Japanese War

At the end of the First Sino-Japanese War, General and soon-to-be Field Marshal Yamagata Aritomo, chief architect of the Japanese war plans, predicted another war over northeastern Asia within the decade. Although Yamagata could not have anticipated the precise circumstances of the Boxer Uprising in China, the Russo-Japanese War came right on schedule. The Boxers were the terrorists of their day. Their revulsion against Western culture and outrage at Western intrusions in their homeland coalesced into a movement to expel all Westerners from China and to kill the stragglers. As part of their rebellion, they tore up much of the Manchurian railway system laid at such great expense by Russia. To defend its investments, in 1900 Russia occupied all of Manchuria, the very area that Japan intended to become the core of its empire. Yamagata also could not have anticipated the Russian failure to honor its international commitments to withdraw these troops once order had been restored, but he clearly foresaw the general outlines of Russian and Japanese foreign policy that put them on a collision course. At issue: which empire would dominate Korea and Manchuria?

Yamagata also could not have anticipated that the young tsar, who assumed the throne upon the sudden death of his forty-nine-year-old father in 1894, would become captivated by the idea of empire in the Orient as the path to

---

[1] Quoted in Roger F. Hackett, *Yamagata Aritomo in the Rise of Modern Japan, 1838–1922* (Cambridge, MA: Harvard University Press, 1971), 163–64.
[2] George H. Rittner, *Impression of Japan* (New York: James Pott & Co., 1904), 142–43.

greatness or that a group of irresponsible noblemen with ambitious but unlikely plans to make money in the East would successfully brief the plan to the impressionable twenty-six-year-old Nicholas II. The irresponsible noblemen had a passion for redundant timber concessions along the Yalu river, in precisely the territory deemed vital by Japan's leaders for their country's national security. Russia, forested from East and West, had no need for more wood, let alone more wood in inaccessible locations.

The Russo-Japanese War would be waged on an unprecedented scale and with unprecedented lethality, both hallmarks of the industrial age. The largest prior Russian engagement had been the Battle of Borodino at the height of the Napoleonic Wars in 1812 when 250,000 combatants had clashed. The numbers at the battles of Liaoyang, Shahe, and Shenyang were 460,000, 580,000, and 620,000 respectively.[3] They anticipated the casualty rates of World War I, something that neither belligerent imagined before, during, or after the war. The Russo-Japanese War reinforced Japan's false and enduring lessons from the First Sino-Japanese War that the generals won the battles and the civilians lost the peace, and that military power alone was sufficient to achieve political objectives.

Underlying and Proximate Causes within a Window of Opportunity

The most fundamental underlying cause of the Russo-Japanese War was a zero-sum competition for empire in Northeast Asia. Just as Japan's leaders believed they required an empire to prosper, so did Russia's. Russia directly threatened Japan's ambitions by coveting the very areas in Northeast Asia deemed central for Japan's imperial plans.

Ever since the Industrial Revolution, the gap between Russian and Western European standards of living had grown. Not only was there a yawning economic gap, but there was also a yawning political gap. When Nicholas II acceded to the throne in 1894, Russia, Turkey, and Montenegro remained the only European states without a parliament. Russia could be classified as a great power not because of its economic or political achievements, but only because of its territorial extent and large standing army to garrison the empire and threaten smaller neighbors. Manchuria became important to the young tsar as an area to extend the empire and thereby to demonstrate his and his country's greatness, and to legitimate autocratic rule.

The First Sino-Japanese War had alerted Russia to a rising power on its least defensible frontier. The ensuing Russo-Japanese arms race only heightened

---

[3] Felix Patrikeeff and Harold Shukman, *Railways and the Russo-Japanese War: Transporting War* (London: Routledge, 2007), 116.

tensions. The war had made Japan an internationally recognized great power and an empire with the acquisition of Taiwan and the Pescadores, had cemented popular loyalties to the new westernized institutions (the army most particularly), and had even earned Japan a profit to pay for a postwar rearmament plan. Thus war had proved to be a highly effective means to achieve political goals. What had worked once should be tried again. This was the second underlying cause of the Russo-Japanese War.

In 1896, immediately after the First Sino-Japanese War, General Yamagata had offered to divide the two countries' respective spheres of influence in Korea along the 38th parallel (a parallel that would become the dividing line half a century later in the Korean War), but the Russians did not want to forgo warm-water ports in the south. In 1898, right after the Russian occupation of Lüshun, the Russians had dismissed a second Japanese request to delineate spheres of influence.

From the Japanese point of view, the problem became acute during the Boxer Uprising (1899–1900) when Russia had invaded Manchuria. In response to the scramble for concessions after the First Sino-Japanese War, the Boxers tried to expel the foreign imperialists from China. In Manchuria, they damaged two-thirds of Russia's railway lines, which had cost the Russian government one-quarter of its budget for a three-year period. The Russian government, given its great-power pretensions essential for continued tsarist rule, would not brook being driven out of Manchuria by Boxer irregulars and so invaded en masse.[4]

From 1900 to 1902 Japanese diplomats had unsuccessfully approached their Russian counterparts with a variety of proposals to delimit spheres of influence that went nowhere. Russia was too busy administering Manchuria, where it had deployed 100,000 troops starting in July 1900 and within three months had occupied its entirety, which exceeded the size of France and Germany combined. Included was the treaty port of Niuzhuang, the major port of entry for Japanese goods, where Russia had taken over the collection of customs even though its own trade was insignificant. Japanese diplomats again approached their Russian counterparts following the latter's failure on 8 April 1903 to meet the terms of Russia's 8 April 1902 agreement signed with China to withdraw its troops from Manchuria.[5]

In the summer of 1903, the Japanese government proposed to allocate Korea to its sphere of influence and Manchuria to the Russian sphere. Russian leaders, however, wanted an exclusive sphere in Manchuria and a mutual sphere in Korea. They procrastinated through the end of the year before rejecting the Japanese proposal. Nicholas II described as "insolent" Japanese demands that

[4] S.C.M. Paine, *Imperial Rivals: China, Russia, and Their Disputed Frontier* (Armonk, NY: M.E. Sharpe, 1996), 239–40, 215.
[5] Paine, *Imperial Rivals*, 212–13, 220–21, 240.

the territorial rights of China in Manchuria be respected. Meanwhile, in the fall, Russian reinforcements arrived at the Korean border. Thereafter, Nicholas II failed to respond to Japan's last negotiating proposal delivered in January 1904.

At this point, Japanese leaders viewed their deadlocked diplomatic approach in terms of a time-sensitive window of opportunity to pursue a military solution. On 2 February, Japan delivered an ultimatum, accusing Russia of negotiating in bad faith and announcing Japan's decision to call off the negotiations and to sever diplomatic relations. The transition from diplomacy to coercion finally became obvious to the Russians with the most proximate of the proximate causes, Japan's headline-grabbing surprise attack on 8 February 1904 on the Russian fleet anchored at Lüshun. Nicholas II had assumed that he controlled whether and when war would break out. Although the proximate causes had been accumulating ever since the end of the First Sino-Japanese War – making Yamagata's prediction of another war not so much prescient as obvious – the Russians failed to analyze either the accumulating tinder or the many lit matches, until the last one finally ignited a bonfire.

The Russians did not appreciate the enormous difference in the value that they, versus the Japanese, attached to control over Korea and Manchuria. While dominance over Northeast Asia would have made a nice addition to the Russian empire, the Japanese, whether rightly or wrongly, considered control over this area as the heart of the future empire, which they deemed vital to their national survival. Whereas the Russians saw any emerging conflict as a war of choice, a war they could choose to avoid, the Japanese considered the brewing conflict a war of necessity. Because war was inevitable, Japan's leaders desired it to occur at a time and place most advantageous for themselves. They perceived a narrow window of opportunity prior to the completion of the Trans-Siberian Railway to settle matters in Northeast Asia or be forever frozen in the status of a third-rate power incapable of defending itself.

The Japanese applied the lessons learned from the First Sino-Japanese War: in order to avoid a repeat of the Triple Intervention depriving Japan of the Liaodong peninsula at the end of the previous conflict, Japanese leaders negotiated Japan's first alliance, the Anglo-Japanese alliance of 1902, in order to isolate Russia diplomatically and to facilitate British assistance financing war loans. This would be Japan's only formal alliance until its far less successful arrangement with Germany and Italy in the 1940s. It allowed Britain to concentrate its limited military assets on the problems most connected with its national security. The rise of German naval power in Europe, stretching the Royal Navy's ability to meet its global commitments; the costly Boer War (1899–1902), constraining the British response to the Boxer Uprising; and the continuing Russian inroads into China, together alerted British leaders to the utility of an ally in Asia.

According to the terms of the Anglo-Japanese alliance, if war came to Asia and more than one non-Asian power combined against Japan, meaning Russia plus one, then Britain would come to Japan's assistance. In effect, this guaranteed a one-on-one conflict between Russia and Japan, since no power wanted to tangle with Britain over Manchuria or Korea. Japan, alone among the powers, valued Manchuria and Korea sufficiently to make these areas the long-term focus of its foreign policy. The treaty went into effect for five years until 1907, opening a five-year window of opportunity to settle matters, while the impending completion of the Trans-Siberian Railway threatened to close that window in the early part of the alliance.

The Japanese applied a second lesson learned from the First Sino-Japanese War: in international affairs, might trumps right. After the war, Foreign Minister Mutsu Munemitsu wrote in his memoirs, "diplomacy shorn of military support will not succeed, however legitimate its aims might be."[6] Others agreed – hence the widespread public support in Japan for the postwar rearmament program. This arms spending peaked in 1901.[7] In other words, from 1901 on, Japan was militarily prepared for war, just as its window of opportunity opened with the Anglo-Japanese alliance. Meanwhile, at the time of the Russo-Japanese War, Russia's own arms buildup had created naval strength in East Asia about three-quarters that of Japan and was scheduled to surpass Japan's soon after 1904, threatening to close Japan's window of opportunity.[8]

At the start of the war, the Trans-Siberian Railway remained unfinished. It had yet to be double-tracked, the Boxers had torn up much of what had been laid in Manchuria, and the link around Lake Baikal remained unbuilt. Lake Baikal approximated the size of Switzerland and so constituted a serious gap. At the onset of hostilities, Russia could transport 20,000 to 40,000 men per month from European Russia to the front. By the Battle of Shenyang (Mukden) at war's end, the number had risen to 100,000 men per month. If this carrying capacity had been available from the beginning, Russia could have maintained numerical superiority from start to finish. To quote a French colonel who wrote a two-volume retrospective on the war, "Never has a railway had, perhaps never will a railway have, such decisive importance in a war."[9]

For all of these reasons – the terms of the Anglo-Japanese alliance, Japan's and Russia's rearmament programs, and the completion of the Trans-Siberian Railway – Japan's civil and military leaders saw the clock ticking, with time on Russia's, not Japan's, side. They concluded: the fate of Korea was central to their national security, therefore Russian expansion in that direction threatened

---

[6] Mutsu, *Kenkenryoku*, 250.
[7] E.L.V. Cordonnier, *The Japanese in Manchuria 1904*, trans. Capt. C.F. Atkinson, vol. 1 (London: Hugh Rees, 1912), 62–64.
[8] Keene, *Emperor of Japan*, 589.
[9] Cordonnier, *The Japanese in Manchuria 1904*, vol. 1, 38.

them. Because they perceived only an extraordinarily brief window of opportunity when they had any chance of dominating Korea before the Russians arrived en masse, it would be now or never. When Russia repeatedly failed to respond to offers to exchange Russian dominance in Manchuria for Japanese dominance in Korea, the Japanese leadership decided to go to war before the window closed.

In a striking parallel to the lead-up to World War II, Japan's civil and military leaders had no confidence that their country could defeat Russia, just as in 1941 their successors would have no confidence that it could defeat the United States. In 1904 the army saw odds of fifty–fifty, while the navy's best-case scenario entailed the loss of half the fleet, which it could not rebuild domestically. Japanese civil and military leaders fixated on the dire nature of the threat and the brief window of opportunity that would soon slam shut forever, and they voted unanimously to go to war.

Japanese Grand Strategy

The Meiji generation, in striking contrast to their World War II-era successors, realized that such a high-risk–high-reward war required a carefully planned exit strategy, which was part of the war plan. Prime Minister Itō Hirobumi regarded American President Theodore Roosevelt, as essential for this purpose. U.S.–Japanese relations had come a long way since the arrival of Commodore Perry's black ships. U.S. intervention in civil unrest in Hawaii in 1893, in Cuba in 1898, and Samoa in 1899 produced U.S. colonies in Asia and aroused growing suspicions in Japan of potential U.S. imperial ambitions in its direction. Nevertheless, the United States remained the preferred destination for Japanese emigrants and elite American and British institutions of higher education boasted key Japanese leaders among their alumni. Japanese leaders leveraged these personal connections.

The day the Imperial Conference voted for war, Prime Minister Itō contacted an old acquaintance of Roosevelt and fellow graduate of Harvard University, Viscount Kaneko Kentarō. Kaneko would remain poised in Washington, to set up U.S. mediation for war termination, which another Harvard alumnus, Baron Komura Jutarō, eventually conducted. Meanwhile a son-in-law of Itō and graduate of Cambridge University, Suematsu Kenchō, went to England to keep the Anglo-Japanese alliance solid.

As had been the case in the First Sino-Japanese War, Japanese strategy went far beyond military strategy to encompass diplomacy, finance, intelligence, psychological operations, and logistics. Diplomatically Japan had isolated the enemy through the Anglo-Japanese alliance and pre-positioned representatives to conduct war termination. Financially it kept the money flowing through internal and foreign loans, which ultimately underwrote half of Japan's war costs, but the foreign loans depended on battlefield success.[10]

Intelligence gathering had begun in the 1880s when the Japanese government had organized students studying in China to collect information, and in 1891 it had established a school in Shanghai to train agents. By the time of the Russo-Japanese War, Japan had such key Chinese generals as Yuan Shikai on the payroll. Yuan would go on to play a starring role in the overthrow of the Qing dynasty and become China's new president. In the meantime, he co-ordinated his mounted forces with the Japanese to observe and harass Russian movements. This made small Russian detachments fearful of leaving camp, which in turn eroded morale. The Japanese also employed such Chinese agents as the barber, who kept the staff of the Russian theater commander, General Aleksei Nikolaevich Kuropatkin, presentable and themselves well informed. Other spies in Lüshun reported whenever Russian naval vessels prepared to sortie so that the Japanese navy always greeted them.

The Japanese also engaged in a variety of psychological operations. They tried to take advantage of the deep class divisions and spreading nationalism in the Russian empire, where there were proliferating demands for political representation among Great Russians and growing aspirations for independence among the many non-Great Russian communities. Japanese strategists hoped to stoke the fires of revolution in European Russia to tie down increasing numbers of troops to protect the tsar from his own subjects. Colonel (and eventually General) Akashi Motojirō co-ordinated Japanese spies from his base at the Japanese Legation in Stockholm, funding Russian, Polish, and Finnish revolutionaries to stir up trouble in European Russia. At the front, Japanese agents tried to promote Russian desertions by distributing postcards of the good life as a prisoner of war in contrast to imminent death as a battlefield casualty. These agents also distributed news accounts of the spreading unrest in Russia and Poland to encourage soldiers to desert to join the revolution. The Japanese used these diplomatic, economic, intelligence, and psychological elements of its grand strategy to predispose military success.

They also keenly understood Russian logistical problems, most particularly the limited carrying capacity of the Trans-Siberian Railway that would leave Japanese forces in a position of numerical superiority in-theater until the railway bottleneck could be overcome. Japanese naval strategy replicated that in the First Sino-Japanese War. Both conflicts began with surprise attacks on the enemy's naval forces in order to drive them from Asian waters and thereby establish immediate command of the sea. Only by doing so could Japan

---

[10] Denis Warner and Peggy Warner, *The Tide at Sunrise: A History of the Russo-Japanese War, 1904–1905* (New York: Charterhouse, 1974), 268, 373; Ian H. Nish, *The Anglo-Japanese Alliance: The Diplomacy of Two Island Empires 1894–1907* (London: University of London Athlone Press, 1966), 289.

deploy its forces at will and guarantee army supply lines. Like the Chinese, the Russians failed to perceive this key Japanese vulnerability and the imperative to target it.

The Imperial Japanese Army General Staff's war plan of the summer of 1903 emphasized speed and initiative so that Japan could leverage its initial, but temporary, numerical superiority in order to occupy key territory before Russia could mobilize. Japanese forces moving rapidly northward up both the Korean peninsula and the railway lines along the Liaodong peninsula would converge in a major battle, perhaps in the vicinity of Liaoyang. The plan envisioned pursuing the retreating Russians to take Harbin and cut the Trans-Siberian Railway, orphan Vladivostok, and, in doing so, make negotiations, rather than further hostilities, palatable to the Russians.

This plan overlooked the naval base at Lüshun, where Russia had concentrated the preponderance of its warships in Asia, and which belatedly became the focus of military strategy for both sides. Those ships were known as the Port Arthur Squadron, Port Arthur being the Russian name for Lüshun. This squadron, together with a much smaller group of ships based in Vladivostok, known as the Vladivostok Squadron, constituted the First Pacific Squadron. Japanese war plans required the neutralization of these squadrons.

On 6 February 1904, Japan cut its diplomatic relations with Russia, a clear cue that something big was brewing. Russia missed the cue. On the night of 8 February, Admiral Tōgō Heihachirō, commander in chief of the Combined Fleet, whose sinking of *Kowshing* had kicked off the First Sino-Japanese War, sent torpedo boats to attack ships of the Port Arthur Squadron anchored at the roadstead (the unprotected anchorage just outside the harbor), damaging two battleships and one cruiser, but leaving unharmed a fleet of five battleships, nine cruisers, twenty-five destroyers, and various gunboats.[11] The Battle of Lüshun continued into the following day, when four additional Russian cruisers were damaged. Damaged Japanese ships included one cruiser and four battleships. The latter constituted two-thirds of Japan's six first-class battleships and probably explains why Tōgō called off the attack. All ships on both sides were subsequently repaired.

Thereafter, no matter how persistently Admiral Tōgō bombarded the harbor, mined the approaches, and blockaded the fleet within, that fleet remained intact, although passive. This Russian fleet-in-being posed a potential threat to Japan's sea lines of communication between the home islands and the

---

[11] David C. Evans and Mark R. Peattie, *Kaigun: Strategy, Tactics, and Technology in the Imperial Japanese Navy 1887–1941* (Annapolis, MD: Naval Institute Press, 1997), 90–91, 97; Vladimir A. Zolotarev and Iurii F. Sokolov, *Трагедия на Дальнем Востоке: Русско-японская война 1904–1905 гг. (Tragedy in the Far East: The Russo-Japanese War 1904–1905)*, vol. 2 (Moscow: Аними Фортудо, 2004), 412.

battlefield. Nevertheless, Tōgō achieved his immediate goal to prevent the enemy squadron from interfering with Japan's initial troop landings.

Simultaneously with the Battle of Lüshun, Japan landed the 12th Division of the First Army at Chemulp'o (today known as Inch'ŏn), the port city for Seoul, for the long northward trek to cross into Manchuria at the Yalu river. The 2nd Division and Guards Division followed over the course of February, completing the deployment of the entire First Army. Russia responded by deploying the Vladivostok Squadron, which sortied twice in February in search of Japanese ships but sank none. At Lüshun, Admiral Tōgō made five unsuccessful attempts to block the narrow harbor entrance, on 24 February, 27 March, 27 April, 1 May, and 3 May. His failure forced him to keep ships on station to maintain a blockade, inflicting major wear and tear on his equipment. The blockade began on 9 May and would continue until the destruction of the opposing fleet.

Russia the Co-operative Adversary

On 20 February the tsar appointed War Minister General Aleksei N. Kuropatkin commander of land forces in Manchuria and Vice Admiral Stepan O. Makarov commander of naval forces in East Asia. Kuropatkin's war plan as of 15 February envisioned an initial contest for command of the sea, and a gradual Russian troop buildup, before the launch of a crushing offensive, culminating in the invasion of Japan and the overthrow of its government. How he intended to execute was another matter. Even Adolf Hitler's blitzkrieg thirty-six years later could not cross the narrow English Channel – a mere twenty-one miles at its narrowest – compared to the thousand plus nautical miles of water separating Japan from the remote and undeveloped Siberian coast that Kuropatkin thought he could traverse.

The tsar did not give Kuropatkin unified command, but rather ambiguous command. In 1903, after nine years on the throne, the thirty-five-year-old Nicholas had begun sidelining his ministers to take control over policy. That year he had created the Viceroyalty of the Far East, with Admiral Evgenii I. Alekseev at its head, making the latter commander in chief of both land and naval forces in theater, as well as emissary in charge of diplomacy with Korea, Japan, and China. In wartime this produced divided command and ambiguous authority over the ground forces in Manchuria. It was unclear where exactly War Minister Kuropatkin, soon to be commander of Manchuria forces, fit in this institutional arrangement. Kuropatkin immediately saw the problem and tried to tender his resignation as war minister, but Nicholas retained him. With the royal fiat creating the viceroyalty, Nicholas gained a free hand in Asia as the final arbiter of the conflicted command structure.

Admiral Alekseev, as the tsar's blood relative, was the trusted one, and General Kuropatkin, as the career military officer, was the one to be watched. Alekseev was an illegitimate son of Alexander II, so an uncle of Nicholas, indeed a favorite uncle. Outside the royal family, Alekseev was hated by career officers and sailors as an arrogant, ambitious, and temperamental royal appointee. By contrast, Kuropatkin had distinguished military qualifications as the valedictorian of his class at the Nicholas Academy of the General Staff; as a veteran of Russia's last major war, the Turkish War (1877–78), as well as of the ensuing wars of colonial expansion in Central Asia; as a major general promoted at the age of thirty-four on the basis of his service in Central Asia; and, most recently, as a full general and war minister. Alekseev had the better access to the tsar, the decision maker who mattered in Russia, while Kuropatkin had the expertise to make better decisions but was exiled to the theater in part to keep him far from the decision maker who counted. As soon as hostilities broke out Alekseev and Kuropatkin were issuing contradictory orders with paralyzing effects on their subordinates.

From the beginning, Kuropatkin and Nicholas II did not see eye to eye on the most fundamental national-security issues. They disagreed on the country that posed the greatest threat and required the preponderance of the Russian defense budget to counter. In 1898 when then General Adjutant Kuropatkin had become war minister, the tsar had told him that troops and resources would be directed from Europe to Asia. Kuropatkin had objected because he believed Russian vital interests lay in Europe, not Asia, and considered Russia's western defenses woefully lacking in the face of a rising Germany. Kuropatkin was right, but the tsar ruled.

Kuropatkin had then sought to maximize his personal power and resisted reformers who advocated copying the Prussian General Staff, which greatly reduced the jurisdiction of the war minister but made wartime co-ordination and the transition from peace to war efficient. Under the Prussian system, the chief of the general staff had responsibility for plans and fighting, while the war minister was limited to administrative functions.

On other issues, Kuropatkin had supported reform. He had recommended large-scale military maneuvers, but imperial relatives liked to observe, interfere, and in effect sabotage them. During the 1902 army maneuvers, he had identified reconnaissance as a key weakness: battlefield information did not reach commanders with adequate speed. He had wished to use the cavalry for reconnaissance, but the cavalry was the virtual preserve of the nobility – those who could afford expensive mounts. His attempts to reform the army alienated both the nobility and the tsar.

When Nicholas made Kuropatkin commander of the Manchurian Army, he deep-sixed a popular war minister in Asia without the necessary staff or streamlined command structure to take effective action. Meanwhile, Alekseev developed war plans of his own relying on his Far Eastern army and navy staffs. No complete army–navy war plans were ever shared with both the war and the navy ministries or with both services' senior commanders. Worse still, Kuropatkin and Alekseev favored mutually exclusive strategies: the military expert wanted to hold for six months while slowly massing troops to achieve numerical superiority before engaging, while the royal favorite envisioned aggressive naval action from the onset and the protection at all costs of Lüshun, which Kuropatkin expected to withstand a long siege. As a result, Kuropatkin became engaged in offensive operations before he was ready and Lüshun did not receive all the attention that Alekseev thought it deserved.

If these were the woes of the Russian army, the Russian navy was even worse off. The navy, with its impressive ships, was the personal toy of the Russian royal family, whose members took detailed interest in naval appropriations without understanding the budgeting trade-offs for a continental power of funding the navy at the expense of the army. The tsar's uncle, Grand Duke Aleksei, general admiral of the Imperial Russian Navy, held the post from 1881 until the disastrous 1905 Battle of Tsushima forced a re-evaluation of his credentials. He was close to his half-brother, Admiral Alekseev, and revered by Nicholas. But Grand Duke Aleksei was neither interested in nor knowledgeable about naval affairs; he was attracted mainly by naval pageantry. His sailors referred to him as "250 pounds of august flesh" in reference to his tonnage, while in Europe he was known as a lover of "fast women and slow ships."[12]

Unlike Japanese commanders, who were veterans of the First Sino-Japanese War, fought a decade earlier in precisely the same theater as the Russo-Japanese War, Russian commanders – army and navy – had little relevant combat experience. The army had fought wars of colonial expansion against preindustrial foes, while the navy had not even done that much. After the war, Kuropatkin ruefully observed that his countrymen could not emulate the Japanese, whose recruits had years of target practice prior to hostilities, for fear that similarly trained Russian soldiers would apply such skills to foment rebellion at home. Russia had long suffered from terrorism aimed at overthrowing the Romanov dynasty. As a thirteen-year-old, future tsar Nicholas had stood at the deathbed of Alexander II, to observe the loss of limbs caused by a bomb tossed at his grandfather's feet. A new wave of terrorism had begun in 1902 that would not subside until after the 1905 Revolution.

If the army rarely engaged in target practice, the navy rarely engaged at all. From the fall of 1903, Japanese sailors participated in daily training at sea, whereas to economize and avoid inclement weather, Russian sailors served ashore from the fall through the spring and had little experience cruising,

[12] Quoted in Constantine Pleshakov, *The Tsar's Last Armada: The Epic Journey to the Battle of Tsushima* (New York: Basic Books, 2002), 21.

let alone fighting, on the high seas. Yet the Russian navy was at least twice the size of Japan's Combined Fleet. While Japan could not build its own largest capital ships, Russia could and did, although it produced ships more slowly, at greater expense, and with inferior technology than the Western countries, which built Japan's best imported ships.

In addition to flawed institutions and practices, the Russian officer corps was overaged and undereducated. Senior officers served until they died. The higher the rank, the greater the percentage of hereditary nobility. In 1903, generals averaged seventy years of age and the eldest was a venerable ninety-two.[13] One specimen, General Nikolai P. Linevich, who commanded the Manchurian Army prior to Kuropatkin's arrival in theater and after Kuropatkin's demotion following the Battle of Shenyang, was sixty-four years old at the opening of hostilities. At that time, he did not know what a howitzer was, could not read military maps, and could not decipher railway movement schedules. Given the institutions, personnel, and practices, small wonder the Russians did not leverage their opportunities.

The Height of Joint Stategy: The Siege of Lüshun

As Japan's First Army laboriously marched through the tortuous geography and bitter cold of wintertime Korea, the Russians had two months to prepare a welcome party on the banks of the Yalu river. River crossings are usually dangerous for armies, particularly when crossing into prepared positions on the opposing bank. In rough terrain, geography and road systems usually limit the choices for where such crossings can occur. Not surprisingly, the Japanese would cross where they had crossed in the last war. Apparently Russian prejudices dismissing the abilities of the Japanese provoked no curiosity to study the last war, which had been fought in precisely the same theater. The British, French, Americans, and Japanese had all produced studies of the previous war that had made clear the key locations, but apparently the research had not tempted Russian readers. So the Russians failed to make geography a force multiplier even though they consistently held the high ground initially.

The Russians sent few troops to the Korean border, prepared no strong positions on the riverbank, and sent few scouts to report on the size and armaments of the approaching Second Army. The latter arrived with howitzers and ample artillery, which the numerically inferior Russian force lacked. The Japanese soon used the big guns to blow the Russians out of their positions in the Battle of Jiuliancheng (also known as the Battle of Kiu-lien-cheng or of

---

[13] Bruce W. Menning, *Bayonets before Guns: The Imperial Russian Army, 1861–1914* (Bloomington: Indiana University Press, 1992), 101; Zolotarev and Sokolov, *Tragedy in the Far East*, vol. 1, 168.

the Yalu) fought between 30 April and 1 May 1904. Russia suffered a multiple of Japanese casualties, when the reverse should have been the case, given the exposure of Japanese troops during the river crossing. Thereafter, the Japanese set to work completing a railway system through Korea to supply their troops.

When Admiral Tōgō failed to destroy the Port Arthur Squadron or to plug the Lüshun harbor entrance, the Imperial Japanese Army came to the rescue. In May it formed a Third Army to invest Lüshun under General Nogi Maresuke, the man who had taken the base in the last war. Japanese war plans called for a battle of annihilation against the Russians in the manner of Prussian victory in the Franco-Prussian War (1870–71). This required all Japanese armies and heavy guns to envelop Russian forces, an impossibility as long as much of Japan's heavy artillery ringed Lüshun and one army out of four remained grounded to conduct the siege. Heavy guns were in such short supply that Japan soon put navy guns on land in order to reduce the fortress.

The same May when the Third Army was formed to invest Lüshun, the First Army crossed the Yalu and headed for Liaoyang, and General Oku Yasukata's Second Army landed at a place called Weasels' Nest (Piziwo), located about fifty miles (seventy-five kilometers) from Dalian on the eastern coast of the Liaodong peninsula, and immediately cut rail and telegraph services to Lüshun. The Second Army would fight the battles of Nanshan and Delisi in order to cut off all Russian overland access to Lüshun before working its way northward up the railway line toward Haicheng to join the First and Fourth Armies.

Also in May, the Fourth Army soon landed at Big Orphan Mountain (Dagushan), located at the top of the Liaodong peninsula about thirty miles (fifty kilometers) from the mouth of the Yalu river. It headed inland directly toward Haicheng, the most contested town of the First Sino-Japanese War, on a route parallel to and fifty miles south of that of the First Army. Haicheng and Liaoyang were both railway stations on the Chinese Eastern Railway in the direction of Harbin, where the north–south line beginning at Lüshun dead-ended into the east–west trunk line connecting Vladivostok with European Russia. The First and Fourth Armies would prepare for a battle of annihilation against Russia's main land forces.

On 26 May the Second Army won the Battle of Nanshan, a hill outside Jinzhou on the narrow neck near the tip of the Liaodong peninsula. Japan suffered more casualties and expended more ammunition at Nanshan than during the entire First Sino-Japanese War.[14] Four days later, the Second Army occupied

---

[14] Y. Tak Matsusaka, "Human Bullets, General Nogi, and the Myth of Port Arthur," in John W. Steinberg, Bruce W. Menning, David Schimmelpenninck Van Der Oye, David Wolff, and Shinji Yokote, eds., *The Russo-Japanese War in Global Perspective: World War Zero*, vol. 1 (Leiden: Brill, 2005), 179–202, 183; Warner and Warner, *The Tide at Sunrise*, 297.

Dalian, which provided the army with an essential logistical hub because the Chinese Eastern Railway serviced the port. That same day, the Second Army, soon to be relieved by the Third Army, began the siege of Lüshun.

In early June, General Nogi's Third Army landed at Dalian, freeing the Second Army to follow the railway northward to Take Profit Temple (variously known as Delisi, Te-li-ssu, Vafangou, Wafangou), another railway station, where Kuropatkin had succumbed to pressure from Alekseev to engage the Japanese before he was ready in order to relieve pressure on Lüshun. Russia lost the Battle of Delisi fought from 14 to 15 June. Thereafter, the Second Army worked its way northward up the Liaodong peninsula.

Russian deployments to Delisi left the Motian Pass vulnerable to attack by the First Army en route to Liaoyang. By geography, had the Russians fortified the pass, they would have inflicted disproportionate casualties on the Japanese, but they were routed instead. General Kuropatkin's plans to delay the Japanese advance by fighting at Jiuliancheng and the Motian Pass had all failed because he had scattered his troops in deference to Admiral Alekseev's insistence that he fight further south at Delisi and Nanshan. He had wished to fight the decisive battle far to the north at Harbin, but Admiral Alekseev and Tsar Nicholas insisted he relieve pressure on Lüshun before he felt he had amassed adequate troop strength.

Back in Lüshun, on 8 March Vice Admiral Stepan O. Makarov had arrived to assume command of the First Pacific Squadron. Russian histories have attempted to lionize him as the tragic hero, who, had he lived longer, might have changed the course of the war, but his main literary effort, *Discussion of Questions in Naval Tactics*, published in 1897, displays an insensitivity to the problem of risk that later cost him his life. Ships, unlike armies, often go down all at once. Capital ships, unlike artillery, take years to build and cost huge sums so that few countries can afford to become naval powers. Naval commanders, even more so than ground-force commanders, must carefully calculate the risks before engaging in battle because ships sink in an instant but often cannot be replaced in a militarily useful time frame.

Makarov was blind to this problem and followed his own cavalier advice: "My rule, if you meet a weaker ship – attack, if equal – attack and, if stronger – also attack ... continue your attack until you destroy the enemy."[15] He went down with his ship on 13 April 1904, just a month after his arrival. The Combined Fleet, which had been bombarding the harbor off and on since February and would continue to do so through mid-May 1904, began laying mines on 13 March, including the one that detonated under Admiral Makarov. The night prior to his death he misidentified Japanese minelayers as Russian ships and ordered his men to hold fire; the following morning he failed to

[15] Cited in Zolotarev and Sokolov, *Tragedy in the Far East*, vol. 1, 341.

order a minesweep of the fairway, and his ship ploughed into a mine with fatal results. Within the week, Nicholas reflagged the Baltic Fleet as the Second Pacific Squadron under the command of the man sleeping with Makarov's wife, Rear Admiral Zinovii P. Rozhestvenskii.

More effective than Makarov's determination to put ships to sea were his own mining efforts. Contrary to Makarov's writings, in the Russo-Japanese War Russia's most strategically effective ship turned out not to be the battleship, but either the minelayer or perhaps the cruiser that the Vladivostok Squadron soon used to great effect. On 15 May, a month after Makarov's death, two of Japan's six battleships sank after hitting mines. Captain Fedor N. Ivanov, in contravention of orders not to proceed ten miles out to sea, had used the First Pacific Squadron's only minelayer to seed mines along the route the Japanese regularly traversed between their base on Elliot Island and Lüshun.[16] During the course of the war, mines sank seven Russian and eleven Japanese warships.[17]

Despite their differences, both General Kuropatkin and Admiral Alekseev considered the preservation of Lüshun to be crucial, but Kuropatkin believed the fortifications sufficient to withstand a long siege and feared that the diversion of troops to Lüshun would undermine his plans for a decisive battle further inland. When Kuropatkin ignored Alekseev's orders to deploy southward, Alekseev complained to his nephew, the tsar. The tsar then convened a highly unusual ad hoc war council comprising the army, navy, and interior ministers. The upshot of the bickering was the deployment of the Second Pacific Squadron to rescue Lüshun, which would surrender while the fleet was under way, removing the rationale for but not continuation of the deployment. Meanwhile, Japan's First, Second, and Fourth Armies converged on Liaoyang, for the envelopment that Kuropatkin both anticipated and feared, while Japan's Third Army besieged Lüshun until it capitulated.

The deployment of the Second Pacific Squadron put the Japanese Combined Fleet on the horns of an unanticipated dilemma. Either maintain the blockade at Lüshun, lest the Russian ships sortie to threaten Japanese sea lines of communication, or prepare for the Second Pacific Squadron's arrival in Asian waters by returning to home ports for vital repairs. Japanese ships could not simultaneously blockade and refit. This put enormous pressure on Admiral Tōgō to take Lüshun as swiftly as possible.

Nevertheless he remained cautious and his actions indicate a much more penetrating mind than that of Vice Admiral Makarov. Unlike his Russian counterpart, if Tōgō lost his fleet, Japan lost the war because Japan required the fleet to reach the theater and to supply its armies there. Because Russian supplies arrived exclusively by land, the loss of its fleet did not directly affect ground

[16] Warner and Warner, *The Tide at Sunrise*, 279–81.
[17] Evans and Peattie, *Kaigun*, 101.

troops in the interior, beyond the psychological impact on morale. So Tōgō had to choose wisely when to risk his fleet. As would be remarked a decade later in World War I concerning British Admiral John R. Jellicoe, Tōgō was the only man who could lose the war in an afternoon.[18] So Tōgō tried to minimize the risk to his fleet until Russia deployed its Baltic Fleet to Asia, when he would suddenly risk all.

The Russians belatedly realized that Lüshun was a useless naval base because its narrow channel permitted warships to leave only during a rising tide (accurate steering required opposing the tide) and the sortie of the entire squadron generally took two tides, making Russian naval movements predictable. While the Port Arthur Squadron had remained port-bound, the Vladivostok Squadron had deployed six times. On the third sortie, from 23 to 27 April, it sank a Japanese merchantman and a troop transport, drowning over 100 soldiers in the vicinity of Wŏnsan. On the fourth sortie, from 12 to 19 June, it sank two more troop transports and heavily damaged another, drowning several thousand Japanese troops and, more importantly, sinking at sea eighteen eleven-inch Krupp siege guns reluctantly removed from Japan's own coastal defenses for shipment to Lüshun.[19] Replacement guns would not be in place at Lüshun for six months. In the meantime, General Nōgi engaged in one bloody and ineffective frontal assault after another, eventually putting the equivalent of an entire army out of action. On 23 June, the Port Arthur Squadron unsuccessfully tried to escape to Vladivostok, but the Japanese drove it back. One Russian battleship suffered damage from a mine but remained afloat. At the next outgoing tide, the squadron fled back to port.

From 28 June to 3 July, the Vladivostok Squadron sortied again to attack merchantmen, and from 17 July to 1 August to cause panic in the waters off Tokyo. Meanwhile, the much larger Port Arthur Squadron sat in port until Nicholas ordered it to Vladivostok. On 10 August, a very reluctant Rear Admiral Vilgelm K. Vitgeft did so and the Battle of the Yellow Sea ensued. The Port Arthur Squadron lost two of its seven battleships, six of its eight armored cruisers, and thirteen of its twenty-five destroyers, and the good admiral lost his life. Again the squadron fled back to Lüshun, where it remained passive for the duration of the war. Soon its guns would be removed to defend the port by land.

---

[18] Winston Churchill, *The World Crisis, 1911–1918*, abridged version (New York: Simon & Schuster, 2005, reprint, first published 1927), 602.

[19] Warner and Warner, *The Tide at Sunrise*, 284–85, 427, 436, 440, 464; John W. Steinberg, "Operational Overview," in Steinberg et al., *The Russo-Japanese War in Global Perspective: World War Zero*, vol. 1, 105–28; Bruce A. Elleman, "Chinese Neutrality and Russian Commerce Raiding during the Russo-Japanese War, 1904–1905," in Bruce A. Elleman and S.C.M. Paine, eds., *Commerce Raiding: Historical Case Studies, 1755–2005* (Newport, RI: Naval War College Press, 2013), 22–23.

The Vladivostok Squadron made a belated sortie from 12 to 16 August, to aid the Port Arthur Squadron that had already lost the Battle of the Yellow Sea. It came into contact with the Japanese navy, which sank a cruiser and heavily damaged and inflicted high casualties on two others, which fled back to Vladivostok and made no further contributions to the war. In Japanese histories this is known as the 14 August Naval Battle of Ulsan because it occurred offshore from the Korean city by that name.

If this was the war at sea, the war on land also focused on Lüshun. The Imperial Japanese Army had equally compelling reasons to take Lüshun as soon as possible because only then could it combine all four armies for the anticipated war-winning battle to the north. Because the Battles of the Yellow Sea and Ulsan did not eliminate the First Pacific Squadron, the Combined Fleet had to maintain the blockade at Lüshun and could not return home to refit. From 19 to 24 August, within a week of the indecisive naval battles, General Nogi launched his first assault on the fortress at Lüshun. The Russians trained searchlights on the nighttime attack with devastating effect. The Japanese suffered an astronomical 16,000 casualties to Russia's 3,000, in the vain hopes of reducing the fortress just prior to the long-anticipated major engagement in central Manchuria.[20]

The Battle of Liaoyang began on 26 August southeast of the city and continued until its fall on 4 September. Three Japanese armies converged on Liaoyang, Manchuria's second-largest city, for the epic battle that Kuropatkin and the Japanese had anticipated and made central to their war plans. The height of the fighting occurred from 31 August to 3 September. The only larger battle in human history had been the Battle of Sedan during the Franco-Prussian War that Japanese officers so wanted to emulate. In the previous land battles, the Japanese had often been the better prepared. This time, the Russians had spent months fortifying the city and outnumbered the Japanese 158,000 to 125,000. The Russian failure to hold the Hongsha Pass to the southeast allowed Japan's First Army to reach the battlefield relatively unscathed. Although the Russians repulsed the Japanese along the entire front, inflicting heavy losses, they grossly overestimated enemy forces and so failed to pursue. Later, when the Japanese maintained their offensive posture, Russian command and control broke down. Units failed to receive orders, others improvised, and confusion and fratricide ensued. General Kuropatkin ordered a general retreat but the Japanese could not pursue because, in addition to exhaustion, they were out of ammunition. Japan suffered 24,000 casualties to Russia's 18,000. Had Kuropatkin fought on, he might have won.[21]

---

[20] Menning, *Bayonets before Guns*, 164–68.
[21] Warner and Warner, *The Tide at Sunrise*, 354–73, 384.

After the Battle of Liaoyang, the military situation turned to Japan's disadvantage. While Russia's troop buildup continued apace, Japan suffered from a desperate lack of munitions, irreplaceable losses of officers, and shortages of horses. Although it sought arms supplies abroad and fielded four new divisions and forty-eight second reserve battalions, it could not fill the necessary slots for officers.[22]

General Nogi made his second costly assault on Lüshun from 19 to 21 September just before the next major battle up north at Shaho, but failed to reduce the fortress. Japan suffered 7,500 casualties to Russia's 1,500 but Nogi learned the importance of 203 Meter Hill, the high ground that alone afforded the unobstructed view of the harbor to allow spotters situated at the top to call in targeting adjustments for the heavy artillery behind the hills. Only after Japan had installed heavy siege guns, like the ones lost to the predations of the Vladivostok Squadron in June, and put spotters on top of 203 Meter Hill could their gunners sink Russia's fleet-in-being hiding in port. Only then could Admiral Tōgō's ships return home to refit in anticipation of the arrival of the Second Pacific Squadron and General Nogi send his army northward to concentrate, at long last, all four Japanese armies along with a new one against General Kuropatkin's forces. The siege of Lüshun was the most joint operation that the Japanese ever conducted. Each service understood the critical importance to itself and to the other service of reducing the fortress.

The Russians responded to Liaoyang by deploying three armies to counterattack; the Battle of Shahe, named for a river crossing the vital railway line between Liaoyang and Shenyang, raged from 5 through 17 October. Unknown to the Russians, the Japanese supply situation verged on collapse. But Russian morale weakened from the effects of gross peculation by officers and inadequate supplies for soldiers, leaving them poorly clothed and cold. Alcoholism was rampant. The Japanese acquired key parts of Kuropatkin's plans from a dead Russian staff officer. During the battle they inflicted twice the casualties – 41,000 to 20,000.[23]

General Nogi responded to the inconclusive Battle of Shahe with a third bloody assault on Lüshun from 26 to 30 October, which also failed and lost another 6,000 Japanese casualties.[24] During the fourth frontal attack on Lüshun from 26 November to 6 December, the Japanese suffered 14,500 casualties to Russia's 6,000 but took the vital 203 Meter Hill on 30 November. By 5 December, they had spotters and 28-centimeter howitzers in place to begin systematically bombarding the ships in port. The guns then sank three battleships

[22] Shumpei Okamoto, *The Japanese Oligarchy and the Russo-Japanese War* (New York: Columbia University Press, 1970), 105–6.
[23] Warner and Warner, *The Tide at Sunrise*, 388–89, 392, 400.
[24] Ellis Ashmead-Bartlett, *Port Arthur: The Siege and Capitulation*, vol. 6 of Ian Nish, comp., *The Russo-Japanese War, 1904–5*, 8 vols. (Folkestone: Global Oriental, 2003), 274, 328.

on 6 December, a battleship and a cruiser on 7 December, and a cruiser and a transport on 8 December. The Russians scuttled the sole surviving battleship on the day of the formal capitulation of Lüshun on 2 January 1905.[25] The Third Army could then depart Lüshun to converge, with Japan's other armies, on Shenyang.

The loss of Lüshun deprived the deployment of the Second Pacific Squadron of its rationale to relieve the First Pacific Squadron, now located on the ocean floor. Rather than cancel the deployment, the tsar reinforced it, sending a Third Pacific Squadron out of the remnants of the Baltic Fleet. It set off on 15 February 1905, four months after the Second Pacific Squadron, which now was ordered to await its arrival before proceeding further, giving the Japanese ample time to refit their ships. What the Second and Third Pacific Squadrons were supposed to achieve and how they were supposed to achieve it remained unclear. The commander, Rear Admiral Zinovii P. Rozhestvenskii, quite correctly believed the deployment to be a gross error of strategy. Russia lacked the basing to support such a fleet, which would arrive greatly weakened, hulls thick with speed-killing barnacles, from the long voyage. The fleet would fight on Japanese terms with the consequences accurately anticipated by Rozhestvenskii. Again, the naval expert's opinion did not matter. The tsar decided.

The Battle of Shenyang and the Decisive Battle of Tsushima

From 25 to 29 January the Russians unsuccessfully tried to envelop the Japanese army during the Battle of Heigoutai (known variously as Black Ditch Tower, Hei-kou-tai or Sandepu), fought to the west of the railway line between Liaoyang and Shenyang. Japan then tried to return the favor further north at Shenyang (Mukden), Manchuria's largest city. The Battle of Shenyang, which took place from 19 February to 10 March 1905, would be the largest in history up to that point.

The Japanese army was desperate for an annihilating battle. Lieutenant General Kodama Gentarō, chief of the general staff, successfully deceived the Russians into thinking that his forces would concentrate in the east, when he actually delivered the main attack on the west. In response to false expectations, mid-battle General Kuropatkin disassembled one of his three armies to scatter it on the field of battle. In doing so, units lost their cohesion so that the sum of the parts became less than the whole. A Chinese interpreter, nominally working for the Russians but actually in the pay of the Japanese, passed along disinformation about Japanese deployments supposedly threatening

---

[25] Viacheslav Shatsillo and Larisa Shatsillo, *Русско-японская война 1904–1905* (*Russo-Japanese War 1904–1905*) (Moscow: Молодая гвардия, 2004), 235; Menning, *Bayonets before Guns*, 170–71.

imminent encirclement. The Russians believed the disinformation and abandoned Shenyang. Japan committed everything it had left, including both those too old and those too young to fight. Even so, it deployed 125,000 fewer troops than did Russia – 250,000 Japanese versus 375,000 Russians. Russia suffered nearly 70,000 casualties and lost 20,000 who became prisoners of war, while Japan suffered over 75,000 casualties.[26] At battle's end, again Japan lacked the ammunition and men to pursue so that Russia retained its armies to fight another day.

The following week, Nicholas relieved Kuropatkin of command and replaced him with the incompetent Lieutenant General Nikolai P. Linevich, who by now presumably knew what a howitzer was. Neither Kuropatkin nor Linevich grasped that Japan verged on exhaustion. In contrast, Russia had an army three times larger and its soldiers in theater, unlike either the initial deployments or the surviving Japanese forces, increasingly consisted of newly arrived crack troops.[27] One more major battle would have finished Japan.

After the Battle of Shenyang, instead of on ground troops, Nicholas II placed his hopes on the Second and Third Pacific Squadrons, which made an eight-month voyage to reach the war zone, despite no chance to refit and great difficulties replenishing coal en route, given the international restrictions precluding neutrals from aiding belligerents. With the fall of Lüshun, the Russian fleet could have but one destination, Vladivostok, and the routes there were predictable, given the intervening location of Japan. There were three choices: Two entailed bypassing Japan to the east, one through the narrow La Perouse Strait between Sakhalin and Japan's northernmost large island of Hokkaido and the other through the Tsugaru Strait between Hokkaido and the main island of Honshū. The third and shorter route that Rozhestvenskii chose bypassed Japan to the west via the Korea Strait. Admiral Tōgō's lookouts immediately reported the choice of the Korea Strait and the refitted, battle-ready Combined Fleet was there to greet the barnacle-covered Russian fleet.

From start to finish, nothing went right for the Pacific Squadron. Upon departure from the Baltic, it had created an international crisis, the Dogger Bank Incident, by firing on British fishing vessels mistaken for Japanese warships, a delusional interpretation of events. Japan had no naval vessels deployed to Europe, where it had neither basing to support them nor any conceivable interest in sending them. En route, Russian crews had become increasingly mutinous from terrible heat below decks, rotting rations, and incompetent officers. Admiral Rozhestvenskii had no faith in the mission but had consistently and correctly advised against it. His parting remarks were, "We have become

[26] Warner and Warner, *The Tide at Sunrise*, 466–80; Okamoto, *The Japanese Oligarchy*, 108–9, 153.
[27] Okamoto, *The Japanese Oligarchy*, 108–9, 153.

miserably weak, and with this general sick weakness, the crazy enterprise of our notorious squadron can hardly count on anything, even on sheer luck."[28] His attitude did nothing to improve morale.

On 27–28 May, the Japanese Combined Fleet made short work of the three Pacific Squadrons in one of the most lopsided naval battles in history, the Battle of Tsushima, named for the eastern channel of the Korea Strait. What did not sink became acquisitions for the Japanese navy. The virtually complete destruction of the Russian navy crushed Russian morale even though the loss had no material effect on the main front, which was Manchuria. The effect was purely psychological but politically debilitating and therefore decisive. A decisive battle leads directly to war termination. While many battles are key, critical or crucial, very, very few are actually decisive. This was one.

The unrelenting succession of Russian losses on land and sea had fueled the already growing revolutionary movement in European Russia. By late 1904 reserves were rioting at their assembly points in European Russia. Back in St. Petersburg, on 22 January 1905, the tsar's troops opened fire on peaceful demonstrators marching toward his palace to petition him to address their economic and political grievances. The day became known as Bloody Sunday and the rapidly spreading unrest became known as the Revolution of 1905. The government feared that the riotous reserves would join rather than suppress the unrest. So rather than form an additional army to fight what would have been a war-winning battle after Shenyang, given Japan's exhaustion of its reserves, the tsar suspended mobilization orders to call up the reserves for the first half of 1905, whereupon the riots subsided. Nicholas sacrificed the war to focus on the restoration of domestic order.

By October 1905, in European Russia the reserves outnumbered by about two to one the regular infantry and the pro-government Guards and Grenadier Corps, poor odds for regime security, or so the royal family thought. Yet once in their units, the reserves were no more mutinous than regular soldiers until the publication in 1905 of the tsar's October Manifesto, promising his people a legislature. In the short term, the manifesto, rather than quelling rebellion, fueled it with cascading mutinies, no longer mere riots, throughout the reserves in Manchuria and European garrisons. One wonders whether a post-Shenyang, war-winning victory might have had the opposite effect on popular loyalties.

At the time of the Battle of Shenyang, Japan's leaders let the Americans know they wanted diplomatic assistance to end the war. In addition to military exhaustion, Japan also verged on financial exhaustion. To maximize its bargaining position, Japan negotiated one final foreign loan the month before the negotiations began and covered one final internal war loan, but only with great difficulty. The Russo-Japanese War cost Japan 8.5 times more than the

---

[28] Cited in Pleshakov, *The Tsar's Last Armada*, 108.

First Sino-Japanese War, nearly seven times more than the ordinary revenues for 1903, and almost twelve times more than the government's tax revenues. Domestic and foreign loans had paid for 80 percent of the war effort.[29]

General Yamagata Aritomo recognized the limitations of Japan's bargaining position: "the enemy will never request peace unless we have invaded Moscow and St. Petersburg" – a scenario he knew to be impossible. He elaborated on Japan's dire situation: "First, while the enemy still has powerful forces in its home country, we have already exhausted ours. Second, while the enemy still does not run short of officers, we have lost a great number since the opening of the war and cannot easily replace them." Yamagata, the man who had wanted to march on Beijing in the First Sino-Japanese War, concluded in the Russo-Japanese War, "We must now be prudent." Chief of Staff of Japan's Manchurian Army General Kodama Gentarō agreed: "If one has started a fire, he must put it out."[30]

Japan took U.S. President Theodore Roosevelt's advice, given in June, to take Sakhalin Island as a bargaining chip in the negotiations. Japan landed troops on Sakhalin on 8 July and rapidly took over. It was far more valuable to Russia than to Japan. For the latter it offered rich fishing grounds, but for Russia ceding territory to any nation, let alone an Asian one given the prevailing racial prejudices, constituted a loss of prestige at home and abroad. Three days later, on 11 July and less than a month and a half after the Battle of Tsushima, Nicholas formally agreed to peace talks.

President Roosevelt played his scripted role to mediate the peace. He invited the belligerents to Portsmouth, New Hampshire, where negotiations took place from 9 to 29 August. Even so, Japan's military leaders found its civil leaders far too slow to act and their political demands excessive so that the talks almost broke down over such secondary issues as an indemnity and possession of Sakhalin Island. Telegrams from Japanese commanders became increasingly desperate for an immediate settlement before the military situation collapsed. At the time, General Kodama expressed his frustration about the prime minister, allegedly saying, "That fool Katsura is still running after an indemnity!"[31]

When the army chief of staff General Ōyama Iwao had departed to take up command of the Manchurian army in July 1904, he had told the navy minister, "I will care for the fighting in Manchuria, but I am counting on you as the man to decide when to stop."[32] In contrast to the First Sino-Japanese War, Japan's military, not civil, leaders sought to avoid making excessive political demands. In the Russo-Japanese War, officers had a much better understanding of the

[29] Okamoto, *The Japanese Oligarchy*, 127.
[30] Cited in Okamoto, *The Japanese Oligarchy*, 111.
[31] Cited in Okamoto, *The Japanese Oligarchy*, 112, 118, 153.
[32] Cited in Okamoto, *The Japanese Oligarchy*, 101–2.

precariousness of the military situation while civil leaders wanted to grasp for more.

Japanese diplomats were about to give up on Sakhalin Island when they learned that the Russians would be willing to cede the southern half, which Japan got. The talks would have broken down had the Russian negotiator, former finance minister Sergei Iu. Witte, followed the order of his sovereign to walk out and had the Japanese negotiator not at long last followed his orders to cease demanding an indemnity. In the First Sino-Japanese War, Japan had made a 50 percent profit from the indemnity; not this time around. The war proved extremely costly for both sides.[33] In the end, Japan's negotiators made demands moderate enough to be acceptable to the Russians and to the other foreign powers capable of intervening.

The Japanese acquitted themselves quite well in the war. They reconfirmed the outcome of the First Sino-Japanese War: Japan, not China or Russia, was the dominant regional power of Asia. The achievements included their immediate war objective of a Russian troop withdrawal from Manchuria. Russia lost influence in Korea, which became a virtual Japanese protectorate. Japan acquired both the southern half of Sakhalin Island and the southern half of the very expensive Russian railway concessions in Manchuria, which provided the beginnings of an empire on the Asian mainland – a key overarching objective of the Meiji generation. Whereas at the outset of the war, Japan had been willing to trade Korea for Manchuria, in the end it got the southern halves of Manchuria and Sakhalin too. Some might also argue that the railway was an indemnity in kind.

The Implications

Japan's strategy of war in the pursuit of national greatness was far more risky than its leaders appreciated. They did not perceive that the favorable outcome reflected not only their wise decisions but at least equally the unwise decisions made by their Russian counterparts. The Russians could have won the war by making a handful of different decisions, all well within their grasp, if not their imaginations.

Russia had nearly three times Japan's population, eight times its gross national product, twice its per-capita standard of living, and seven times its armed forces.[34] It missed numerous opportunities to employ its material

---

[33] Peter Duus, *The Rise of Modern Japan*, 2nd edn. (Boston: Houghton Mifflin, 1998), 142, 148.

[34] B.R. Mitchell, *European Historical Statistics 1750–1970*, abridged edn. (New York: Columbia University Press, 1978), 7; Nish, *The Russo-Japanese War, 1904–5*, vol. 1, 19; Zolotarev and Sokolov, *Tragedy in the Far East*, 162, 202; Ono Keishi, "Japan's Monetary Mobilization for War," in John W. Steinberg, David Wolff, Steve Marks, Bruce W. Menning, David Schimmelpenninck van der Oye, and Shinji Yokote, eds., *The Russo-Japanese War in Global Perspective: World War Zero*, vol. 2 (Leiden: Brill, 2007), 253.

superiority with decisive cumulative effects. Japan had barely enough men to fight the Battle of Shenyang, when it committed virtually everyone it could put in a uniform. Had Japan suffered additional prior troop losses, Russia would have won the battle, the revolution at home would have fizzled with visions of victory and revenge around the corner, and, if not Shenyang, then certainly one more battle would have trounced Japan when its armed forces and supplies collapsed.

Inflicting such casualties was easily within Russia's grasp. First, the Russians failed to study the First Sino-Japanese War, despite their huge railway investments in Manchuria, the theater of the prior war that was now Russia's to defend. Japanese lines of advance followed the same routes in both wars because the geography remained the same. These lines ran through the same dangerous chokepoints, which, if the Russians had bothered to study the prior conflict, they could have prepared and defended. Neither Alekseev nor Kuropatkin kept the other informed of their minimalist and inconsistent efforts to defend at the Yalu river. Neither diverted significant firepower to contest the Japanese river crossing during the two months when the Japanese were making the arduous march up the Korean peninsula. Likewise, Russia never bothered to fortify the mountain passes separating Korea from the Manchurian plain and the location of Russian railway lines. Russia could have. The most notorious was the Motian Pass. The Motian, Fenshui, and Daling (Taling) passes all fell between 26 and 30 June 1904, the first to the Fourth Army and the last two to the First Army, with negligible Japanese casualties.[35] The Russians could have exacted a high price to cross these naturally fortified points. Or, more effective still, they could have stopped the progress of both the First and Fourth Armies in the mountains protecting the Manchurian plain and the Russian railway system. This would have left the Second Army exposed to Russian troop concentrations. The Russians should also have been aware that the Liaodong peninsula has a very narrow neck. Take it and Dalian falls – an important port adequate to supply large armies – and once Dalian falls, Lüshun is next.

Second, Russia could have deployed its available naval assets differently. Like the Russian Army, the First Pacific Squadron displayed incredible passivity and reluctance to make obvious moves. Although Vladivostok was farther from the war theater than Lüshun and required icebreakers to remain open in the winter, it possessed key advantages. Rather than concentrating the First Pacific Squadron in Lüshun, which lacked easy egress, the facilities to repair cruisers or battleships, and the space to accommodate all the ships in the secure inner harbor, the Russians could have deployed more of the fleet to Vladivostok for commerce raiding. Attacking vulnerable cargo ships and

---

[35] [Charles à Court Repington], *The War in the Far East*, vol. 5 of Nish, *The Russo-Japanese War, 1904–5*, 265.

transports favored conventional naval ships on the hunt and would have targeted a critical Japanese vulnerability: its comparative shortage of soldiers and war materiel of all types. Surely drowning troops at sea or as they disembarked had advantages over fighting them on land.

Third, the Russians could have held out longer at Lüshun. The siege pinned approximately 200,000 Japanese troops, who suffered 110,000 casualties, and cost the Imperial Japanese Navy fifteen ships and seriously damaged sixteen others maintaining the naval blockade.[36] General Nogi Maresuke's Third Army became available only after the Battles of Liaoyang and Shahe, but before the Battle of Shenyang. What if his army had not been available at Shenyang? Major General Roman I. Kondratenko, in command of Lüshun's land defenses, had been determined to hold out as long as possible. Given the increasingly grim conditions within the fortress, the nobleman and royal favorite in town, Lieutenant General Baron Anatolii M. Stoessel, manipulated the politics for an early surrender. Even after the fall of 203 Meter Hill, Kondratenko insisted that the fortress could last several more months given the 3,500 edible horses within. But on 15 December, a shell took Kondratenko's life and with him went the only powerful advocate for holding out. At the surrender the Japanese inventoried a long list of food and munitions sufficient for at least another month, including stockpiles of grain and 207,855 rounds of different caliber.[37] Apparently those inside the fortress perceived their own sacrifices but not the strategic effects on Japan as long as the fortress remained battered but undefeated. What if the fortress had held out another month and a half – after the Battle of Shenyang? How many more assaults would General Nogi have launched and at what cost? Without Nogi's army, Russia would have possessed overwhelming numerical superiority at Shenyang.

Nogi had a sense of the disaster that he had almost brought upon his country. Of the 89,000 casualties suffered by men under his command, including the deaths of his two sons, over 64,000 had occurred at Lüshun. After its fall, he requested permission from the Emperor Meiji to commit suicide. The emperor ordered him to live, but Nogi and his wife committed suicide the day the emperor died five years later.[38]

What if, as recommended by a British military observer on the Japanese side, the Russians had fortified 203 Meter Hill with a permanent fort, trenches, and overhead cover?[39] Russia had several months to make the preparations.

[36] Zolotarev and Sokolov, *Tragedy in the Far East*, vol. 1, 485.
[37] Zolotarev and Sokolov, *Tragedy in the Far East*, vol. 1, 485; Shatsillo and Shatsillo, *The Russo-Japanese War 1904–1905*, 236; Ashmead-Bartlett, *Port Arthur*, 459–60, 473–74, 503–5.
[38] Keene, *Emperor of Japan*, 645–46; Ashmead-Bartlett, *Port Arthur*, 336–37, 399, 474; Matsusaka, "Human Bullets," 201, Warner and Warner, *The Tide at Sunrise*, 544.
[39] Ashmead-Bartlett, *Port Arthur*, 310.

Would Japan ever have been able to take the hill? And if so, at what additional cost in men and materiel? Had the blockade been protracted, how many more Japanese ships would have sunk in the Russian minefields protecting the port? As it was, Japan lost to mines ten important ships, including two, or one-third of its total of six, first-class battleships.[40]

Fourth, the tsar could have declined to deploy the Baltic Fleet to Asia and saved himself a prestige-searing loss. Rear Admiral Zinovii P. Rozhestvenskii believed the deployment to be a "crazy enterprise."[41] The Anglo-Japanese Alliance meant Russia's exclusion from Britain's coaling stations en route. Rozhestvenskii believed that the objectives were not feasible because the fleet would arrive in need of extensive repairs after such a long deployment, without the necessary repair facilities available at either Lüshun or Vladivostok under the best of circumstances. As it was, he did not believe he would make it into either port, and while he was en route Lüshun fell, eliminating the nearer destination. Russia lacked the bases to accommodate the Second and Third Pacific Squadrons, so in effect Nicholas delivered the rest of his fleet to the Japanese for destruction, rather than taking advantage of his growing numerical superiority in land forces. Even with Russia's failure to take any of these four alternative courses of action, the Imperial Russian Army put the equivalent of an entire Japanese army out of commission at the Battle of Shenyang.

Moreover, if Nicholas II had been a competent strategist, he would have understood that his country was a continental, not a maritime, power whose defenses depended not on the navy but on the army. Rather than making the huge naval investments that he chose, he should have followed the advice of Russia's finance minister from 1892 to 1903, Sergei Iu. Witte, to spend the money on the army and the means to deploy that army by rail. The money that went into capital ships could have double-tracked the Trans-Siberian and other railway lines. This would have yielded numerical superiority of ground troops from start to finish. As it was, Russia increased its troop levels in theater from 98,000 in February 1904 to 149,000 in August 1904 at the Battle of Liaoyang, when its numbers surpassed those of Japan by 20,000 men, and reached 788,000 in August 1905, just one month before the conclusion of the Portsmouth Peace Treaty. At that time, Russia had deployed just 40 percent of its army to the Asian mainland, while Japan had deployed 670,000, virtually its entire army.[42]

If Russia mangled its wartime strategy, Japan mismanaged its postwar strategy. In December 1906, the hero of Tsushima, chief of the navy general staff,

[40] 田中健一 (Tanaka Kenichi) and 氷室千春 (Himuro Chiharu), eds., 東郷平八郎目でみる明治の海軍 (The Meiji Navy in the Eyes of Tōgō Heihachirō) (Tokyo: 東郷会社・東郷, 1995), 84–85.
[41] Cited in Pleshakov, The Tsar's Last Armada, 108.
[42] Ono, "Japan's Monetary Mobilization for War," 253.

Admiral Tōgō Heihachirō, told a joint committee of army field marshals and navy fleet admirals that the Imperial Japanese Navy would never give up independent command to the army. Naval representatives argued that their service had its own understanding of national security and so should have the same freedom as the army to focus on its likely adversary. Naval representatives believed that the army's choice of Russia as the main adversary would undermine navy budget requests for expensive ships. The navy preferred to make the United States its enemy of choice – a self-fulfilling prophecy, as it turned out. Each service chose the enemy that required high-end purchases. The most pressing national-security problem was neither Russia nor the United States, but China, the neighboring failing state on whose economic welfare Japan's own economic health depended. China never became the subject of either service's main war plans, although China was always where they fought.

Inter-service rivalries in Japan produced war plans, force structures, and inter-service tensions ill-suited to national needs. From 1907 onward, the army and navy developed mutually irrelevant war plans focused on different enemies. They ignored the China problem in the manner that the Russian armed services had ignored the Japan problem prior to the Russo-Japanese War. Although virtually any war would require army–navy co-ordination, neither service made peacetime preparations to do so nor attempted to understand the strengths and weaknesses of the other service to allow Japan to leverage its strengths and compensate for its weaknesses.

The two stunning victories in the First Sino-Japanese War and the Russo-Japanese War spelled the end to grand strategy in Japan. When the generation that had practiced it with such dexterity died off, they left behind no score to guide their successors. Just as China's phenomenal success as the dominant civilization in Asia set it up for failure in the nineteenth century, likewise Japan's phenomenal success in its two wars of Russian containment set it up for failure in the mid-twentieth century. Each rested content on its achievements without inquiring into its shortcomings, let alone into the ambitions of its neighbors. The ancient Greeks long ago identified the fatal flaw of hubris that has destroyed so many gifted peoples.

Photo 3 Takahashi Korekiyo (1854–1936)
www.ndl.go.jp/portrait/e/datas/122_1.html (National Diet Library, Japan)

4   The Transition from a Maritime to a Continental Security Paradigm

> I believe few countries' politicians' lives are in such danger as ours are in Japan ... Military men are fond of saying, "We risk our lives for society." ... [M]ilitary men, particularly those of higher rank ... have few opportunities to die in war ... Looking back, I think one can safely say that since the Restoration there have hardly been any politicians equivalent to four-star generals and field marshals who have not become targets of assassins.[1]
>
> Ozaki Yukio (1858–1954), Diet member from 1890 to 1954, Cabinet minister

The Industrial Revolution brought trade of global scope and wealth of unimaginable scale. It heralded an incoming maritime world order, which gradually supplanted the outgoing continental world order of empires underlying so many great civilizations. Formerly, land had been the currency of power. It produced the agricultural commodities to be sold and the peasant conscripts to field mass armies. In the nineteenth century, commerce became the juggernaut of wealth creation, which in turn underwrote high standards of living and expensive ambitions, armaments, and allies. The Meiji generation lived at the transition between two global orders but they charted a course to the outgoing one, then at high tide, because they and so many others did not yet apprehend the incoming one just beyond the horizon. It is only with the perspective provided by long retrospect that such tectonic changes become clearer. At the time, people saw great change but not its cumulative direction.

Continental and maritime powers face different security problems that have far-reaching military, economic, and political ramifications. Continental powers border on their historic enemies, which pose their most lethal national security threats. The more numerous the potentially dangerous neighbors, the more difficult the problem of national security becomes. Continental powers require large standing armies to ward off neighboring threats. They do so often by deploying their armies to dominate surrounding buffer zones, which over time become national territory so that the army assumes a crucial domestic garrisoning function. Large standing armies also tend to have a palpable presence

---

[1] Ozaki Yukio, *The Autobiography of Ozaki Yukio: The Struggle for Constitutional Government in Japan*, trans. Hara Fujiko (Princeton: Princeton University Press, 2001), 391.

in the capital, where they often exercise great political influence. They tend to support economic policies that fund the army, produce conscripts, and efficiently exploit buffer zones for military purposes; as a result, they often favor extensive state planning.

Maritime powers have an oceanic moat, which precludes neighbors from easily invading. Therefore they do not need large standing armies, nor do they require a large army presence in the capital shaping government institutions. Instead, the comparative security afforded by the sea allows maritime powers to focus on economic growth and wealth accumulation. Those with political influence tend to support institutions that promote wealth creation. This wealth can then fund a large navy to prevent invasion and to protect the sea lines of communication over which the wealth-producing trade flows. A maritime national security strategy rests not on fighting on the main front but on generating the wealth to fund and arm allies fighting on the main front engulfing their borders and impinging directly on their economies. Time is on the side of the sea power coalition in a fight against a land power. Because the fighting occurs on the territory of the land power while the oceans give the sea power both sanctuary at home and access to the world, the gap in relative productive capacity grows over time and shifts ever more in favor of the sea power. This positions it to withstand a protracted conflict.

Sea powers tend to have many allies, whereas land powers tend to have few – another element of sea powers' resilience. This is because the evolving maritime global order favored by sea powers is a positive-sum order in the pursuit of economic growth, which all members can share. The maritime order is based on freedom of navigation, freedom of trade, and a growing body of international law and set of international institutions to regulate the transportation, communication, and diplomacy that the trade requires.

In contrast, continental powers generally have few friends because theirs is a negative-sum global order based on the domination of territory by one country at the expense of another. The sum is negative because the damage incurred in the fighting means that one side's gain of damaged territory is less than the other side's loss of a once pristine possession. Indeed, fighting does not create but destroys wealth at a brisk rate. Continental powers find national security through the destabilization, vivisection, domination, and absorption of neighbors – also not wealth-generating activities. Gain comes from what can be confiscated from others. Therefore continental powers envision the world in terms of exclusive spheres of influence to be closed off and sucked dry. Continental empires were highly effective until the Industrial Revolution, when wealth creation suddenly became far more lucrative than wealth confiscation, and until the advent of nationalism, when local peoples much more persistently resisted outside domination. A negative-sum global order guarantees conflict, if not immediately, then eventually. Industrial-era armaments then made such conflicts deadly.

The Industrial Revolution, not by intent but in effect, produced a spreading maritime global order, which gradually embraced many former land powers, which acquired the security denied by geography through an expanding maritime alliance system and growing body of international laws and set of international institutions. But the push back from both aspiring and traditional continental powers has been enormous and at the root of terrible wars: France in the Napoleonic Wars, Germany in two world wars, and the Communists during the Cold War. The Meiji generation remained ambivalent. On the one hand, they emulated Britain and its emphasis on trade and naval power. On the other hand, they eschewed Britain's democratic political institutions in favor of Prussia's, which, in the absence of brilliant statesmanship, ultimately put the army in charge.

At the turn of the century, the United States and Japan were moving along opposing trend lines. Until the conquest of western North America, the United States had followed the precepts of a continental power and the Monroe Doctrine enunciated in 1823 came from this continental tradition of exclusive spheres of influence. In the 1890s, Captain Alfred Thayer Mahan wrote the most widely read classic on naval strategy ever published, *The Influence of Seapower upon History*, which influenced naval budgets immediately and globally. He popularized the notion that wealth and power were a function of commerce. At home he made the case for a big navy, by persuasively arguing that the United States was a maritime power by geography, economic structure, government, and the commercial proclivities of its people. Americans embraced his ideas and over the next several presidencies traded their continental past for a maritime future. Manifest destiny was out and the free-trade doctrines of the Open Door were in and have remained so ever since. Japan initially embraced the emerging maritime world order, but support atrophied after the Russo-Japanese War, when it gradually reverted to its samurai land-power traditions, in part because of a changing international environment.

The Receding Permissive International Environment

The Meiji generation lived in a permissive international environment characterized by decline in China and Russia and soon by revolutions in both, so that the neighbors' attentions turned inward as Japan's turned outward. Japan, fresh from its two stunning victories, then took an increasingly firm approach to its neighbors, starting with Korea, the tinder of these conflicts.

After the Russo-Japanese War, confirming that Russia had no place in Korea's immediate future, Japan signed three agreements supportive of its special relationship with Korea. These were with the United States (the Taft–Katsura memorandum of July 1905 trading Japanese recognition of U.S. dominance over the Philippines for U.S. recognition of Japanese dominance over Korea), Britain (the renewal of the Anglo-Japanese alliance in August 1905), and Russia (the Portsmouth Peace Treaty of September 1905). This set the stage for Japan to establish a residency general in Seoul. The oligarchs intended to reform Korea along the lines of their own westernizing reforms in order to benefit both countries. They appointed Itō Hirobumi, their most experienced civil leader, for this delicate task under the framework established by the 17 November 1905 Korean–Japanese Protectorate Treaty and a 22 November 1905 declaration by the Japanese government. Itō then worked to minimize interference by the Japanese government, particularly the army, by arguing that the resident general should be the supreme Japanese civil and military authority in Korea. He believed that reform required Korean support and that this could not be had with clumsy meddling by the Foreign Ministry, let alone the army. In other words, he left himself maximum latitude; but by minimizing the institutional restraints on this authority, he also left no institutional framework to constrain less gifted successors.

Despite Itō's light touch (relative to the army's), in 1907 King Kojong rejected Japan's intrusions, sought great-power help, and was requited by Japan with a forced abdication in favor of his mentally disabled son. Korea's Cabinet nominally forced the abdication, but Japanese diplomacy and pressure made the nominal actual. The Western powers saw a realpolitik choice for Korea – either Russian or Japanese domination – and they favored the latter as more enlightened or, in the terminology of our own day, more conducive to economic growth.

Itō recognized the growing anti-Japanese sentiments among Koreans. He referred to Toyotomi Hideyoshi (1536–98), Japan's national hero but Korea's foreign desecrator: "When Hideyoshi attacked Korea, his followers murdered many Koreans and today Koreans remember this. Propagandists of anti-Japanese feeling argue, 'Though the Japanese say their purpose is to help Koreans, their real purpose is to annihilate them.' "[2] Itō's disbandment of the Korean army in a rescript dated 1 August 1907 precipitated a wave of riots and a peninsula-wide insurgency that resulted in over 14,000 Korean deaths between July 1907 and October 1908 and ever more brutal Japanese reprisals.[3] Yet he continued to resist calls for annexation spearheaded by Marshal Yamagata Aritomo and his protégé, General (and soon to be prime minister

---

[2] Quoted in Conroy, *The Japanese Seizure of Korea*, 364.
[3] Stewart Lone, *Army, Empire and Politics in Meiji Japan: The Three Careers of General Katsura Tarō* (New York: St. Martin's Press, 2000), 138, 164; Conroy, *The Japanese Seizure of Korea*, 365–68; Carter J. Eckert, Ki-baik Lee, Young Ick Lew, Michael Robinson, and Edward W. Wagner, *Korea Old and New: A History* (Seoul: Ilchokak Publishers, 1990), 255–56.

again) Katsura Tarō, the man who had almost scuttled termination of the Russo-Japanese War by insisting for too long on an indemnity.

At the height of Japan's infighting over Korea policy, a Korean nationalist shot Itō to death at the Harbin, Manchuria railway station on 26 October 1909. Itō's dying words were "What a fool!" The assassination brought about the opposite of its intended outcome: annexation. Unwittingly the assassin cleared the decks for the army by eliminating the man who understood the prerequisites for economic development.[4] Itō saw the ends: transformation of Korea into a stable and productive country both to foster trade and, more importantly, to preclude a hostile power from invading Japan via the peninsula. He had a sophisticated understanding of the integration of multiple instruments of national power – finance, trade, diplomacy – and the centrality of naval over land power, given Japan's island geography and trade dependence. In contrast, the Imperial Japanese Army fixated on the operational means of military occupation and operational ends of killing those who resisted, with ever less understanding that this strategy precluded any conceivable desirable outcome. Military operations are a means for political ends; never the reverse. Those who miss this simple equation set up their country for ruin.

Itō, the Meiji generation's pre-eminent civil leader, and Yamagata, its preeminent military leader, had repeatedly disagreed over policy. But Yamagata outlived Itō by fourteen years. Although Itō had appointed a younger protégé, Saionji Kinmochi, the only oligarch of aristocratic heritage, Saionji lacked Yamagata's stature. Saionji and his realist protégés favored party prime ministers, foreign policy in co-operation with the maritime powers (Britain and the United States), civilian control over the military, and constitutional monarchy with rule through the popularly elected House of Representatives of the Diet. In opposition, the continentalists favored national mobilization under military leadership, non-party cabinets, rule through the ministries and increasingly through the War Ministry on the basis of imperial prerogatives, and eventually foreign policy in co-operation with the Axis powers in pursuit of spheres of influence. Politically both the realists and the continentalists shared the goal of maintaining Japan as a great power and, after the Russian Revolution in 1917, resisting communism at home and in China. They differed on strategy. Institutionally, by the 1920s, this had become a disagreement over the supremacy of the legislature versus the bureaucracy. Internationally, one was consonant with and the other antithetical to the emerging global maritime order.

---

[4] Cited in Nakamura Kaju, *Prince Ito: The Man and Statesman: A Brief History of His Life* (New York: Japanese–American Commercial Weekly, 1910), 92–93; Donald Calman, *The Nature and Origins of Japanese Imperialism: A Reinterpretation of the Great Crisis of 1893* (London: Routledge, 1992), 153–54.

In 1910 General and War Minister Terauchi Masatake, a Yamagata protégé, became Itō's successor in the position of resident general, soon upgraded to governor-general. On 22 August 1910 the Yi dynasty ended with the Treaty of Annexation transforming Korea into a Japanese colony. Terauchi pacified the countryside and prohibited all Korean newspapers, political organizations, and public gatherings. He also "Japanized" the educational system. Although Japan invested massively in infrastructure and resource development, Korean hatred metastasized so that soon virtually all Japanese actions were perceived as heinous. Japan's liberals, who had once promoted democracy at home, championed aggressive imperialism abroad. Both liberals and continentalists agreed on Japan's civilizing mission in Asia.

With Russia neutralized in Asia, Marshal Yamagata favored Japanese expansion beyond the Great Wall, posing a direct threat to China's capital, located fifty kilometers to the south. By May 1911, on the eve of the Chinese Revolution toppling the Qing dynasty, an Imperial Japanese Army memorandum recommended the occupation of the Yangzi river valley, the heart of the British sphere of influence. With the outbreak of World War I in August 1914, these visions for empire expanded into an Asian Monroe Doctrine, initially outlined in a letter that month by General Terauchi. Just as U.S. president James Monroe had informed the great powers that they had better stay clear of Latin America, likewise increasing numbers of Japanese favored making East Asia their exclusive preserve. By 1915 Terauchi believed, "Eventually all of Asia should be under the control of our Emperor."[5]

China the failed state constituted both a threat and an opportunity. No longer did Japan face a great-power neighbor, which gave it great latitude in foreign policy, yet Japan's economic health depended on trade with the mainland, which required the very stability China so conspicuously lacked. As China imploded, the Japanese army gravitated toward a continental, sphere-of-influence solution. After the Russo-Japanese War, Japan negotiated a series of sphere-of-influence agreements with Russia: the secret Russo-Japanese Political Convention of 30 July 1907 made Manchuria part of the Japanese and Outer Mongolia part of the Russian sphere of influence. Another secret agreement in 1910 promised that neither would hinder the other from developing its sphere. A third secret agreement in 1912 recognized western Inner Mongolia as part of the Russian sphere. In 1916 a fourth secret agreement promised co-operation to prevent any other great power from dominating China.[6] The secret convention to the 1916 treaty paralleled the earlier

[5] Cited in Frederick R. Dickinson, "Japan Debates the Anglo-Japanese Alliance: The Second Revision of 1911," in Phillips Payson O'Brien, ed., *The Anglo-Japanese Alliance, 1902–1922* (London: RoutledgeCurzon, 2004), 101–2.

[6] Paine, *Imperial Rivals*, 274–76.

Anglo-Japanese Alliance, in that each promised to aid the other in the event of a war with China plus one.

Russia had its own continental plans. It took advantage of the collapse of the Qing empire in 1911 to negotiate agreements with Outer Mongolia, in 1912 and 1913.[7] Mongolia eagerly sought independence from China, envisioning Russia as a counterbalance. In the fall of 1914, Russia presented China with twenty-one draft resolutions that would have transformed Outer Mongolia into a Russian protectorate had not World War I intervened to consume its attention.[8]

Chinese instability, however, worsened and threatened to spill over into Manchuria, the focus of Japanese overseas investments. With the fall of the Qing dynasty in 1912, China disintegrated into a long civil war that lasted until the Communist victory in 1949. Three revolutions followed in rapid succession and engulfed the country: the first revolution from 1911 to 1912, a second in 1913, and a third in 1916, when the government in Beijing lost control for the duration of the long civil war. South and north China attempted to establish competing governments in the 1910s and early 1920s. The warlords of north China eviscerated each other in a succession of wars of shifting coalitions – the Anhui–Zhili War (1920), the First Zhili–Fengtian War (1922), the Second Zhili–Fengtian War (1924), the Fengtian–Zhejiang War (1925), and the Fengtian–Feng Yuxiang War (1925–6). By 1926, this had opened an opportunity for the reunification of China from the south.

As the Imperial Japanese Army considered what to do about instability first in Korea and then in China, it failed to consider the reactions of the other great powers to its continental ambitions. In order of increasing determination, Russia, Britain, and the United States all opposed the annexation of Korea. Russia soon became preoccupied with a succession of Balkan wars, which would culminate in World War I. The Romanov dynasty did not survive the war, eliminating, for the time being, Japan's second most potentially threatening neighbor and providing even more foreign-policy latitude.

Although Japan and Britain had renewed their 1902 alliance in 1905 and strengthened it in 1907, Britain looked askance at Japanese imperialism in Korea. The head of the Far Eastern Department of Britain's Foreign Office observed in 1919 that the "Japanese do exactly the reverse" of Britain, which tried to administer colonies "in the interest of the natives with a view to educating them to take a larger share in the government."[9] In 1919 Foreign Secretary Lord Curzon bluntly told the Japanese ambassador, "it seemed to me a great

---

[7] Paine, *Imperial Rivals*, 292–98.
[8] Bruce A. Elleman, *Wilson and China: A Revised History of the Shandong Question* (Armonk, NY: M.E. Sharpe, 2002), 13–14.
[9] Cited in Phillips Payson O'Brien, "Britain and the End of the Anglo-Japanese Alliance," in O'Brien, *The Anglo-Japanese Alliance, 1902–1922*, 273.

mistake that the Japanese, in their administration of Korea, so entirely ignored the natives of the country they were endeavoring to rule."[10] Within the British government, civil and military support for continuation of the alliance with Japan disappeared as they concluded that Japan's ambitions in China were political domination and the economic exclusion of other powers.

Meanwhile, the United States rejected the existing treaty port system based on concession areas. Starting in 1899 it promoted the Open Door Policy in opposition to the colonial powers' attempt to divide China into spheres of influence. Rather, China's door to trade should remain open to all. The British agreed. Ever since, the United States has applied this maritime, economic vision in opposition to a continental, spheres-of-influence approach. In 1922 at the Washington Conference, Britain and Japan jettisoned their alliance in favor of the Four-Power Treaty with the United States and France to uphold the status quo in the Pacific. The Nine-Power Treaty then guaranteed the Open Door in China. Finally, the Washington Naval Treaty set a 10–10–6 capital-ship tonnage ratio for Britain, the United States, and Japan respectively, infuriating much of the Imperial Japanese Navy. The limitations, which followed U.S. wishes, did not necessarily leave the Imperial Japanese Navy dominant in Asian waters and permitted Britain and the United States navies global reach. The Diet was excluded from the negotiations and so felt free to criticize the treaty. A bitter and politically destabilizing domestic debate ensued.

The treaty followed a series of events that the Japanese people saw as reducing their country to an inferior status: the U.S. failure to join the League of Nations, Japan's return to China of Germany's former Shandong concessions in 1922, and U.S. renunciation of the 1917 Lansing–Ishii agreement recognizing Japan's special interests in China and the end of the Anglo-Japanese alliance, both in 1923. During the popular outrage, the military raised the issue and won the right of supreme command to veto future Cabinet decisions related to national defense. The United States would have done better with more generous tonnage terms for Japan. Then, in 1924, as a sop for nativist voters, the United States passed the Immigration Act excluding Japanese immigration to the United States, infuriating Japanese in general.

Foreign Minister Shidehara Kijūrō (1924–7, 1929–31) became an increasingly solitary supporter of the Versailles settlement of World War I and the Washington Naval Conference treaty system. He was Japan's first career diplomat to become foreign minister on the basis of the civil service examination. But the army soon trumped his preferred foreign policy of nonintervention in China. So just as the period of Anglo-Japanese co-operation was ending, a period of intensifying U.S.–Japanese hostility was dawning. The international environment had been relatively benign from Japan's point of view: declining

---

[10] Cited in O'Brien, "Britain and the End of the Anglo-Japanese Alliance," 274.

great-power neighbors, and relatively supportive great powers located further afield. But this era was coming to a close.

The Passing of the Oligarchs

With the passing of the anomalous Meiji generation and of a benign international environment, Japan gradually returned to its continental and martial roots, with dire consequences for all. The Constitution laid out broad imperial prerogatives, which, as the Meiji generation died off, each bureaucracy increasingly tried to hijack to further its own aims. During the Meiji period, there were approximately nine oligarchs who set policy. Most came from Chōshū (Yamaguchi), particularly in the army; Satsuma (Kagoshima), particularly in the navy; and a minority from Tosa (Kōchi) and Hizen (Saga), a minority that became further marginalized in 1881. In the military, rank structure then perpetuated the Chōshū and Satsuma dominance.

While the oligarchs lived, they were the key players determining national policy. They chose each new prime minister, a position virtually all had held themselves and had monopolized from 1885 to 1913 (minus a five-month hiatus in 1898). Many had held a variety of Cabinet positions. These civil, military, and court leaders knew each other well and had broad experience crossing the boundaries of civil and military institutions, so that consensus was possible and indeed was their preferred modus operandi. Together four palace leaders (the imperial household minister, the grand chamberlain, the chief aide-de-camp, and the lord keeper of the privy seal), the leaders of the executive branch (the privy councilors and the ministers of state), the leaders of the armed forces, and finally those who had formerly held these positions together negotiated the consensus. Once their grand bargain was reached, they presented it to the emperor for his ratification. The palace leaders and retired senior statesmen, who were expected to focus on national rather than bureaucratic interests, played the guiding role in this process. The oligarchs in control of civil power set a realist path and in the 1880s and 1890s suppressed the liberals, who favored a more democratic approach to governance. But the continentalists, with a growing army following, gained strength thereafter.

The power of the oligarchs came from what the Meiji Constitution left unsaid. They wielded enormous influence but the power was informal because the Meiji Constitution was silent on their jurisdiction. This allowed them to rule unfettered by constitutional limitations. The constitution also lacked articles outlining the responsibilities of the Cabinet or the prime minister. The Meiji generation leveraged the large voids in the written law and the structural weakness of the prime minister's authority to rule on the basis of their personal ties with each other, forged in the revolution that had put them in charge. This worked well enough as long as people of broad experience, sound judgment, and enormous prestige served as oligarchs. Their ties crossed civil and military boundaries to create interinstitutional cohesion that disappeared with their deaths in the first quarter of the twentieth century. Nor did their informal modus operandi solve the problem of succession, a key measure of institutionalization and political stability. Indeed, however convenient it was for their generation to exercise power unencumbered by legal limitations, they could not transfer to others the prestige that allowed them to operate autonomously, so their special status died with them. This would leave power to its most thoroughly institutionalized source: the army.

Itō Hirobumi, the author of the Meiji Constitution, played an instrumental role in marginalizing the imperial court from governance. This gave the oligarchs a monopoly on decision-making that facilitated their rule while they lived. Yamagata Aritomo, the most influential oligarch on matters military, insisted on the separation of civil and military power. This was his takeaway from the Satsuma Rebellion of 1877, when the old samurai tried to reassert their traditional privileges. In 1882 he had the emperor issue the Imperial Rescript to Soldiers and Sailors ordering them to stay out of politics. Yet Yamagata was instrumental in creating institutions following the Prussian model that gave the war and navy ministers and chiefs of staff direct access to the emperor, bypassing the prime minister, and separated army administration (now under the war minister) and operations (now under the chief of the general staff). But bypassing the prime minister and the other Cabinet ministers meant bypassing those with expertise in all the nonmilitary instruments of national power that nevertheless came into play in wartime as well as in peacetime.

The Prussian system also deprived the army of effective unity of command and gave only a symbolic variant to the emperor. The requirement, added in 1900, that both war and navy ministers be in active service gave the senior officer, Yamagata until his death, control over the appointment of the war minister, and de facto control over all Cabinet appointments and policies, because either service, by declining to appoint a minister or by ordering one to resign, forced the resignation of the prime minister and the formation of a new Cabinet. Although by logic the War Ministry should have controlled all appointments as a personnel issue, in practice the army chief of staff made all ministerial appointments. In 1907 army and navy ministers could bypass the prime minister on administrative issues by issuing imperial orders in the name of the emperor. Yamagata, the creator of this system, then purged his opponents and promoted loyalists. Thus, while he lived, he could exercise unity of command. By the time of his death in 1922, his consistent appointments over a lifetime had thoroughly skewed government institutions in favor of army domination and the narrow perspective of army officers without broad educations or broad career experience in nonmilitary institutions.

After Yamagata's death, the war minister and the chief of the general staff became potential political rivals. Yamagata's institutional legacy left the military accountable only to one man, a figurehead emperor isolated in his palace under the thumb of the Imperial Household Ministry. The Prussian system lacked an institutional mechanism to force civil and military leaders to consider the integration of all instruments of national power – the numerous nonmilitary prerequisites for and consequences of military operations – most particularly finance, production, commerce, and diplomacy. Japanese institutional structures giving pre-eminence to active-duty officers prevented civil interference in military affairs, but did not limit military interference in civil affairs, which soon overwhelmed civil authority.

After the Russo-Japanese War, the army countered the Foreign Ministry's attempt to return the empire to civil administration with "the right of military command." The army established parallel institutions to supplant the Foreign Ministry's jurisdiction: the Advisory Council on Foreign Relations in 1915, the Colonial Ministry in 1929, and finally the Asian Development Board in 1938. The Foreign Ministry, with a budget of 17 million yen in 1931 in comparison to the military's budget of 590 million yen, did not have a prayer in this struggle.[11] In Japan's two successful wars, the war and navy ministers had consulted with the foreign and finance ministers. The passing of the oligarchs allowed the war and navy ministers and chiefs of staff to act without accountability to the electorate, to their fellow Cabinet ministers, to the prime minister, or to the emperor. Soon the military would put aside the oligarchs' pro-Anglo-American inclinations consonant with a maritime global order and direct their pro-emperor-system inclinations toward a continental world order.

Ironically, the nominal head of state, the emperor, had no autonomous role. He was a legitimator of decisions made by others, not an independent political actor. On paper, he made war and peace; commanded the armed forces; appointed all generals, admirals, Cabinet ministers, and prime ministers; legislated with the assent of the Diet; and concluded treaties. In practice, these prerogatives were parceled out among the relevant ministries whose decisions he then ratified. He operated under a separate bureaucracy, the Imperial Household Ministry, and his family under a separate constitution, the Imperial House Law. The lord keeper of the privy seal served as the senior palace official keeping the emperor informed about politics. The military, and increasingly the army, appointed and the emperor accepted his and his family's aides-de-camp. While the chamberlains served as the emperor's liaison with the bureaucracies of the imperial household and government, the aides-de-camp served as his liaison with the military. Conversely, both served as the civil and military filters of

[11] Barbara J. Brooks, *Japan's Imperial Diplomacy: Consuls, Treaty Ports, and War in China 1895–1938* (Honolulu: University of Hawaii Press, 2000), 1, 8, 42–43, 140, 165.

information reaching him. Thus the emperor reigned but did not rule. He symbolized authority but did not exercise power. He served as the ratifier-in-chief.

The oligarchs of the Meiji period agreed on the policy objective – maintain Japan as a great power and foster economic growth – but they disagreed vehemently on the strategy most likely to produce this outcome. Nevertheless, after much bickering they cobbled together highly effective strategies that reflected their various viewpoints and expertise. As the oligarchs succumbed to mortality – half died within a decade of the Russo-Japanese War – decision making spread beyond their numbers to their protégés, whom they had infiltrated throughout the bureaucracy. As a result, consensus became an ever-scarcer commodity.

Unlike those who assumed control over policy after their deaths, the oligarchs were the creators not the creatures of Japan's modern political institutions. They were the founding fathers of modern Japan. Their competition was personal, not institutional. After their deaths, the creatures took over from the creators and the competition became institutional both among institutions over their respective jurisdictions and within institutions among factions, which then reached out to like-minded factions in other institutions.[12]

Competing oligarchs increasingly organized segments of the population to push their agendas at the expense of others'. This produced short-term wins at the price of the gradual devolution of power to groups outside their numbers. Some oligarchs reached out to political parties. By the second decade of the twentieth century, key decision making in civil institutions (but not in military institutions) had devolved from the oligarchs to professional politicians. This eroded the oligarchs' ability to set cabinets, which produced party cabinets, which precluded oligarch rule on the basis of imperial orders between Diet sessions. The oligarchs most concerned with civil rule lost control over the judiciary, the police, and the bureaucracy in general; meanwhile Marshal Yamagata consolidated his control over the army, further shifting power from civil to military institutions.

The Rise of Political Parties

In the late nineteenth century, the prime minister had alternated between representatives from Satsuma and Chōshū, although after the First Sino-Japanese War the oligarchs did include certain vetted party leaders in the Cabinet. In the first decade of the twentieth century, the office of prime minister alternated between the protégés of Itō (Saionji Kinmochi) and Yamagata (Katsura Tarō). This alternation between civil and army leaders broke down with the death of

---

[12] The phraseology comes from David Anson Titus, *Palace and Politics in Prewar Japan* (New York: Columbia University Press, 1974), 317–18, 325.

the Meiji emperor. There followed a succession of an unpopular admiral, an unpopular septuagenarian, and then an unpopular general. Their unpopularity with voters contributed to a period of party cabinets, dominated not by oligarchs but by leading bureaucrats, bankers, and diplomats. Party cabinets produced a destabilizing succession of prime ministers, which gave more de facto decision-making power to the enduring bureaucracy.

Under the Taishō emperor (r. 1912–26), the main task confronting Japan's leaders changed from building a great power to corking the domestic unrest arising from industrialization and urbanization – another factor contributing to party cabinets. Due to the emperor's failing health, his son Hirohito became prince regent in 1921. Mass political participation began in the form of riots, starting with the Hibiya riots of 1905 in opposition to the Portsmouth Peace Treaty. To channel political participation, the government expanded the franchise only gradually. Under the Elections Act of 1889 only about 2 percent (450,000) could vote because of the exclusion of women and those below a minimum tax threshold. The 1900 Elections Act extended the vote in the 1902 elections to 3.9 percent (983,000) by lowering the tax threshold and adding urban districts. By 1917, eligible voters had grown to 4.8 percent (1.4 million). Nationwide Rice Riots erupted in August and September 1918 over the doubling of rice prices during World War I. The ensuing widening of the franchise ushered in party government when further reductions in the tax threshold in the 1919 Elections Act increased the electorate to 10.2 percent (8 million) in 1920 elections, and finally to universal male suffrage – 19.1 percent of the population (12.4 million) – in 1925.[13]

Democracy requires a combination of broad electoral participation, fair elections, and voter control over political office. Electoral participation did grow, fostering the development of political parties, which exercised their power through the popularly elected lower house of the legislature, the House of Representatives. Its key power lay in the authority to approve the budget. Nevertheless the oligarchs could get around the Diet via an imperial rescript and the electorate never controlled political parties. The parties developed not as mass organizations, but as vehicles to represent rural elites, who controlled voting patterns in their areas, and then leveraged the power of the lower house to veto the budget and tax increases in order to strike compromises with other elites. Key institutions not subject to public control included the upper house of the legislature, the House of Peers, composed of hereditary members and

---

[13] Harukata Takenaka, *Failed Democracy in Prewar Japan: Breakdown of a Hybrid Regime* (Stanford: Stanford University Press, 2014), 49, 58; J. Mark Ramseyer and Frances M. Rosenbluth, *The Politics of Oligarchy: Institutional Choice in Imperial Japan* (Cambridge: Cambridge University Press, 1995), 42, 45, 47, 49; Leonard A. Humphreys, *The Way of the Heavenly Sword: The Japanese Army of the 1920s* (Stanford: Stanford University Press, 1995), 42–43.

imperial appointees, with infusions of officers appointed after each war; the Privy Council, appointed by the emperor to advise him on constitutional and legal matters, including treaties; and most significantly the military, the oligarchs, and the emperor. Finally, a wide franchise, fair elections, and voter control over political institutions required an impartial and empowered judiciary. Japan's courts never were independent, but successively controlled by the oligarchs, the parties, and then the military.

In 1900 Itō Hirobumi, over the objections of Yamagata Aritomo, formed his own party, the Rikken Seiyūkai or Friends of Constitutional Government. Yamagata worked to sideline Itō from party politics thereafter and Itō's appointment in 1905 to administer Korea fit the purpose. In December 1904, Hara Kei, a Seiyūkai leader, cut a deal with Prime Minister Katsura Tarō, the so-called "tiger of the bureaucracy." In return for the Seiyūkai's support, Katsura agreed to support as his successor Itō's protégé, Saionji, and, in the meantime to garner the support of the Kenseihontō, the second-largest party, despite its leader Inukai Tsuyoshi's antipathy toward the political dominance of the Satsuma and Chōshū clans. Katsura was drifting away from his ties to Yamagata, the embodiment of Chōshū loyalties, and came around to support political parties during his third cabinet and just before his sudden death, when, to counter the Seiyūkai, he formed the Dōshikai from his bureaucratic connections.[14]

The Imperial Japanese Navy, in its eternal competition with the army over appropriations, became a major supporter of the Seiyūkai. The navy, as the junior service in politics and practice, had worked tirelessly since its formation to equal the status, budget, and political power of the army. By 1922 it would become the world's third-largest navy, a major accomplishment of the Taishō years. Although it closed the gap on the budgetary front, it never succeeded on the crucial political front. After Itō's death and the 1912 elections, favoring the Seiyūkai and the liberal Kokumintō, the army decided to break the Seiyūkai–navy alliance. In 1925, a Yamagata protégé, Tanaka Giichi, would become the head of the party.

The passing of the oligarchs had far-reaching implications for the balance between civil and military power and the ability of the military services to conduct joint operations. No formal institutional links forced the army and navy to co-ordinate war plans. Yet joint army–navy operations had been essential for Japan's victories in the First Sino-Japanese War and Russo-Japanese War. The leaders of each service had understood the critical needs and capabilities of the other through their personal contacts as the founding fathers of modern Japan. These connections died with them. In the tight budgetary environment of the 1920s, the two services became bitter enemies in the struggle to hog the

---

[14] Peter Duus, *Party Rivalry and Political Change in Taishō Japan* (Cambridge, MA: Harvard University Press, 1968), 30–31, 35–36, 38, 40, 42, 49.

national budget, and they soon excluded civilian experts in finance from the debate.

In the post-oligarch era, each ministry had an internal career path closed to outsiders. Those within each ministry saw clearly how their own ministry contributed to the national interest but not how the others did, let alone how the combined work of many ministries could be optimized for policy formulation and strategy implementation. They failed to appreciate the negative space of the many things they did not know and the career experiences that they did not have, nor did they seek it out in others. Instead institutional loyalties increasingly hindered policy formulation. Sectionalism in the bureaucracy became the civil equivalent of the growing factionalism in the military.[15]

The most stovepiped career track of all was that of military officers. While some civil ministers had served in the Diet, each of the two armed services did not appreciate the role played even by the other. Navy officers at least saw the world. Army officers saw only the empire. Over time, army officers increasingly dominated cabinet positions – closing down the diversity even of the stovepipes. Process stovepipe sabotaged the old way of consensus building that had required an understanding of the contributions of all parts of the government to national policy. And it utterly skewed power away from civil institutions in favor of military institutions and the army above all.

In 1913 both the Dōshikai and the Seiyūkai parties acquired new leaders, Katō Kōmei and Hara Kei respectively. This generational change ended the Saionji–Katsura era. Foreign Minister Katō Kōmei, a member of the Dōshikai, tried to seize the political and commercial opportunities opened by World War I, which removed Europe from an active role in Asia. To maximize his freedom of maneuver, he minimized sharing secret diplomatic records with the oligarchs. He then revamped his country's China policy without their consultation and, as its turns out, without their wisdom.

On 18 January 1915, he responded to Russia's twenty-one draft resolutions to China concerning Outer Mongolia with his own, much more famous Twenty-One Demands requiring China (1) to relinquish to Japan German concessions, (which Japan had just occupied as a member of the World War I Allies), (2) to grant mining and commercial privileges along the Yangzi river (in the heart of the British sphere of influence), (3) to cede a sphere of influence in Manchuria and Inner Mongolia (to counterbalance Russia), (4) to forswear alienating further coastal areas to others (so Japan could keep on going), and, most controversially of all, (5) to populate its government and police with numerous Japanese advisers. Katō's freelancing not only outraged the Chinese, but also alienated the Americans and British, with whom he had failed to share

---

[15] The terminology comes from Gordon Mark Berger, *Parties out of Power in Japan 1931–1941* (Princeton: Princeton University Press, 1977), 80.

the complete list of demands, which they soon received from China. Japan responded to the ensuing great-power hullabaloo by dropping its demands for the German concession in Shandong, for the sphere of influence in Fujian province, and for advisers throughout the government and police. Katō was out of a job within the year but over a century later his handiwork continues to sour Sino-Japanese relations. To this day, the Twenty-One Demands (Japan's, not Russia's) remain a watchword in China for infamy. It turns out foreign policy is a dangerous vocation for amateurs.

The end of World War I brought false and rapidly dashed hopes to those on the receiving end of imperialism. American President Woodrow Wilson's Fourteen Points nowhere promised (though many interpreted them to promise) national self-determination. The Versailles Peace Treaty did not make good on the promise that was never made and this failure deeply disappointed the colonized worldwide. On 1 March 1919, Koreans demonstrated for independence throughout the peninsula. This became known as the March First Movement. The unrest overwhelmed the police, Japan deployed the army, and hundreds, if not thousands, of Koreans died, creating yet another iconic event to crystalize their hatred of Japan and another bloody milestone in the development of Korean nationalism. On 4 May 1919, Chinese also demonstrated against the Versailles settlement, as well as Japan's failure to return Germany's Shandong concession with adequate dispatch. Suppression did not suppress. Instead the movement that began in Beijing became national and, as in Korea, a bloody milestone in the development of Chinese nationalism. To the present, Chinese herald the May Fourth Movement as a key way station on their path to national liberation. Both movements were intensely anti-Japanese, which did not bode well for future commercial or diplomatic relations.

China's iconic event rested on a misrepresentation of the facts. Contrary to what the demonstrators publicized, at issue was never the return of Germany's former concessions in Shandong to China. All agreed to their return. Rather at issue was a matter of "face," whether Germany or Japan would be the bearer of returned territory. Chinese dignity required the largesse from Germany, a great European power, not Japan, a despised Asian rival, whereas Japanese diplomacy and international law gave Japan the honor. China's cash-starved government had signed treaties and loan agreements making Japan's legal case ironclad, but it played the racism card against Japan with great finesse, since Japan had done much for the Chinese to hate. So the Chinese demonstrated against the Japanese, the unrest delayed the return of Shandong until 1922, and the demonstrations fed the young a full diet of anti-Japanese hatred, with cascading repercussions to follow.

Warfare in north China coincided with the Russian Civil War (1917–22) that brought to power the Communists (then called Bolsheviks). Tsarist Russia's defection from the Entente in World War I stranded in Siberia 40,000 Czech forces en route to the European front as well as over 200,000 Central Power prisoners of war. France immediately pressured Japan to intervene and it eventually agreed to U.S. plans for a combined Allied force to extricate the Czechs and the prisoners of war from the spreading Russian Civil War.[16] The World War I Allies also deployed troops to prevent German confiscation of war materiel stockpiled in Archangel and Murmansk. Japan, which had signed up to provide up to 12,000 of the planned total of 24,000 Allied troops, unilaterally sent 73,000, to the shock of allies and enemies alike.[17] From 1918 to 1920, the Allied powers deployed over 100,000 soldiers from fourteen countries. The Czechs soon joined with the White Guard (anti-Bolshevik) forces in the Russian Civil War.[18] After many complications, on 1 September 1920, the last of the Czechs boarded ships bound for home, removing the original rationale for Japan's intervention.

Some Japanese army planners had envisioned not a simple rescue of some Czechs but the establishment of a buffer state in Siberia east of Lake Baikal. So they had deployed a multiple of the forces anticipated by the United States and soon they too aided the White Guards. After the end of World War I, disagreement erupted among Japanese leaders over whether to withdraw from Siberia or to continue on the mission to establish a buffer state. Russian actions then delayed the withdrawal.

On 28 March 1920, when Bolshevik forces had taken Nikolaevsk, a town located near the mouth of the Amur river separating Siberia from Manchuria, they violated the surrender agreement to massacre all surrendering Whites. The Bolshevik forces eventually delivered the same fate to all of the town's Japanese soldiers. Then in late May, when the Bolsheviks learned of approaching Japanese reinforcements, they murdered, dismembered, and pitched into the river the bodies of the nearly 700 remaining Japanese civilians. In all, they killed half of the town's population and the massacre poisoned the rapidly deteriorating relations between the two countries.[19] On 3 July 1920, Japan responded by securing Nikolaevsk and occupying the Russian half of Sakhalin

---

[16] Humphreys, *The Way of the Heavenly Sword*, 25–28; A. Morgan Young, *Japan under the Taisho Tenno 1912–1926* (London: George Allen & Unwin, 1928), 178.

[17] Young, *Japan under the Taisho Tenno 1912–1926*, 35.

[18] Paul E. Dunscomb, *Japan's Siberian Intervention 1918–1922: "A Great Disobedience against the People"* (Lanham, MD: Rowman & Littlefield, 2011), 102–3; Edward J. Drea, "Kurihara Yasuhide and the Tokyo Young Officers Movement 1918–1936" (Ph.D. diss., University of Kansas, 1972), 6; Nicholas V. Riasanovsky, *A History of Russia*, 5th edn. (New York: Oxford University Press, 1993), 483; George F. Kennan, *Soviet–American Relations, 1917–1920*, vol. 2, *The Decision to Intervene* (Princeton: Princeton University Press, 1958), 415.

[19] George Alexander Lensen, *Japanese Recognition of the U.S.S.R.: Sino-Japanese Relations 1921–1930* (Tallahassee, FL: Diplomatic Press, 1970), 8–9; *Japan's Siberian Intervention 1918–1922*, 115–19.

Island as redress. Simultaneously, it began withdrawing from the area between Lake Baikal and Harbin.

By this time, the Siberian intervention had become deeply unpopular in Japan. The Americans, British, and French had begun withdrawing their troops in 1919 but Japanese troops remained until 1922, when the end of the Russian Civil War removed any legal pretext for lingering, and on northern Sakhalin Island until 1925. Sakhalin had long been a bargaining chip in Russo-Japanese relations. In 1875 Russia and Japan had agreed to Russian sovereignty over the island and Japanese sovereignty over the Kuril Islands. But in 1906 Japan had acquired the southern half in the settlement for the Russo-Japanese War, until 1945, when another war redrew the boundaries yet again.

At the time of the Siberian intervention, Finance Minister Takahashi Korekiyo, who served seven terms in that position, presented "A Personal View of National Policies at Home and Abroad" to Prime Minister Hara Kei. Takehashi advocated civil control over the military in order to execute grand strategy over the operational focus preferred by the military. He wrote,

The army does not stop at planning to send troops abroad for military reasons, but interferes in diplomatic and economic decision making as well, so that our country does not have a unified policy ... Because the army's general staff interferes with other state organs we should abolish it and unify the army's administration [under the war ministry]. The navy's general staff happily does not have the same invidious effects as the army's, but it is an unnecessary organ. We should abolish both general staffs at the same time.[20]

Needless to say, the military strongly disagreed.

The power of the Diet peaked in the 1920s, a period of antimilitarism after the Imperial Japanese Army's expensive Siberian intervention and suppression of the Rice Riots. Diet leaders formed a coalition with the Home and Finance Ministries and hard-pressed oligarchs turned from outside their ranks to Hara Kei, the leader of the Seiyūkai, as the only viable candidate for prime minister, to form Japan's first party cabinet. Prime Minister Hara soon appointed civilians over military officers to serve as governors of the key colonies of Korea, Taiwan, and Manchuria. Over the objections of the army, War Minister Tanaka Giichi supported Prime Minister Hara's desire to reduce Japanese forces in Siberia in 1918. Tanaka trumped the army's opposition by securing the emperor's prior approval. The army did not allow itself to be trumped again and continued to develop plans to take Russian territories east of Lake Baikal eventually.

The Seiyūkai's decision under Hara to defeat the 1920 universal suffrage bill radicalized the labor and student movements. Then Hara's murder in 1921 and Yamagata Aritomo's death in 1922 ended a stabilizing relationship of two

---

[20] Cited in Dunscomb, *Japan's Siberian Intervention 1918–1922*, 140.

powerful political opponents who strove to work together. The army used the Great Kantō Earthquake of 1 September 1923 that burned to the ground two-thirds of Yokohama and half of Tokyo to recoup some of its lost popularity by restoring order and providing prompt disaster relief. It also took advantage of the post-quake chaos to murder 6,000 Koreans and assorted political radicals. Nevertheless, from 1924 to 1932 prime ministers were party leaders and party members dominated but did not monopolize Cabinet positions.[21]

The State Shintō Answer to a Treacherous International Environment

Great disagreement remained over the role that the legislature should play. At the turn of the century, Professor Minobe Tatsukichi (1873–1948), a leading jurist at Tokyo Imperial University, developed theories justifying a constitutional monarchy and, by extension, an important role for political parties. He defined the emperor as an organ of state whose person but not prerogatives were sacred. The emperor must exercise power through his ministers, who then assumed accountability for decision making. The military, however, defined the emperor as sacrosanct in order to hijack his supreme command and, in doing so, to eliminate civil interference. By the 1930s, it criminalized Minobe's interpretation. In 1935, the public uproar over his views led to his expulsion from the House of Peers and from his professorship at Tokyo Imperial University, and to persecution thereafter.

Even as the power of political parties grew, no new theories emerged in support of democracy. Instead, the ideological support for party government atrophied. Shintō, however, received a makeover by Uesugi Shinkichi (1878–1929), who transformed it into an ideology of mass appeal, justifying terrorism in the name of the state in order to eliminate the defilers of the polity. He defined the Japanese state as the "ultimate morality" with its "god incarnate" emperor, who alone stood above selfish interests and therefore alone could represent the best interests not just of Japanese, but of humanity. He rejected westernization and constitutional monarchy to advocate totalitarianism with Japanese characteristics. His works formed part of the curriculum at military schools and his views greatly influenced unit officers – those who did most of the killing and the dying. Increasingly, education at the Military Academy emphasized not practical military training but ideology and the special relationship between the officer corps and the emperor. Army indoctrination then became embedded in public-school curricula.[22]

---

[21] Berger, *Parties out of Power in Japan 1931–1941*, vii.

[22] Walter A. Skya, *Japan's Holy War: The Ideology of Radical Shintō Ultranationalism* (Durham, NC: Duke University Press, 2009), 239; Humphreys, *The Way of the Heavenly Sword*, vii–viii, 97, 102, 122–24, 126; Theodore Failor Cook Jr., "The Japanese Officer Corps: The Making of a Military Elite, 1872–1945" (Ph.D. diss., Princeton University, 1987), 105–8, 114, 167, 170–71.

State Shintō discounted science, technology, weapons systems, rationality, institutions, and material factors in warfare. It villainized urbanites, industrialists, politicians, and foreigners, and yet advocated foreign expansion on the basis of an apocalyptic, social Darwinist interpretation of international relations. The emperor-centric nation-state required the complete subordination of the individual to a strategy of aggressive territorial expansion in pursuit of the collective goal of a Japanese global order, a Pax Japonica. These ambitions had two possible but antithetical outcomes: total victory or utter annihilation. Adherents had undue optimism about the first possibility, but were dead right about the second.

State Shintō emphasized two characteristics unique to Japan: the longevity of the ruling dynasty and the ethnicity (defined through bloodlines) of the people. It heralded a special role for the Japanese to play in history, a message that resonated with Japanese from all walks of life and motivated them to act and achieve in ways that shocked others. It galvanized nationwide, unquestioning support for the military in the name of their emperor and a Pax Japonica to come. In the 1930s, a generation of highly motivated officers, who became known as the Young Officers, operationalized state Shintō through a domestic strategy of assassination, hybridized the traditional samurai's contempt for the merchant class with a Marxist bloodlust for class warfare, and planned an inversion of the social pyramid, all packaged in a mystical assurance in Japan's destiny. On the basis of World War I, they concluded that Japan must prepare for total war. They did not examine their country's geographic position as an island defended by nature from attack by an oceanic moat. Nor did they examine their country's economy: its utter dependence on trade for survival – it could not even feed itself. Instead they chose courses of action that predisposed the very apocalyptic outcome that they most feared.

The decline of party influence coincided with the end of the long prevailing permissive international environment. When the Communists won the Russian Civil War, they transformed the political landscape of Asia. They immediately set about founding communist parties all along their borders, including in Japan and its neighbors, adding a volatile ideological dimension to recent Russo-Japanese imperial rivalries. The Russian Communists became deeply involved in China and a major supporter of the Nationalist Party and its efforts to create a credible military force to reunite China from the south. Russia provided essential funds and expertise to found the Whampoa Military Academy that educated some of the finest officers in both the Nationalist and Chinese Communist armed forces. As part of the aid package, Russia brokered the First Communist Party–Nationalist Party United Front in 1923 in an attempt to infiltrate communist political commissars into the Nationalist Party and military structure to take over the Nationalist government from within.

In 1926, the Russian-trained Nationalist armies swept northward to reunite China. Although the Nationalists halted the Northern Expedition (1926–28) mid-campaign in 1927, to eliminate the Communist presence in urban China by summary execution, thus ending the First United Front, Japan perceived a growing Communist influence inimical to its national security. The Nationalist Party's reunification of north and south China then raised the prospects of a rising power on Japan's doorstep, an eventuality considered dangerous by the Imperial Japanese Army.

Japanese military intervention moved south during the Northern Expedition. On 3 May 1928 when Nationalist forces approached the former German concessions in Shandong, Japanese and Nationalist forces clashed in Jinan, the provincial capital of Shandong. Certainly hundreds, if not thousands, of Chinese soldiers died – including those promised safe passage by the Japanese. This became known as the Jinan Incident in the growing Chinese lexicon of Japanese infamy.[23]

In response to the civilian government's earlier Siberian intervention fait accompli, which had forced a withdrawal from Siberia, this time the army produced the Zhang Zuolin fait accompli and hijacked foreign policy for good. As Nationalist forces swept northward, the Manchurian warlord, Zhang Zuolin, attempted to retreat from Beijing back home. Colonel Kōmoto Daisaku, in defiance of his government's promise to allow Zhang and his army safe passage, but in conformity with the Kantō Army's insistence that it take control over Manchuria minus the warlord and warlord army, arranged on 4 June 1928 to detonate Zhang's railway carriage with the desired fatal results for both Zhang and the Japanese government, which fell as a result. The Kantō Army (also known as the Kwantung Army) was Japan's army in Manchuria. For many years Zhang had attempted to eliminate Russian influence in Manchuria – principally by trying (and failing) to take control of tsarist-era railway concessions from Russia – a goal that Japan supported. But Zhang equally desired to eliminate Japanese influence and assume control over their railway concessions, and this cost him his life. Thereafter, the army protected Kōmoto from prosecution.

The Kantō Army's fears of a growing Nationalist influence in Manchuria and the erosion of Japanese privileges that had inspired the pre-emptive action paradoxically guaranteed these outcomes. When General Chiang Kai-shek's forces reached Beijing, they overthrew the internationally recognized government there, and soon cut a deal with Zhang's opium-addict son, Zhang Xueliang, now fearful of Japan after his father's murder. The deal produced a very nominal reunification of China and marked a northward expansion of Nationalist influence – a highly undesirable turn of events from the point of

---

[23] Jonathan Fenby, *Chiang Kai-shek: China's Generalissimo and the Nation He Lost* (New York: Carroll & Graf, 2003), 177–78.

view of the Kantō Army. On 19 July 1928 the Nationalist government uni-laterally renounced its 1896 commercial treaty with Japan, promising to end Japanese commercial privileges in China, including Manchuria.

The Zhang assassination took place in the context of spiraling financial cri-ses and dislocations: the post-World War I depression of 1920, the Great Kantō Earthquake of 1923, an expanding boycott of Japanese goods by Chinese con-sumers, the 1927 depression, and the capstone event, the Great Depression of 1929 that tanked trade globally for the next decade. The Hamaguchi Osachi Cabinet under the Minseitō party then bungled economic policy with a most ill-timed return to the gold standard in January 1930 that magnified the downward economic spiral. Thereafter it refused either to maintain government spending or to alleviate the hardships of the growing ranks of the unemployed, who increasingly gravitated toward Communism. Instead, the government treated the symptoms of economic collapse with nationwide arrests of communists in 1928, 1929, and 1930.

Desperate times inspired desperate actions. Assassinations of business lead-ers began in 1921 with the murder of Yasuda Zenjirō, the president of the com-pany of his name, Yasuda, not by the left wing, as one might expect, but by the right wing – state Shintō beliefs marked both communists and capitalists for doom. In 1932, members of the Fraternity of Blood (Ketsumeidan), a secret ultranationalist society, murdered Inoue Junnosuke, a former finance minis-ter and current brother-in-law of the president of Mitsubishi, as well as Dan Takuma, the director of the Mitsui Bank. Owners of *zaibatsu* (large holding companies) responded by hiring guards for themselves and delivering payoffs to right-wing groups.

Simultaneously, corruption scandals plagued political parties: the Matsushima Club Scandal from 1926 to 1927 engulfed the leadership of the three main political parties; concurrent allegations of lenient treatment of the Korean would-be assassin of the prince regent (Hirohito serving for his mentally ill father) allowed two parties out of power to impugn the party in power, tarnishing the reputation of party government in general. Meanwhile, Tanaka Giichi, who had so recently outraged the army by sup-porting the withdrawal of troops from Siberia, found himself at the center of allegations that he, as president of the Seiyūkai, had his hand in the army's till.

The Great Depression also coincided with a series of escalating politi-cal crises perpetrated by Young Officers, beginning with navy outrage over Prime Minister Hamaguchi Osachi's signing of the 1930 London Naval Treaty, which modified upward the tonnage ratio in Japan's favor to 10–10–7. This did not mollify the Imperial Japanese Navy, whose hotheads insisted that the minimally acceptable ratio did not actually apply to all categories of ships, so Japan had been cheated yet again. Hamaguchi paid with his life, dead in April 1931 from a gunshot wound inflicted by Young Officers of the navy the previous year. The army coup that never occurred (the March Incident) was called off for insufficient support from War Minister Ugaki Kazushige, the supposed coup beneficiary, who still found himself out of a job within the month. Young Officers of the army upped the ante to regional war when they arranged the pretext to invade and occupy all of Manchuria, the so-called Manchurian Incident of 18 September 1931, and ignored a succession of Wakatsuki Reijirō Cabinet orders to cease and desist. While the invasion was ongoing, the Young Officer masterminds of the coup that never was then rescheduled for October (the October Incident), but General Araki Sadao, this coup's supposed beneficiary, refused to go along, supported their arrests but leniency thereafter, and, in so finessing, became war minister by the end of the year. Araki was the leader of the devout state Shintōists of the Imperial Way faction of the army, whose followers came mainly from the feudal domains of Hizen and Tosa.

On 15 May 1932 (the May 15 Incident), came the party-government-terminating assassination of Prime Minister Inukai by Young Officers of the navy desirous of an undefined Shōwa Restoration. (Shōwa was the era name for Hirohito's reign.) The army was more inclined to arrest than support the assassins, although the sentencing was light. The Control faction of the army then negotiated a solution. (The Imperial Way faction apparently coined the term Control faction to deride army officers, who insisted on following the chain of command instead of delegating key matters of national strategy and policy to junior officers.) The Control faction cobbled together a coalition including sympathetic naval officers and bureaucrats from the civil ministries to make an admiral, Saitō Makoto, the new prime minister. The navy, but not the army, then purged its Young Officers. The emperor's younger brother, Prince Chichibu, was a particularly dangerous supporter of the Young Officers since he presented an alternative to his older brother. Apparently he and perhaps other members of the royal family were complicit in the 1932 coup.

Both the domestic and international environments had turned treacherous. Russia and China, both failed states, were in the process of restoration. This potentially put two great powers on Japan's doorstep. Nationalism in China and Korea, and communism in Russia, were all anti-Japanese. Japanese investments concentrated in Korea and China, the two countries that despised Japan the most, and the communism peddled by Russia found a receptive audience among Japan's unemployed workers and idealistic students, struggling in the deepening economic depression. Although the army suppressed its coups, the Manchurian Incident hijacked foreign policy and soon domestic policy by opening a Fifteen Year War that would ruin imperial Japan. From the assassinations of the 1930s onward, those who dared support constitutional monarchy did so at the risk of their lives.

Both Japan and China required stability in China in order to foster prosperity through commerce and economic development. Yet their peoples and militaries failed to perceive this overarching and vital common interest and, instead, became divided over secondary but emotionally charged issues. Japanese diplomats understood the inversion of priorities but, as diplomatic incidents accumulated, became increasingly powerless vis-à-vis their military, which at home was assassinating its way to political domination. So instead of a positive-sum co-operation in the pursuit of economic growth, both countries soon became consumed by a zero-sum competition to undermine the other, producing a negative-sum and eventually a catastrophic lose–lose outcome.

In Japan, neither party government nor civil authority survived the deluge of economic and political crises. Japan's institutions were incomplete – its state building had been partial and dependent on a brilliant generation of leaders operating in a permissive international environment. The brilliant leaders had died and the environment had turned treacherous despite Japan's activist foreign policy, so the army turned the clock back to samurai rule.

The Point of No Return

Zhang Zuolin's assassination in 1928 was the first Shintō ultranationalist act of high-visibility terrorism. It was also the first instance in the new trend of army governance by fait accompli that soon undermined civilian control. Just six years of carefully targeted terrorism – assassinating two serving and two former prime ministers, and unsuccessfully targeting two others – changed the political landscape of Japan. At the time, Hugh Byas, a journalist and resident of Japan for twenty-three years, called it "the gangster decade."[24] By the 1930s, the key players in national politics came from a much broader group of people. They did not necessarily know each other and, judging from their increasing resort to assassination, did not believe that consensus was possible even within their own bureaucracy, let alone among bureaucracies.

Shintō ultranationalists then attempted to purge the military leadership with the murder in 1935 of Major General Nagata Tetsuzan, head of the Military Affairs Bureau of the War Ministry in charge of army modernization. Although originally a supporter of General Araki Sadao, the leader of the Imperial Way faction, he increasingly differed as to strategy to become the purported leader of the opposing Control faction. Like Araki, he supported a fully mobilized state, but negotiated through coalition building, not through assassination. Nagata's emphasis on command and control got in the way of the Young Officers' plans for a Shōwa Restoration to make the emperor's rule global. Never before had an active-duty, field-grade officer assassinated his superior.

---

[24] Hugh Byas, *Government by Assassination* (New York: Alfred A. Knopf, 1942), 368.

This assassination took place against the backdrop of the highly publicized trials of the Young Officers who had assassinated Prime Minister Inukai. As one of the defendants testified, "The Imperial Way should be spread through the world, the Asiatic nations being first consolidated into a unit and thereafter the rest of the world."[25] Such views rhymed with orthodox Fascism, totalitarianism, and Islamism – all are messianic justifications for a continental world order bent on territorial control, ideological uniformity, and antipathy toward a maritime rules-based order focused on mere wealth creation and base self-interest.

The Minseitō party won the general election on 20 February 1936. The 26 February 1936 Incident, or Young Officers' Revolt, took place the day after the announcement of the election results and during the widely covered, politically charged trial of the assassin of Nagata Tetsuzan. An attempt to transfer to Manchuria the First Division – in which most of the hotheads of the Young Officers movement served – triggered rather than defused a revolt. Unlike the aborted army coups of 1931, this one took.

In the manner of the Marxist general uprising, the plotters assumed that once they had assassinated key political leaders, opposition to the government would spontaneously coalesce and army sympathizers would take power. For an institution normally given to meticulous planning, such as the army, a reliance on spontaneity seems highly out of character. The plotters and over a thousand subordinate troops fanned out over Tokyo before sunrise on 26 February 1936 in search of their quarry. They occupied the Diet and War Ministry and killed Finance Minister Takahashi Korekiyo, Lord Privy Seal Saitō Makoto, and Inspector General of Military Education Watanabe Jōtarō, but found little support in naval or financial circles. Finance Minister Takahashi understood that Shintō ultranationalist plans for continental empire would not work out well for a resource-dependent country separated from the necessary resources by expansive seas dominated by the maritime powers. He knew that military power required a foundation of economic power and had tried to keep down military budgets in order to foster economic growth. He paid with his life for speaking truth to power.

The immediate hitch in the coup was Hirohito's abhorrence of Shintō ultranationalist plans; the Shōwa Emperor opposed the Shōwa Restoration: "They have killed my advisers and are now trying to pull a silk rope around my neck … I shall never forgive them, no matter what their motives are." On 27 February he threatened to take command of the Imperial Guards Division and personally restore order if the army remained paralyzed.[26] Rumors circulated that Prince

---

[25] Cited in Skya, *Japan's Holy War*, 243.
[26] Cited in Ben-Ami Shillony, *Revolt in Japan: The Young Officers and the February 26, 1936 Incident* (Princeton: Princeton University Press, 1973), 173.

Chichibu had been slated to replace Hirohito. The navy helped restore order instead.

The War Ministry downplayed events in a comparatively bland official announcement:

The purpose of the uprising, as stated in the manifesto of these officers, is to uphold our moral principles and manifest the national polity, by destroying the traitorous *genrō* [oligarchs], senior statesmen, financial magnates, military clique, bureaucrats and politicians, who, at a time of external and internal dangers, were undermining our national structure.

Only 124 of the 1,483 participants were prosecuted. Others were soon transferred to Manchuria. Unlike the high-visibility public trials of the assassins of Inukai and Nagata, those for the 26 February assassinations were secret; seventeen received death sentences, five received life sentences, and fifty others received varying terms.[27]

During the Young Officers' Revolt, Saionji lost the struggle for governance on the basis of liberalism and party rule at home, and co-operation with the maritime powers abroad. Already assassinated in 1931 and 1932 respectively were two recent prime ministers favored by Saionji, Hamaguchi Osachi and Inukai Tsuyoshi. Together this overturned not only party leadership but also the palace leadership, producing stability in the palace for the duration of imperial rule but at a price of complete subordination to the army.

Saionji's counterargument to continentalism had been rebutted and although the navy had not joined the revolt, it had joined the continentalists. The navy had purged its Young Officers after the assassination of Inukai, but the Fleet faction, so-named for its insistence on building a large fleet, had remained up in arms against the 1922 Washington and 1930 London naval treaties. Naval officers increasingly detested the Treaty faction responsible for those treaties. The 26 February hit list had included three Treaty faction admirals, Lord Privy Seal Saitō Makoto, who died; Grand Chamberlain Suzuki Kantarō, who survived severe wounds; and Prime Minister Okada Keisuke, who survived in a case of mistaken identity for which his brother-in-law paid with his life instead.

By the 1930s an inner cabinet system emerged with five or fewer ministers, depending on the Cabinet, who made crucial decisions. The army and navy ministers, but not necessarily the prime minister, always belonged to the inner cabinet. The finance minister and the foreign minister might serve, but again not necessarily. The consistent army and navy attendance, in contrast to the sporadic presence of the different civilian ministers, shifted the internal balance of power further toward the military, making it far more powerful at home and abroad than in the Meiji era. Particularly after the assassination in 1936

---

[27] Cited in Shillony, *Revolt in Japan*, 161, 198, 201

of Takahashi Korekiyo, the brilliant and outspoken finance minister, civilians feared for their lives with good reason and became reluctant to criticize the preferred policies of the army or navy. By the 1930s, civil appointments rolled with the cabinets. The military alone was immune.

Shintō ultranationalism played the ideological role in Japan that Nazism and Fascism did elsewhere. By 1937 it became orthodoxy with the government's publication of *Fundamentals of Our National Polity*, outlining a winner-take-all cosmic war against the Western maritime global order in order to eradicate individualism and notions about the universality of logic. As the journalist Hugh Byas wrote in 1942, "Japan's spiritual malady is the same as Germany's – a false philosophy. It is a belief that the Japanese race and state are one and the same and that it has unique qualities that make it superior to its neighbors and give it a special mission to perform."[28]

The Misidentification of Japan as a Continental Power

In addition to incomplete institutions and cascading crises, Japan's leaders ultimately misidentified their country as a great continental power. In doing so, they overlooked the great gift of geography that allowed them to become a maritime power as well as the great geographic vulnerability that precluded their becoming a continental power.

Starting in the 1890s, in recognition of Japan's unusual geography as an island power, Admiral Yamamoto Gonbee (1852–1933), who served as navy minister (1898–1906) and prime minister (1923–24), tried to make the navy the dominant military service. He believed that overseas empire was not essential to Japan's national defense and could be jettisoned in time of war. Predictably, the army leadership adamantly disagreed in the ensuing bitter debate, and the navy came around to the idea of maritime empire. His opposite number in the army, Field Marshal and eventually Prince Yamagata Aritomo, had already coined the term "absolute lifeline," to describe Manchuria's vital security relation to Japan in his famous edict on Japanese foreign policy.[29] The army looked to the Asian mainland for Japanese security and justification for its proportion of the budget.

Vice Admiral Satō Tetsutarō (1866–1942), president of Japan's Naval War College and among Japan's most influential naval thinkers, wrote, "Among the Powers in the World, there are only three countries that can defend themselves

---

[28] Byas, *Government by Assassination*, 331.
[29] 金安泰 (Jin Antai), "'九一八'事变与美国外交" ("The Manchurian Incident and U.S. Foreign Policy"), 史学集刊 (*Collected Papers of Historical Studies*) (1983), 12 no. 3, 73; Marius B. Jansen, "Japanese Imperialism: Late Meiji Perspectives," in Ramon H. Myers and Mark R. Peattie, eds., *The Japanese Colonial Empire, 1895–1945* (Princeton: Princeton University Press, 1984), 67.

primarily with navies. They are the UK and the US and Japan." Given the gift of geography as an island state, Japan should not maintain a large and expensive army.[30] He considered the United States to be Japan's most likely enemy on the basis of U.S. naval capabilities rather than on the basis of likely U.S. intentions, setting Japan on the path toward self-fulfilling prophesies. Like the army, the navy's preferred enemy justified its portion of the budget.

During World War I, the army embraced an Asian Monroe Doctrine. In 1928, it gravitated to a Japan First Policy, rejecting diplomacy either in co-operation with Britain and the United States, or in co-operation with China and Russia. Even Prime Minister Tanaka Giichi, who had served as war and foreign minister in the 1920s and had supported Japan's withdrawal from Siberia in 1922, argued that Japan should "free itself from previous conditions of being an island and develop its national future as a continental power."[31] As prime minister, he called for the detachment of Manchuria and Mongolia from China, guaranteeing hostile Sino-Japanese relations. He anticipated that future wars would be protracted; success would depend on economic mobilization and the resources of a continental empire on the Asia mainland. He failed to grasp that Japan's economic survival depended not on resources per se, but on trade, meaning co-operation with others. He never examined the problem of protecting the sea lines of communication to connect the resources and the empire with the home country. Britain in its era of dominance possessed on the home islands the iron and energy resouces (coal at the time) necessary to build and sustain a navy. Japan did not. Whereas, in World War II, the British understood that they could not fight their main oil supplier (the United States), the Japanese did not.[32]

The long-serving navy minister (1915–23) and short-serving prime minister (1922–23), Admiral Katō Tomosaburō, who signed the 1922 Washington Naval Treaty, understood the economic prerequisites for military power. He had argued, "National defense is not a monopoly that belongs to military men ... no war can be fought without money." He saw the United States as the only potential adversary, but believed Japan could never win such a war. His logic: "Even if we could match the US in terms of military power ... where would we get the money? ... Thus, war with the US is simply impossible."[33] Shintō ultranationalists detested his conclusions and the logic leading to them. So they rejected the entire field of logic and, like many other people in similarly untenable positions, planned to substitute will power instead. They turned to

[30] Cited in Tadokoro Masayuki, "Why Did Japan Fail to Become the 'Britain' of Asia?", in Steinberg et al., *The Russo-Japanese War in Global Perspective*, 301–2.

[31] Cited in Tadokoro, "Why Did Japan Fail to Become the 'Britain' of Asia?" 304–5.

[32] Anand Toprani, "Oil and Grand Strategy: Great Britain and Germany, 1918–1941" (Ph.D. diss., Georgetown University, 2012), 1–3.

[33] Tadokoro, "Why Did Japan Fail to Become the 'Britain' of Asia?" 221–22.

bushido, the code of the samurai, emphasizing the ability of will power to trump economic factors in warfare. By 1932 the Imperial Japanese Navy had developed a formula: Japan's naval power equaled the product of the size of its fleet multiplied by the square of the quality of its sailors and officers. It measured their quality in terms of their superior "morale, efficincy, endurance, discipline, etc."[34] The mathematics did not work out well in practice.

A closer study of the Napoleonic Wars – involving logic, of course – would have revealed that Britain's comparatively narrow moat, the English Channel, had proved sufficient in combination with the Royal Navy to keep the largest and finest armies of continental Europe away. Depending on the enemy, Japan's moat was at least twenty-five miles (to Sakhalin Island), and China and Korea were hardly capable enemies. A better understanding of the British economy would have revealed that trade, not war, formed the basis for British prosperity and its position as a great power. The Royal Navy was a means to protect the trade and defend the homeland against invasion, not to fight distant naval powers. Negotiation, not war, was a more useful instrument of national policy to deal with the West, particularly since Asia was a secondary interest at best for the West and a primary interest for Japan, giving Japan leverage to encourage the West to back down.

The opinions of Yamamoto Gonbee, Satō Tetsutarō, and Katō Tomosaburō became increasingly marginalized as the Fleet faction gained strength. By the 1935 London Naval Conference, the Imperial Japanese Navy forced a Japanese walkout from the negotiations; the arms limitations then expired at the end of 1936, and Japan began building its super-battleships, *Yamato* and *Musashi*, which had nearly twice the displacement of any ship on the planet.

Generals Yamagata, Terauchi, and Tanaka and the Imperial Japanese Army in general failed to understand the unique advantage that geography gave Japan. Geography provided a moat and unfettered access to the high seas along its long coastline, affording security from invasion in times of war and access to the world's markets in both war and peace. In contrast to countries like Russia and Germany, whose vessels reached the high seas only after traversing blockadable chokepoints, or China, whose many ports all opened onto seas cluttered by occupiable islands and near neighbors, Japan's long eastern coastline was extraordinarily difficult to blockade. As a result, maritime powers such as Japan possessed a level of national security unattainable for a continental power, whose contiguous neighbors could suddenly invade.

---

[34] Document from Bruce A. Elleman. LT E.T. Layton, U.S. Naval Attache in Peiping, China, "Mathematics of Naval Warfare as Applied to Naval Disarmament as Expressed in the Writings of Messrs. Ikezaki, Ozaki, Hirata and Kawaishi," December 1932, File No. XTAV, accession no. 1934-106, Military and Technical Intelligence, U.S. Naval War College Archives.

They also failed to understand the key prerequisite for a continental power. It must be able to access essential resources contiguously, most importantly energy. Otherwise, the dominant maritime power will deny essential resources by sea through blockade, commerce raiding, and fleet-on-fleet engagements, operations which geography and the maritime alliance system position the maritime alliance to win. Japan's energy dependence positioned it poorly to survive a protracted war against the maritime powers. Therefore the Japanese decision to follow the Imperial Army's inclination to act as if Japan were a continental power was a gross strategic error that produced a cascade of undesired and undesirable effects.

Map 4 Second Sino-Japanese War

松 岡 全 權 の 近 影

Photo 4 Matsuoka Yōsuke (1880–1946)
http://www.ndl.go.jp/portrait/e/datas/333_1.html (National Diet Library
of Japan)

5   The Second Sino-Japanese War (1931–1941)

> Communism has already invaded China, and the alarming extent and success of the invasion is far too seldom realized. A communized China would constitute a problem for Europe and America beside which other questions would pale into insignificance.[1]
>
> 1933, as Japan withdrew from the League of Nations

The military eclipse of civil authority marked a return to the pre-Meiji Restoration balance between civil and military institutions.[2] During the shogunates, the army had ruled. But army rule was a throwback to a system no longer adequate to navigate the problems Japan faced. Its modern army missed the strategic advantages conferred by an island location to misidentify Japan as a continental, not a maritime, power. This led to a succession of errors of commission: the universal answer to problems in China became escalation. This produced a protracted war for control of the Asian mainland that need never have been fought. There were better ways to achieve the policy objective of restoring domestic prosperity and maintaining Japan as a great power.

The Sino-Japanese conflagration that broke out in 1931 ignited an accumulation of highly combustible grievances. World War I had destroyed the European political system and the Great Depression had destroyed the global economic system. Both the Great War and the Great Depression were of unprecedented scale. Botched military strategy in the former followed by botched economic strategy in the latter put Fascism and Communism on the march as the only two political systems apparently capable of restoring economic health. As the countries of the world tried to navigate these turbulent uncharted waters, they became increasingly focused on their own dire situations and ever less cognizant of the equally dire situations of their neighbors. This blinded them to

---

[1] Japanese Foreign Ministry Archives, A.1.1.0-21-35, 満州事件　満州事件及上海事件関係公報集 (Manchurian Incident: Collection of Public Announcements on the Manchurian and Shanghai Incidents), vol. 2, 満州事件及上海事件関係発表集（五）(Announcements on the Manchurian and Shanghai Incidents, part 5), Report of the Assembly [of the League of Nations], 31 March 1933.

[2] This chapter is based on S.C.M. Paine, *The Wars for Asia 1911–1949* (Cambridge: Cambridge University Press, 2012).

the interests of others and to the likely countermeasures to their own policy choices. Escalation became the name of the game.

Army leaders, their many civilian supporters, and the Japanese public perceived no alternative to an aggressive foreign policy in China in order to overcome the Great Depression and to counter Russian territorial and ideological expansion. They faced an intractable dilemma: good citizenship in the prevailing global order promised economic disaster with the collapse of international trade caused by Western protectionism. Failure to play by the rules, however, risked diplomatic isolation and possibly war. Japanese leaders perceived Communism to be on the march and their options narrowing by the minute. They had compelling reasons to intervene in China.

Underlying and Proximate Causes

The Chinese refused to recognize that Japan had become the dominant regional power. Japanese leaders remained adamant that others should treat them in accordance with their great-power status, which the Western powers more or less did, but which China most conspicuously did not, still referring to the Japanese in official communications as dwarf bandits or *wokou* (倭寇), murdering Japanese businessmen at higher rates than they did Westerners, and violating Japan's commercial treaties. Japanese furor over the ill-treatment might have gratified the Chinese, but when the furor turned to coercion, the Chinese had their turn at infuriation when they became the victims of Japanese provocations and invasions. This escalatory spiral, although at times abating, has never ceased but remains an enduring source of tinder for Sino-Japanese conflict. Some might call it racism.

Competing Chinese and Japanese nationalisms became another source of tension. China was determined to expel the imperialists – Japan most of all – in order to regain full sovereignty over its territory and set out on the road to national restoration. A Rights Recovery Movement began in the twilight years of the Qing dynasty. One offshoot focused on the nationalization of the railway system to create a unified transportation grid. No foreign power with concessions and railway investments looked forward to China's full sovereignty over them, least of all Japan, which considered concession areas as benchmarks of its own status. By 1931, Chinese and Japanese leaders increasingly viewed their goals as mutually exclusive: only one country could dominate Asia. China was as determined to reverse the outcome of the First Sino-Japanese War as Japan was to reaffirm it. In the short run, China could do little, while Japan did far too much.

In addition to mutual hatred and a shared negative-sum approach to the Asian balance of power, the long Chinese Civil War constituted a third underlying cause of the Second Sino-Japanese War. The unrest unraveled the Chinese economy; threatened to engulf Manchuria, the focus of Japanese investments; and produced an environment unconducive to economic development and trade. Since the beginning of the Meiji Restoration, Japan had tried to conduct its foreign policy within the framework of Western international law and diplomatic norms. Manchuria was the focus of its foreign investments, where the local warlord family, the Zhang clan, gutted the economy by devoting 80 percent of government revenues to fund an army in an eternal struggle to overthrow the internationally recognized government in Beijing.[3] Neither pressure nor bribes, nor even the assassination of the clan patriarch, Zhang Zuolin, in 1928 produced the desired salutary effect. Regardless of what Japan did, the unrest worsened, Chinese hostility to Japan grew, and the Communists made further inroads. Japan observed what Western powers did in such situations – the United States occupied various insolvent Caribbean countries for decade-long intervals to re-establish fiscal responsibility, while the European powers sent punitive expeditions to colonies to stifle unrest, so the Japanese government felt well within international norms to deploy troops to protect its interests. As Japan and Russia stood to lose the most from unrest in China, unsurprisingly they intervened the most aggressively.

Russia's quest for empire in the East was the fourth underlying cause. Although World War I, the Russian Revolution, and the Russian Civil War had gravely weakened Russia economically, it sprang back with unaccountable vigor armed with a communist ideology that resonated globally among colonized and downtrodden peoples. It peddled the ideology most effectively in China, where it funded multiple sides in the Chinese Civil War. It aided the Nationalists, their dire enemies the Chinese Communists, and a variety of regional warlords bordering on Russia. Its ultimate goal was a much reduced China with Russia in possession of Xinjiang, Mongolia, and Manchuria. These plans left no place for Japan. Worse still from Japan's point of view, the ideology resonated among Japan's poor, threatening political stability on the home islands.

The incomplete institutions left by the oligarchs became the final source of tinder. Or conversely, the crippling of civil institutions put the fire department out of business. The post-Meiji generation had an inadequate knowledge of the diplomatic, financial, and economic elements of grand strategy, let alone any expertise in their integration. Rather, the military leaders who dominated the government applied operational military solutions to foreign-policy problems. No institutional mechanisms forced officers out of their career comfort zone to

---

[3] 西村成雄 (Nishimura Shigeo), "日本政府の中華民国認識と張学良政権 – 民族主義的凝集性の再評価" (The Japanese Government's Recognition of the Republic of China and Zhang Xueliang's Sovereignty: A Reappraisal of National Cohesion), in 山本有造 (Yamamoto Yūzō), ed., 「満洲国」の研究 (Research on "Manchukuo") (Tokyo: 緑蔭書房, 1995), 5, 12–14, 19–21.

join in a difficult debate with those who understood the many other elements of grand strategy. Instead officers assassinated those who raised the most persuasive objections.

Thus Sino-Japanese hatred, the Sino-Japanese competition for dominance in Asia, anarchy in China, the Soviet attempts to export Communism to Asia, and the inadequacy of both Japanese leaders and institutions together constituted the volatile underlying causes of the Second Sino-Japanese War. A long series of proximate causes finally ignited it into a conflagration of unprecedented scale even by Chinese standards.

From the Japanese point of view, the first match with serious candlepower was the nominal reunification of China including Manchuria as result of the Northern Expedition. In order to solidify domestic support for the new government, the Nationalist Party relied on nationalism (not surprising given the name of the party) in combination with a deeply felt and widespread hatred of Japan. As part of the many domestic reforms, the Nationalist government introduced new educational materials that fomented anti-Japanese sentiments. Japan had its own anti-Chinese propaganda at home. As both added lighter fluid, emotions seethed.

The new Nationalist government put all foreign powers on notice: the period of unequal treaties and scrambled concessions was over. Japan refused to comply. China refused to back down. Both applied more lighter fluid. On 7 December 1928, the Nationalists unilaterally announced tariff autonomy as of 1 February 1929, with the goal of increasing customs revenues. The changes in the tax law greatly increased the levies on bulk items (i.e. items shipped by rail), which were taxed by quantity – promising major repercussions on Japanese businesses. The United States agreed to the Nationalist demand that China, not outside powers, should set its tariffs. The Western nations followed suit. Japan resisted until the end of 1930, when it finally backed down so that on 1 January 1931 the Nationalists assumed control over their tariffs. A major upward revision of tariffs soon followed with another increase in 1933. Chinese customs revenues skyrocketed from 46 million yuan in 1927 to 385 million in 1931.[4]

Meanwhile, beginning in late October of 1929, a mishandled stock market crash on the New York Stock Exchange triggered a worldwide economic depression, which soon created bonfires of discontent. From peak to trough, the Dow Jones Industrial Average lost 89 percent of its value – wiping out capital, lifetime savings, livelihoods, and hope – not just in the United States, but soon globally as a capital vacuum destroyed the interconnected web of international commerce. The crash reverberated through Japan, already hit hard by the

---

[4] 张生 (Zhang Sheng), "南京民国政府初期关税改革述评" (A Discussion of Customs Reform in the Early Nanjing Nationalist Government), 近代史研究 (*Modern Chinese History Studies*) 74 no. 2 (March 1993), 208–20.

depressions of 1920 and 1927. It caused an immediate 10 percent pay reduction for civil servants and military officers above the rank of second lieutenant – two essential pillars of political stability – and hit agriculture particularly hard.[5] Between 1929 and 1931, Japanese exports then halved.[6]

On 17 June 1930 the United States erected the most formidable tariff barrier in a century. Predictably, U.S. trade partners followed suit. Together they waged an international tariff war that tanked international trade, leaving trade-dependent countries like Japan with no hope for recovery. Western protectionism not only threatened to undo the Meiji generation's transformation of Japan into a great power, but also discredited Japan's many civil leaders, who had consistently promoted co-operation with the West. In the hour of need, the West abandoned them. Given the Western origin of the global economic collapse, many concluded that the Western liberal economic and political model was too deeply flawed to save. Japan must look elsewhere. In the short and medium term, only the Fascist and Communist governments found an effective response because they did not shy away from government spending. It is no coincidence that the Kantō Army invaded Manchuria a year after the Hawley–Smoot Tariff Act set U.S. tariffs at historic highs.

The bad economic news coincided with a deteriorating geopolitical situation. In 1929, the Manchurian warlord, Zhang Xueliang, son of the man so recently blown up by the Kantō Army, tried to force the Russian Communists to make good their promise to return all tsarist concessions. When Zhang took over the Chinese Eastern Railway, Russia responded by deploying over 100,000 men to retake it.[7] Japan observed in horror as Zhang lost the 1929 Railway War, fought from July to December, and the Nationalists did nothing to counter the aggression. The Russian victory portended another round of territorial expansion southward, requiring another round of Japanese containment. Reinforcing this conclusion was the peace settlement that allegedly included a June 1931 railway purchase agreement, which would have exempted Russian but not Japanese railway traffic from Chinese tariffs and applied the amount toward the eventual Chinese purchase of the railway. This would have undercut Japanese trade, already in critical condition from Western protectionism Three months later, the Kantō Army invaded and rendered the purchase agreement moot.

The divisiveness of the tariff issue reflected not only a disagreement over the allocation of the profits from trade, but also Japan's declining terms of trade in Manchuria. The Japanese particularly condemned China for the construction of railway lines potentially competing with theirs and its unwillingness to link up

[5] Humphreys, *The Way of the Heavenly Sword*, 125.
[6] Richard J. Smethurst, *From Foot Soldier to Finance Minister: Takahashi Korekiyo, Japan's Keynes* (Cambridge, MA: Harvard University Press, 2007), 250.
[7] Bruce A. Elleman, *Modern Chinese Warfare, 1795–1989* (London: Routledge, 2001), 182.

all railways to create a unified transportation grid. This problem became acute between 1928 and 1930 when nearly 90 percent of the Chinese-built railway lines came into operation.[8] The Japanese also feared other forms of Chinese economic competition. Since 1905 Japan's trade with Manchuria had exceeded China's, but the gap had narrowed so that in 1930 Chinese trade was poised to turn the tables. Then, in March 1931, the Nationalists unilaterally renounced their unequal treaties – meaning the treaties imposed on China by Japan and the West. In the spring of 1931, they made the nationalization of the Japanese railway concessions in Manchuria a cornerstone of their foreign policy.

In the Manchurian hamlet of Wanbaoshan (萬寶山), located about 100 kilometers southwest of Harbin, on 2–3 July 1931 Chinese farmers clashed with Korean farmers, but the latter, as colonial subjects of Japan, had the protection of Japanese police. No one died. This became known as the Wanbaoshan Incident in Chinese lore because of what followed. Japanese propaganda emphasizing Chinese brutality helped trigger anti-Chinese rioting in Korea (3–9 July), where the Japanese military and police stood by while over 100 Chinese lost their lives. Japanese and Chinese diplomats, but not the Japanese military, wanted a diplomatic resolution of the crisis.[9] The Chinese people boycotted. All sides threw matches.

The Chinese public discovered a counterstrategy that struck vital Japanese economic interests. In response to Japan's growing interference in China's domestic affairs – the Twenty-One Demands (1915), its covert support for Zhang Zuolin in the north China warlord infighting (mid-1920s), the Jinan Incident (1928), the Zhang Zuolin Bomb Incident (1928), and most recently the Wanbaoshan Incident (1931) – the Chinese waged a series of boycotts. Between 1908 and 1931, they conducted eleven boycotts for periods of three to thirteen months each, averaging one boycott per year between 1925 and 1931. Most centered in south and central China, the seat of Nationalist influence, and safely outside the range of the Kantō Army, which apparently fumed at its inability to stop them. Chinese consumers' refusal to buy Japanese goods ruined Japanese trade, the basis for Japanese interests in China. Sadly, the operational effects did not produce the desired strategic effects: far from moderating Japanese imperialism, the boycott strategy elicited increasingly aggressive reprisals.[10]

[8] 満史会 (Manchurian History Committee), ed., 満州開発四十年史 (*A Forty-Year History of Manchuria Development*), 2 vols. and supplement (Tokyo: 謙光社, 1964–65), vol. 1, 357.

[9] Donald A. Jordan, *Chinese Boycotts versus Japanese Bombs: The Failure of China's "Revolutionary Diplomacy," 1931–32* (Ann Arbor: University of Michigan Press, 1991), 24–25; 日本近現代史辞書編集委員会 (Japanese Modern History Dictionary Compilation Committee), ed., 日本近現代史辞書 (*Japanese Modern History Dictionary*) (Tokyo: 東洋経済新報社, 1978), 628.

[10] Japan, Defense Agency, Defense Research Archives, 満洲 ： 地誌資料１０満洲事変関係、地図各国新聞, "The Origin and History of the Anti-Japanese Movement in China," *Herald of Asia*, Library of Contemporary History, no. 7 (Tokyo: Herald Press, 1932), ii; Sandra Wilson,

Meanwhile another incident was brewing. On 27 June 1931, Chinese forces had executed Captain Nakamura Shintarō and his companions, who were conducting reconnaissance for Japan's General Staff Headquarters in preparation for a possible war against Russia. The Japanese Army's stock war plan entailed a Siberian land grab, known as the Northern Advance Plan. Nakamura and friends were investigating strategic areas around the Xing'an Mountains, a part of Manchuria close to the Japanese sphere of influence. Apparently his disguise as a Mongol agricultural specialist did not work. Japanese military authorities confirmed the deaths a month later and the so-called Captain Nakamura Incident was born when the military went public on 12 August. An emotionally charged public debate on Manchuria policy ensued.

By this time, national outrage infused both sides. The Kantō Army then engineered a fait accompli of such scale that it precluded backing down and so became a pivotal event irrevocably upending the status quo. Its junior officers ignited a fifteen-year war. On 18 September 1931, when saboteurs destroyed a few meters of easily repairable track of the South Manchurian Railway line in the vicinity of Shenyang, the Kantō Army launched a full-scale invasion soon encompassing all of Manchuria. By the end of February 1932, Japan had occupied all of Manchuria as well as northeastern Inner Mongolia and Barga, the easternmost portion of Mongolia. The Japanese and Chinese called this event the Manchurian Incident. Yet the Imperial Japanese Army's own investigation soon concluded that the Kantō Army had conducted the sabotage and then blamed it on the Chinese to create a pretext for war. Army officers chose the ultimate solution in keeping with their Shintō ultranationalist, apocalyptic vision of world politics. Theirs was a self-fulfilling prophecy.

The North China Campaign

If the West would not trade, then Japan would turn to the alternative economic model of the time, autarky, or economic self-sufficiency. Since Japan lacked the resources to become self-sufficient, it needed an empire of adequate size to become so, which is where Manchuria came in. On 18 September 1931 the Japanese army launched its full-scale invasion of Manchuria. On 21 September, the Chinese government appealed to the League of Nations, which on 4 January 1932 sent an investigatory commission. On 13 December 1931, the Japanese Cabinet fell over its inability to force the army to conform to the government foreign policy emphasizing co-operation with neighbors, not their invasion. Two days later, the Chinese government also collapsed. Not until

The Manchurian Crisis and Japanese Society, 1931–33 (London: Routledge, 2002), 173; Jordan, *Chinese Boycotts versus Japanese Bombs*, 32, 259; Henry L. Stimson, *The Far Eastern Crisis: Recollections and Observations* (New York: Harper & Brothers, 1936), 111.

mid-January 1932, after virtually all of Manchuria had fallen to Japan, did the competing factions of Chinese high politics finally cobble together a government. In Japan, after two failed assassination attempts against the new prime minister, Inukai Tsuyoshi, in February and March of 1932, army and navy militants got their quarry on 15 May, precipitating the formation of yet another cabinet, this time under an admiral, Saitō Makoto. Inukai had been trying to negotiate with the Nationalists to arrange for a peaceful resolution, but the military was interested in retribution, not peace.

Meanwhile, the Japanese military opened a secondary front, or peripheral operation, in Shanghai, to divert Western attention away from the focus of Japanese investments and military operations (Manchuria) to the focus of Western investments (Shanghai), and to threaten the Nationalist financial center in order to force a settlement on Japanese terms. The Imperial Japanese Army used a brawl on 18 January 1932 between Chinese and Japanese nationals (including some Buddhist monks) fomented by its own hired agents provocateurs to create a pretext for military operations. This became known as the Buddhist Monk Attack Incident in Japanese iconography. More scuffles occurred two days later and the Mitomo Industries Attack Incident became another entry in Japanese iconography.

With these pretexts, fighting broke out between main units on 28 January, and soon the Imperial Japanese Navy landed reinforcements. This initially became known as the Shanghai Incident, but after the much more serious "incident" in 1937, it became known as the First Shanghai Incident in a series of two. Whereas the invasion of Manchuria was an all-army act, Shanghai allowed the navy to showcase its repertoire and in doing so justify its proportion of the defense budget. The Japanese military hoped to trade Chinese recognition of Manchurian independence for a promise to withdraw from Shanghai. When the Nationalists rejected the trade, Japan retaliated by having Manchuria declare independence on 1 March as the world's newest puppet state of Manchukuo and enthroning the deposed Qing dynasty emperor, Puyi, as its emperor on 9 March. Japan deployed 150,000 soldiers, who in just five months took Manchuria, dispersed the main guerrilla resistance within a year and a half, and expanded the borders to incorporate Rehe (Jehol), an area the combined size of Virginia, West Virginia, and Maryland, by 1933.[11]

Thereafter Japan invested massively in Manchukuo, focusing initially on infrastructure development with a rapid expansion of the railway and road

[11] Alvin D. Coox, *Nomonhan: Japan against Russia* (Stanford: Stanford University Press, 1990), 55; Edward Bing-Shuey Lee, *One Year of the Japan–China Undeclared War* (Shanghai: Mercury Press, 1922), 320; William Henry Chamberlin, *Japan over Asia* (Boston: Little, Brown, 1938), 27; Yūzō Yamamoto, "Japanese Empire and Colonial Management," in Takafusa Nakamura and Kônosuke Odaka, eds., *Economic History of Japan 1914–1955: A Dual Structure*, trans. Noah S. Brannen (Oxford: Oxford University Press, 1999), 224.

systems. It started by nationalizing Chinese railway lines and their many asso-
ciated industries. The Kantō Army managed these investments through the
South Manchurian Railway Company, an umbrella organization for the verti-
cally integrated railway as well as for the many related industries such as coal,
steel, telegraph, electric power generation, and so on. After infrastructure, the
Japanese government turned to investments in resource development, particularly in the areas of heavy industry and mining necessary to produce the war
materiel essential for managing an expanded empire. It also made significant
investments in education.

Incredibly, the Japanese economic development program proved remarkably successful. After the Russo-Japanese War, when Japan had acquired the
railway in lieu of an indemnity, company investments increased over fifty
times between 1907 and 1930. Prior to 1931, Japan accounted for 72 percent
of Manchuria's foreign investments and Russia 24 percent. Great Britain, the
next-largest foreign investor, controlled just 1 percent.[12] Industrial development in the rest of China lagged far behind Manchuria, which accounted
for 90 percent of China's oil, 70 percent of its iron, 55 percent of its gold,
and 33 percent of its trade.[13] By 1943 Manchuria produced 49.5 percent of
all Chinese coal, 78.2 percent of its electricity, 87.7 percent of its pig iron,
93 percent of its steel, 66 percent of its concrete, and 99 percent of its oil.[14] By
1945 it had a per capita income 50 percent higher than the rest of China and
had become the most industrialized part of Asia outside the Japanese home
islands, outproducing even Shanghai and the Yangzi river valley, long the heart
of China's modern economy.[15] Japan could not have prosecuted its long war
against China, let alone the Pacific Ocean war against the United States, without these resources.

As Japanese investments poured into Manchuria and as employment rolls
expanded, Japan's own urban economy rapidly recovered in contrast to the

---

[12] Manchurian History Committee, *A Forty-Year History of Manchuria Development*, vol. 1,
79–80.

[13] 金安泰 (Jin Antai), "'九一八'事变与美国外交" (The Manchurian Incident and U.S. Foreign
Policy), 史学集刊 (*Collected Papers of Historical Studies*) 12, no. 3 (1983), 73.

[14] Manchurian History Committee, *A Forty-Year History of Manchuria Development*, vol. 2, 537–3
9; Japan, Defense Agency, Defense Research Archives, "満洲全般１４８満洲における電力
事業に関する調査" (Survey of the Manchurian Electric Power Industry), April 1951, *passim.*

[15] Christopher Howe, *The Origins of Japanese Trade Supremacy* (Chicago: The University of
Chicago Press, 1996), 403; A.M. Ledovsky, *The USSR, the USA, and the People's Revolution in
China*, trans. Nadezhda Burova (Moscow: Progress Publishers, 1982), 102; Lloyd E. Eastman,
Seeds of Destruction: Nationalist China in War and Revolution 1937–1949 (Stanford: Stanford
University Press, 1984), 224; O. Borisov, *Советский Союз и маньчжурская революционная
база 1945–1949* (*The Soviet Union and the Manchurian Revolutionary Base 1945–1949*)
(Moscow: Издательство «Мысль», 1975), 49, 53–54, 56; Thomas R. Gottschang and Diana
Lary, *Swallows and Settlers: The Great Migration from North China to Manchuria* (Ann
Arbor: University of Michigan, 2000), 45.

West, where unemployment rates remained high. This economic about-face, in combination with deeply felt nationalism, contributed to strong public support for the military. Although Japan rapidly stabilized the Manchurian economy and soon laid infrastructure that would benefit future generations, its trade imploded when Chinese citizens launched a nationwide boycott, anti-Japanese sentiments across China went viral, and these widely shared sentiments increasingly forced an anti-Japanese agenda on any Chinese government that hoped to retain or gain power.

None of this impressed the League of Nations, which on 24 February 1933, with Siam abstaining and twelve others absent, voted forty-two to one (Japan being the one) to denounce the occupation of Manchuria as a violation of Japan's many treaties with China and the West, not to mention the Charter of the League of Nations. The Japanese withdrawal from the League on 27 March signaled their rejection of the global order and, in the stroke of a pen, transformed Japan into a diplomatically isolated nation. Japan's withdrawal marked the end of its long and constructive role in international affairs.

After the conquest of Manchuria, Japan continued military operations to occupy China north of the Yellow river, whose valley forms the cradle of Han civilization. With the Great Wall Campaign from 5 March until 30 May 1933, the Great Wall became Japan's line of control. In early April it broke through the Great Wall to move into the core area of Han civilization, starting with Hebei. The Nationalists sued for peace and signed the Tanggu Truce on 31 May 1933, whereby Japanese troops withdrew north of the Great Wall and Chinese troops withdrew from eastern Hebei, leaving a neutral zone between them. In the Umezu Yoshijirō–He Yingqin Agreement of 10 June 1935, the Nationalist government agreed to withdraw all troops and party offices from the rest of Hebei. General He Yingqin served as the Nationalist war minister from 1930 to 1944. His counterpart, General Umezu Yoshijirō, commander of the China Garrison Army, would go on to clean house after the Young Officers' Revolt. That year, Japan bought the Russian-owned railway lines in Manchuria, and on 18 June 1937 it finished standardizing the track to the Chinese gauge, creating a unified transportation grid just in time for its upcoming invasion of coastal China the following month.

In the meantime, on 14 May 1935, the Kantō and China Garrison Armies, under the command of Generals Minami Jirō and Umezu Yoshijirō respectively, decided to detach the five north China provinces of Hebei, Shandong, Shanxi, Chahar, and Suiyuan. On 13 January 1936 the Cabinet in Tokyo confirmed this decision.[16] After the Young Officers' Revolt, Minami would be exported to Korea, where he served as governor-general until 1942.

---

[16] 石島紀之 (Ishijima Noriyuki), 中国抗日戦争史 (*A History of China's Anti-Japanese War*) (Tokyo: 青木書店, 1984), 34, 38; Takafusa Nakamura, "Japan's Economic Thrust into North

As Japan gradually extended its counterinsurgency operations throughout north China, a proliferation of armies ruled the expanding territory through a growing list of puppet governments and regional development companies modeled on the Kantō Army's rule via the mother puppet government of Manchukuo in combination with the South Manchurian Railway Company. After 1937, the new North China Area Army oversaw north China's economic development, while the Kantō Army managed not only Manchuria but Inner Mongolia and Shanxi as well. In 1938 the Japanese established the North China Development Company, as well as a parallel Central China Development Company. The opening move in these takeovers was the seizure of Chinese-owned assets – a program not designed to win hearts and minds.

Nevertheless, from 1938 to 1946, north China production increased from 12.8 to 60 million tons of coal, from 68,000 to 870,000 tons of iron, from 17,000 to 407,000 tons of aluminum, from 247,000 to 597,000 tons of cotton, and from zero to 1 million tons of liquid fuel. Significant proportions of these resources went directly to Japan.[17]

The Road Not Taken

Back in Tokyo, Finance Minister Takahashi Korekiyo cut a lonely figure. Takahashi was one of the most distinguished finance ministers in Japanese history and has sometimes been called Japan's John Maynard Keynes, for his rapid turnaround of the urban economy to full employment and full capacity by 1935–36, a decade ahead of the United States, despite a weather-induced famine in 1934. Keynes was the brilliant British economist whose theories prescribed the antidote to the Great Depression that did not become generally accepted until after World War II. Agricultural incomes in Japan, however, did not reach their 1920 highs until after 1945, leaving a gap between urban and rural prosperity, acutely felt by the army, whose recruits came primarily from the countryside. Japanese military leaders interpreted their conquests as the reason for Japan's economic turnaround. In fact, economic indicators

China, 1933–1938," in Akira Iriye, ed., *The Chinese and the Japanese* (Princeton: Princeton University Press, 1980), 226, 232–33; Ian Nish, *Japanese Foreign Policy 1869–1942: Kasumigaseki to Miyakezaka* (London: Routledge & Kegan Paul, 1977), 212–13; Shimada Toshihiko, "Designs on North China, 1933–1937," in James William Morley, ed., *The North China Quagmire: Japan's Expansion on the Asian Continent 1933–1941* (New York: Columbia University Press, 1983), 195; 解学诗 (Xie Xueshi) and 宋玉印 (Song Yuyin), "'七・七'事变后日本掠夺华北资源的总枢纽" (The Fulcrum of Japan's Plundering of North China's Resources after 1937), 中国经济史研究 (*Research in Chinese Economic History*) 4 (1990), 44–57.

[17] 中村隆英 (Nakamura Takafusa), "北支那開発株式会社の成立" (The Formation of the North China Development Joint-Stock Corporation), in 井上清 (Inōe Kyoshi) and 衞藤瀋吉 and (Etō Shinkichi), eds., 日中戦争と日中関係 (*The Sino-Japanese War and Sino-Japanese Relations*) (Tokyo: 原書房, 1988), 359, 362.

did not improve in 1931, they stagnated after 1937, and they plummeted after 1941, the critical years of the military escalation. Although military production peaked in 1944, output of food and basic necessities peaked in 1937, with enormous implications for the general standard of living.[18]

Japan's economic recovery, however, fully coincided with Takehashi's final three terms (out of seven) as finance minister from 1931 to 1936, when he finished his career at eighty-two years of age. The hallmarks of his term were departure from the gold standard, devaluation of the yen to stimulate exports, increase of the money supply to raise consumption, deficit financing to allow government spending, public-works investments, civil control over military spending, co-operation with the West, and resistance to the dismemberment of China but support for its economic development. After restoring the urban economy to prosperity, he tried to hold firm on defense spending. Although it remained a steady 6.55 percent of the gross national product from 1933 to 1936, it grew from 27 percent of the government budget in 1931 to 46 percent of a much larger budget in 1936.[19]

Takahashi argued vehemently against this trend. His ideas represented an alternative to the path demanded by the military. He lost his life in the Young Officers' Revolt in 1936 and thereafter finance ministers were sidelined. The military budget for 1937 tripled the average for the 1934–36 period. In 1939 it doubled again. Rampant inflation produced a 1944 military budget seventy times larger than that of 1936. The military got the planned economy it coveted as well as the hyperinflation and the resource bottlenecks that Takahashi had predicted.[20]

The Chinese resisted Japanese expansion during the North China Campaign. The Nationalist government used diplomacy to rally the international

[18] Ann Rasmussen Kinney, *Japanese Investment in Manchurian Manufacturing, Mining, Transportation, and Communications 1931–1945* (New York: Garland, 1982), 25, 152–55; *The Manchoukuo Year Book 1942* (Hsinking, Manchoukuo: Manchoukuo Year Book Co., 1943), 66, 254–55, 271, 326–30, 425, 490, 492–93, 500, 531–32, 539–40; Kungtu C. Sun and Ralph W. Huenemann, *The Economic Development of Manchuria in the First Half of the Twentieth Century* (Cambridge, MA: Harvard University Press, 1969), 86–87; Kang Chao, *The Economic Development of Manchuria: The Rise of a Frontier Economy*, Michigan Papers in Chinese Studies no. 43 (Ann Arbor: The University of Michigan Center for Chinese Studies, 1982), 83; Kerry Smith, *A Time of Crisis: Japan, the Great Depression, and Rural Revitalization* (Cambridge, MA: Harvard University Press, 2001), 242, 251; Mikiso Hane, *Peasants, Rebels, Women, and Outcasts: The Underside of Modern Japan*, 2nd edn. (Lanham, MD: Rowman & Littlefield, 1982), 114–15; Kozo Yamamura, "The Japanese Economy, 1911–1930: Concentration, Conflicts, and Crises," in Bernard Silberman and H.D. Harootunian, eds., *Japan in Crisis: Essays on Taishō Democracy* (Princeton: Princeton University Press, 1974), 304; Wilson, *The Manchurian Crisis and Japanese Society*, 219; Takehiko Yoshihashi, *Conspiracy at Mukden: The Rise of the Japanese Military* (New Haven: Yale University Press, 1963), 113–15.
[19] Smethurst, *From Foot Soldier to Finance Minister*, 268, 274, 294.
[20] Smethurst, *From Foot Soldier to Finance Minister*, 3–4, 6, 238, 297.

community and involve the League of Nations, but reserved its own military operations for the Chinese Communists. From 1930 to 1934 the Nationalists fought a succession of five encirclement campaigns that finally expelled the Communists from south China on the Long March to desolate Yan'an, Shaanxi, much nearer Russia, their great benefactor from the north. The Nationalists were primarily a south and central China phenomenon. The Chinese of north China, however, fought a persistent guerrilla campaign against the Japanese, who raised a succession of new armies to conduct counterinsurgent operations. The geographic scope of the instability did not diminish, but grew.

Japanese military officers not only failed to understand the economic essentials for military power, emphasized by the late finance minister, they also confused a potential ally with their primary adversary. The primary ideological threat to both Japan and Nationalist China was Communism. Chiang Kai-shek had demonstrated his skill at annihilating Communists, a skill the Japanese should have fostered. In grand strategy, normally a common primary enemy forms the basis for a coalition. But the Imperial Japanese Army's strategy was anything but grand. Its officers increasingly saw the world in terms of zero-sum operational wins against the Chinese that served to make Chinese of all political persuasions ever more anti-Japanese. Rather than use flame retardants, the Japanese army relied on accelerants.

The Japanese assumed that if they took enough territory, surely the Nationalists would formally recognize Manchuria's detachment and thereby legitimize Japan's activities. They guessed wrong. Unlike the Han conscripts of the First Sino-Japanese War, who felt little connection with their Manchu overlords, or the Russian conscripts of the Russo-Japanese War who felt no connection with Manchuria, in the Second Sino-Japanese War Chinese conscripts and guerrillas felt a deep connection with the land which the Japanese were taking and the people whom the Japanese were uprooting and killing. Instead of leveraging common interests with the Nationalists, Japanese actions conjured the most unlikely opposing alliance, composed of parties which under normal circumstances would have focused on fighting each other. The Chinese agreed that they hated Japan even if they could agree on nothing else.

The Second United Front

Although the Chinese Communists and Nationalists each ultimately intended to destroy the other, from at least 1935, if not earlier, both had been trying to secure military aid from Russia in order to fight Japan. Both understood that full-scale war required conventional military equipment such as tanks, aircraft, and artillery that China lacked. Russia cultivated contacts with the many power brokers along its borders, including the Communists, the

Nationalists, and an array of warlords, but had provided little aid since the demise in 1927 of the First United Front in a Communist bloodbath courtesy of the Nationalists.

On 25 November 1936, Germany and Japan signed a treaty of alliance known as the Anti-Comintern Pact aimed at neutralizing Russia's international propaganda arm called the Communist International, or Comintern for short. Within a fortnight, Russia played every one of its carefully cultivated contacts in China to broker the Second United Front at Xi'an in order to avoid a two-front war against Germany in the West and Japan in the East. The last tsar had failed to fight off Germany despite the enormous military efforts of his great-power allies, France and Britain. Russia had neither fully recovered from World War I and the ensuing Russian Civil War nor fully institutionalized its new government. Its plans to communize the world had alienated the West, so it had no great-power allies. It desperately needed some power to deflect either Germany or Japan, and preferably both. Yet none of the Western powers, where protectionism and domestic considerations ruled the day, showed any signs of going beyond words to contain either.

So Joseph Stalin immediately turned to Asia. When Chiang Kai-shek traveled to Xi'an to organize a final encirclement campaign against the Communists holed up in Yan'an since the Long March, his north China generals mutinied and took him hostage on 12 December 1936. This became known as the Xi'an Incident. Both the Chinese Communists and the Nationalists made Russian military assistance a precondition for co-operation, while Russia made a formal United Front a precondition for arms. The Japanese saw Russian machinations behind the incident and threatened Chiang with harsh reprisals if he allied with the Communists. They saw spreading Communism in China, their perennial nightmare, and were determined to stop it with their usual military antidote of escalation. In 1937 all parties made good their promises. The Chinese also expected Russia to join the war against Japan. They got it backward: once they were in, Russia was out.

Since 1931, Nationalist and Japanese troops had repeatedly clashed but the Nationalists had always backed down because they preferred to fight one enemy at a time, starting with the Communists. With the Xi'an Incident, they changed strategy to focus instead on resisting Japan's unrelenting territorial expansion. On 7 July 1937, a Japanese company lost track of a single sol-dier during night maneuvers near the Marco Polo Bridge on the southwestern outskirts of Beijing. To find him, the Japanese demanded to search the posi-tion of China's 29th Army. The Chinese refused. Someone fired and then both sides fired. The Japanese called in reinforcements and remained on the attack. Meanwhile, the missing soldier turned up unharmed. No matter. The Japanese demanded that the Chinese withdraw the garrison. They began to do so, but with inadequate dispatch, so the Japanese bombarded it on 9 July. These events became known as the Marco Polo Bridge Incident to the Chinese and the North China Incident to the Japanese.

Prime Minister Konoe Fumimaro and the army leadership in Tokyo, including General Ishiwara Kanji and General Tada Hayao, did not desire to escalate the crisis because they preferred to concentrate on the economic development of the resources they had already seized, in preparation for the long-expected war against Russia. They failed to understand that all the choices were not theirs to make. Unlike past altercations, this time the Chinese did not choose to back down. The Nationalists honored the deal brokered at Xi'an to fight Japan under a Communist–Nationalist alliance armed by Russia. The Japanese reacted viscerally; they sent reinforcements of three army divisions in July, followed by two more in August after the hostilities spread to Shanghai. They did not anticipate a dire struggle. War Minister Sugiyama Gen expected a Nationalist capitulation in one month; others thought three. Their predictions were not remotely accurate. By the end of 1937, Japan had suffered 100,000 casualties, doubled the number of divisions deployed in China to twenty-one, and committed 600,000 men. A year later, Japan struggled to raise twenty new divisions.[21] By the end of 1938 Japan had thirty-four divisions totaling 1.1 million men, and, by 1941, fifty-one divisions, and still the Chinese refused to capitulate.[22]

On 28 July 1937, Japan began its general attack on China over an area roughly equivalent to the United States east of the Mississippi river. On 30 July, Beijing and Tianjin fell. The main thrust followed two parallel railway lines southward into Nationalist country: Japan's First Army followed the Beijing–Wuhan Railway toward the inland center of industry in Wuhan, while the Second Army followed the Tianjin–Pukou Railway toward the capital in Nanjing and, for logistical reasons, both lines of attack remained within 150 to 180 miles of the tracks. No bridge spanned the Yangzi, so a ferry service linked Nanjing on the southern bank with Pukou on the facing northern bank. On 26 August 1937, the North China Area Army was activated under Count Terauchi Hisaichi (the son of former War Minister Terauchi Masatake) to assume overall command. A third, smaller campaign left from Beijing northwest along the Beijing–Suiyuan Railway into Chahar, Inner Mongolia toward Communist country. Elements of the Kantō Army and the First Army launched the Taiyuan Campaign to take the capital of Shanxi. The Communist Eighth Route Army participated in the fighting in order to defend the base area in neighboring Shaanxi province. On 13 September Datong fell, followed by a

---

[21] Michael A. Barnhart, *Japan Prepares for Total War* (Ithaca: Cornell University Press, 1987), 91, 95; Edward J. Drea, *Nomonhan: Japanese Soviet Tactical Combat* (Honolulu: University Press of the Pacific, 1981), 13.

[22] F.F. Liu, *A Military History of Modern China 1924–1949* (Port Washington, NY: Kennikat Press, 1972; first published 1956), 205; Harries and Harries, *Soldiers of the Sun*, 260.

three-week battle to take Xinkou, which fell on 13 October, and Taiyuan on 9 November, putting most of the Shanxi railway system in Japanese hands. In early 1938, the Nationalists and Communists responded by establishing the Border Government of Hebei, Shanxi, and Chahar, with Hebei under the authority of the Nationalists and Shanxi under the Communists. Together they sponsored numerous guerrilla attacks to harass the Japanese.

This campaign threatened to cut China's vital supply route to Russia, which was on the verge of making good its promise to provide essential military equipment. So in August 1937, the Nationalists disrupted Japanese plans by opening a second front in Shanghai, the so-called Second Shanghai Incident. The fighting would threaten Western investments and would perhaps even bring a Western ally into the war. From 13 August until 12 November, fighting raged in Shanghai. The campaign was among the largest of the war. Chiang Kai-shek's second in command, General Chen Cheng, faced General Matsui Iwane, recently recalled to active duty at age fifty-nine to remain in service through the Rape of Nanjing. By the time the city fell, 9,115 Japanese soldiers had died and 31,257 had been wounded. Chinese forces suffered 187,200 casualties, including 70 percent of Chiang Kai-shek's young officers. Afterward, Chiang concluded that he should have retreated sooner.[23]

Russian military equipment began arriving in September 1937. From 1937 to 1941 Russia sent 1,235 planes, 1,600 artillery pieces, 50,000 rifles, over 14,000 machine guns, over 300 advisers, over 2,000 pilots, over 3,000 engineers and technical experts, and thousands of drivers to deliver the goods. Russian pilots flew from Nanjing, Wuhan, Chongqing, Chengdu, Lanzhou, Xi'an, and other places.[24] Over 200 Russian pilots died in China.[25] The Nationalists relied on Russian planes until 1942, when U.S. generosity took over.

On 11 July the Japanese army and navy had divided their responsibilities, with the army in charge of north China and the navy of the air war over central and south China. On 14 August, the Nationalists made their first air raid. Instead of Japanese ships, they hit the International Settlement and French

---

[23] Yang Tianshi, "Chiang Kai-shek and the Battles of Shanghai and Nanjing," in Mark Peattie, Edward J. Drea, and Hans van de Ven, eds., *The Battle for China: Essays on the Military History of the Sino-Japanese War of 1937–1945* (Stanford: Stanford University Press, 2011), 153–54; Stephen R. MacKinnon, *Wuhan 1938: War, Refugees, and the Making of Modern China* (Berkeley: University of California Press, 2008), 23.

[24] 王真 (Wang Zhen), "论抗战初期苏联援华政策性质" (The Nature of the Soviet Policy to Assist China Early in the Anti-Japanese War), 中共党史研究 (*Research on the History of the Chinese Communist Party*) 53 (1993), 48–54; Sergei Leonidovich Tikhvinskii, ed., *Русско-китайские отношения в XX веке* (*Russo-Chinese Relations in the 20th Century*), vol. 4 (Moscow: «Памятники исторической мысли», 2000), part 1, 1937–45, 11–12; part 2, 1945, 473.

[25] Iu.V. Chudodeev, *По дорогам Китая 1937–1945: Воспоминания* (*Along the Roads of China 1937–1945: Memoirs*) (Moscow: Издательство «наука» главная редакция восточной литературы, 1989), 61, 147.

Concession of Shanghai. That day, the Japanese Third Fleet, based in Shanghai and under the command of Admiral Hasegawa Kiyoshi, seized the opportunity to showcase its aviation capabilities, which were superior to those of the army. On 15 August, Imperial Japanese Navy planes began bombing Nanjing and the Nationalists ordered a general mobilization. On 16 August Japan blockaded Shanghai and Guangzhou, on 25 August it extended the blockade to China's entire east coast with the exception of foreign treaty ports, and over the fall it bombed dozens of Chinese cities. In October, Japan put the Central China Expeditionary Army under the command of Matsui Iwane to prosecute the Shanghai Campaign. By late October, Japan had more troops deployed in the Shanghai Campaign than in all north China and had retroactively upgraded the North China Incident to the China Incident.

Provincial capitals fell like dominoes: Baoding (Zhili) on 24 September, Shijiazhuang (Hebei) on 10 October, Taiyuan (Shanxi) on 9 November, Hangzhou (Zhejiang) on 24 December, and Jinan (Shandong) on 26 December. Provincial capitals were important. They were transportation hubs. Upon taking Shanghai, Japanese troops moved up the Yangzi, launching the Nanjing Campaign on 1 December and occupying the former capital on 13 December. The Chinese, rather than capitulate, as the Japanese had assumed, traded space for time in keeping with plans drawn up after the first Battle for Shanghai in 1932. These plans anticipated a protracted war of attrition fought deep inland to force Japanese overextension and impose unsustainable costs.

After the fall of Nanjing, Japan's North China Area Army, under General Terauchi, again deployed southward on two axes following the main north–south railway lines, one toward the junction at Zhengzhou and the other toward the junction at Xuzhou, where the Central China Expeditionary Army under General Matsui converged from the south. The Xuzhou Campaign, fought between December 1937 and 19 May 1938, was one of the largest campaigns anywhere in the 1930s or 1940s, involving some 600,000 combatants. The city sits at the midpoint of the north–south Tianjin–Pukou Railway connecting Manchuria with Shanghai and serves as the junction with the major east–west railway line, connecting Zhengzhou with the sea (at Shanghai) and linking up with the other north–south line, the Beijing–Wuhan Railway.

After the Russian equipment ran out, Xuzhou fell on 19 May 1938, but unlike the disorderly retreats after the fall of Shanghai, Nanjing, and Jinan, Chinese troops conducted an orderly retreat. In an act of desperation to halt the Japanese progress inland, on 5 and 7 June of 1938 the Nationalists, not the Japanese, committed one of the worst atrocities of a war famous for atrocities: Chiang Kai-shek ordered the breach of Yellow river dikes at Huayuankou, Henan, near the key railway junction at Zhengzhou. The dikes were actually breached in multiple places, including at the junction with the Grand Canal. This inundated 70,000 square kilometers of mainly prime farmland.[26] Nearly 900,000 people perished and almost another 3.9 million became refugees.[27] In this one act, Chiang Kai-shek killed more Chinese than had the Japanese despite all their atrocities.[28] For the next decade the Yellow river ran outside its dikes, leaving a wake of misery. Although the flood prevented the Japanese from taking the railway junction at Zhengzhou to reach Wuhan by rail, they rapidly improvised to reach the city by boat via the Yangzi river.

With the failure to surround and annihilate the Nationalist army at Xuzhou, the Japanese again targeted China's economy and transportation network. Wuhan was the great distribution and processing center for China's agricultural commodities as well as its inland industrial center. It was also the point where the Yangzi river became wide – with the confluence of the Hanshui river – and could not be easily crossed all the way east to Shanghai, thereby forming a powerful barrier between north and south China and the armies caught on either bank. From Yibin, located upriver from Wuhan, no bridges spanned the Yangzi to the east until 1957, with the completion of the railway bridge at Wuhan, and a decade later with a second railway bridge crossing at Nanjing.

In 1938 Wuhan became the staging area for the two million Nationalist troops defending the central Yangzi valley.[29] The Japanese launched a triple pincer, with one prong sweeping up the Yangzi river toward Wuhan and the capital of Chongqing further upstream, another prong reaching down the coast to Guangzhou in order to cut the railway terminus and supply lines in the south, and the last sweeping southward down the railway system to break Nationalist control from Wuhan to Guangzhou and east to the coast.

Japan took Yangzi river cities in succession: on 15 June 1938 Anqing fell, followed by Jiujiang on 26 July. Meanwhile, in May, the Imperial Japanese Navy launched an air campaign over the new Nationalist capital at Chongqing, which it bombed more than any other city, mainly from May to October when the cloud cover lifted. Japanese pilots called their route the "Chongqing Milk Run." When they dropped incendiary bombs and watched Chongqing burn, little did they dream of how much more flammable their own cities were should anyone return the favor.

---

[26] Diana Lary, *The Chinese People at War: Human Suffering and Social Transformation, 1937–1945* (Cambridge: Cambridge University Press, 2010), 61; Fenby, *Chiang Kai-shek*, 320.

[27] Diana Lary and Stephen R. MacKinnon, eds., *Scars of War: The Impact of Warfare on Modern China* (Vancouver: UBC Press, 2001), 3, 112; Edward J. Drea, *Japan's Imperial Army: Its Rise and Fall, 1853–1945* (Lawrence: University Press of Kansas, 2009), 201.

[28] Diana Lary, "A Ravaged Place: The Devastation of the Xuzhou Region, 1938," in Lary and MacKinnon, *Scars of War*, 112; Odoric Y.K. Wou, "Food Shortage and Japanese Grain Extraction in Henan," in Stephen R. MacKinnon, Diana Lary, and Ezra F. Vogel, eds., *China at War: Regions of China, 1937–1945* (Stanford: Stanford University Press, 2007), 177.

[29] MacKinnon, *Wuhan 1938*, 1.

Japan temporarily suspended the Wuhan Campaign not because of the flooding but because of fighting on the Korean–Russian–Manchukuo border at Zhanggufeng, where, from 11 July to 10 August 1938, Japanese and Russian troops fought a pitched battle. This became known as the Zhanggufeng (Chōkohō) Incident for the Chinese and Japanese or the Battle of Lake Khaisan/Khasan for Russians. Russian–Japanese border incidents had occurred with regularity since 1931. This time the Russians chose to escalate at a place of their choosing, seventy miles south of Vladivostok. Events seemed to be moving toward Chiang Kai-shek's long-awaited Russo-Japanese Armageddon. The Russians deployed a force of 21,000 against 3,000 Japanese with predictable results.[30] They accused Japan of territorial encroachments, and deployed the air force, but after a month of fighting the Japanese withdrew and both sides signed a cease-fire agreement. The Russian price for peace was a swath of Chinese territory. Afterward, the Russians deported to Kazakhstan 200,000 Koreans, who had farmed the area and given cover to Japan's main espionage base in Siberia.[31]

Despite this delay, in the fall of 1938 Japanese forces closed in on Wuhan via the Beijing–Wuhan Railway from the north, the Yangzi river from the southeast, and overland from the east. Russia had provided 602 planes in early September, but by 28 October only eighty-seven remained.[32] While the military equipment lasted, the Chinese fought well. The Nationalists removed Wuhan's munitions factories to Sichuan before the city fell on 25 October. Again the Nationalists conducted an orderly retreat after a hard-fought, ten-month campaign. Their attrition strategy had done what it was designed to do: survive to fight another day and overextend the Japanese militarily and financially in the meantime.

Victory put Japan in possession of all of north China and the Yangzi river valley, the most prosperous and developed parts of the country. Japan set up two major air bases, one in Wuhan and the other in Yuncheng, Shanxi. The former facilitated the bombing of Nationalist interests in Chengdu, Chongqing, Kunming, and Guilin, while the latter facilitated the bombing of the Communist

[30] Coox, *Nomonhan*, 135, 136.

[31] 香島明雄 (Kashima Akio), 中ソ外交史研究１９３７–１９４６ (*Research on Sino-Soviet Diplomatic History, 1937–1946*) (Tokyo: 世界思想社, 1990), 32; Maochun Yu, *The Dragon's War: Allied Operations and the Fate of China 1937–1947* (Annapolis, MD: Naval Institute Press, 2006), 19.

[32] K.P. Ageenko, P.N. Bobylev, T.S. Manaenkov, R.A. Sabyshkin, and I.F. Iakushin, *Военная помощь СССР в освободительной борьбе китайского народа* (*Soviet Military Aid in the Liberation Struggle of the Chinese People*) (Moscow: Military Press of the Ministry of Defence, 1975), 77; Chudodeev, *Along the Roads of China*, 67; MacKinnon, *Wuhan 1938*, 25; Edward J. Drea, "The Japanese Army on the Eve of the War," in Peattie, Drea, and Van de Ven, *The Battle for China*, 114–15; Boris Grigor'evich Sapozhnikov, *Китайский фронт во Второй мировой войны* (*The Chinese Front in the Second World War*) (Moscow: Издательство «наука» Главная редакция восточной литературы, 1971), 161–62.

headquarters in Yan'an and Lanzhou, the terminus of the 1,816-mile highway specially built by the Russians to convey their aid and the location of their air base to train Chinese pilots. Yet still the Chinese fought on.

After Wuhan crumbled, Russia again relieved pressure on the Nationalists by opening a second front. In May 1939 fighting broke out between Japanese and Russian forces, this time in Nomonhan, Mongolia, in what became known as the First Nomonhan Incident to the Japanese. In June renewed fighting at Nomonhan escalated into pitched tank battles that raged until the exchange of a cease-fire agreement in September. The Russian price was another piece of Chinese territory. The battle became known as the Second Nomonhan Incident. Russian tanks under the command of the soon-to-be legendary Georgii K. Zhukov, future savior of Russia, obliterated Japanese forces, killing or wounding an astounding 79 percent of front-line Japanese troops and, in the process, gutted the Imperial Japanese Army's long-standing war plan (really its only war plan): the Northern Advance on Russia.[33] The plan had called for a rapid conquest of Siberia as far west as Lake Baikal to eliminate the Communist threat to Asia.

At this point the Second Sino-Japanese War stalemated. Japan had run out of accessible targets either along the railway lines or on the coast. After the destruction of the Chinese economy proved insufficient to bring the Nationalists to terms, the Japanese again attempted to occupy Chongqing. In March of 1939 Japan won the Nanchang Campaign, taking the railway spur connecting Nanchang, the capital of Jiangxi, to the Yangzi river between Wuhan and Nanjing and also to the east–west Zhejiang–Jiangxi Railway. Japan engaged in successive campaigns further west in May 1939 at the Battle of Suixian–Zaoyang, Hubei; and in the fall of 1939 at Changsha, Hunan.

Over the winter of 1939 to 1940 the Nationalists retaliated with the Winter Offensive, a massive counterattack involving eighty divisions in southern Shanxi and along the Yangzi that widened into south China when the Japanese threatened Sichuan from the south in the Battle of Southern Guangxi. On 23 November, Japan won the Nanning (Yongning) Campaign far to the south in Guangxi in an attempt to sever trade via Hanoi. Trade was not severed but only diverted to Bose (Paise), Guangxi. The Nationalist victory in the Battle of Kunlun Pass saved the supply route.

The Japanese also lost the Battle of Changsha, near the southernmost point on the north–south railway line from Beijing to Changsha via Wuhan. South of Changsha, the railway connected with the major east–west line running from Shanghai to Liuzhou. The Nationalists successfully defended the city three times, from April to October 1939, from September to October 1941, and from December 1941 to January 1942. These are known as the First, Second, and

---

[33] Coox, *Nomonhan*, 914–16; Yu, *The Dragon's War*, 19.

Third Battles of Changsha. The Nationalists did not lose the city until 1944 in Japan's Ichigō Campaign.

In the spring of 1940, the Japanese launched the Zaoyang–Yichang Campaign up the Yangzi river toward Chongqing. On 12 June, the Nationalists halted the Japanese advance at the Yichang rapids in the Yangzi gorges, the gateway to Sichuan and Chongqing, but the campaign cost them Hunan, a key source of rice. By the fall of 1940 the Chinese Communists had built up their conventional forces sufficiently to wage their only conventional campaign of the Second Sino-Japanese War. They suffered the kind of enormous casualties that the Nationalists had endured throughout. The Hundred Regiments Campaign from August to September 1940 contested the territory that Japan had taken in the Taiyuan Campaign in the late fall and winter of 1937.

The Hundred Regiments Campaign boomeranged as badly as any Japanese strategy. General Okamura Yasuji responded with the Three Alls Campaign, the Chinese abbreviation for "kill all, burn all, and pillage all," but which the Japanese insisted was actually the Three Prohibitions Campaign, admonishing the Chinese not to burn, commit crimes, or kill. Whatever the name, the Japanese waged a war of annihilation, including the use of poison gas. Beyond all of the killing, they stripped the countryside of food, causing indescribable civilian misery, while temporarily reducing the population under Communist control from 44 million to 25 million.[34]

In 1941, Japan conducted three offensives, the fruitless Battle of Southern Henan in which it gained no territory, the unsuccessful Battle of Shanggao in which it lost nearly half its force, and its only operational success in the Battle of Southern Shanxi, where it forced the Nationalists to withdraw at the cost of opening north and central China to Communist infiltration. Japan inadvertently relieved the Nationalist blockade of the main Communist base areas – a strategic blunder given Japan's belief that Communism constituted the main threat.

The Second United Front had already ended in January 1941, when the Communist-led New Fourth Route Army defied Chiang Kai-shek, who ordered it to deploy north of the Yangzi river. In 1940, the New Fourth Route Army had destroyed the Nationalists' largest army operating behind Japanese lines. Nationalist forces retaliated and tried to drive it into the Japanese-dominated north. They wiped out a 10,000-man column, and captured the commanding officer Ye Ting, but proved unable to disband the army. In Chinese Communist

---

[34] Ishijima, *A History of China's Anti-Japanese War*, 171; 江口圭一 (Eguchi Kei-ichi), "中国戦線の日本軍" (The Japanese Army on the China Front), in 藤原彰 (Fujiwara Akira) and 今井清一 (Imai Seiichi), eds., 十五年戦争史 (*A History of the Fifteen-Year War*), vol. 2 (Tokyo: 青木書店, 1989), 60–62; Edward L. Dreyer, *China at War, 1901–1949* (London: Longman, 1995), 253–54; Dagfinn Gatu, *Village China at War: The Impact of Resistance to Japan 1937–1945* (Vancouver: UBC Press, 2008), 357–60.

lore this became known as the New Fourth Army Incident (also known as the South Anhui Incident).[35]

Despite numerous Japanese offensives, after 1938 they failed to hold the new territory. As soon as their main units departed for battles elsewhere, Chinese forces returned. In the second half of 1937, Japanese forces had advanced 17.4 kilometers per day; this declined to 7.6 kilometers per day in 1938, to 1.1 kilometers in 1939, to 0.6 kilometers in 1940.[36] The Second Sino-Japanese War had stalemated.

China's Illusive Center of Gravity

Over the course of the Second Sino-Japanese War, the Japanese targeted a succession of centers of gravity in order to force the Chinese to capitulate. In military terminology, a "center of gravity," once correctly targeted, causes the enemy to collapse like a building with charges properly laid at the foundations. Initially, the Japanese considered the Nationalist capital to be China's "center of gravity." They believed that if they targeted that center of gravity the edifice of Nationalist control would collapse. In 1937 they occupied the historical capital, Beijing, and the Nationalist capital, Nanjing, and in 1938 they took the interim capital at Wuhan. Each time, the Nationalists moved their capital inland, settling in 1938 in Chongqing, Sichuan, a province beyond the railhead on which the Japanese way of war depended, behind mountains that the Japanese could not cross, and upstream of rapids that made the Yangzi river difficult to navigate.

In 1937, as Japanese forces moved up the Yangzi river in the direction of the capital at Nanjing, they also targeted a second presumed center of gravity, the Chinese will to resist. *Bushidō*, or the code of the samurai, treated will power as the trump card in warfare. Naturally, as Shintō ultranationalists believed their will power to be indomitable, they targeted that of others. So they brutalized occupied populations to undermine the will to resist. On the trip upriver to Nanjing, Japanese troops had orders to treat all Chinese outside Shanghai as belligerents, kill them, and destroy their homes. They burned Zhenjiang, a city located on the Yangzi river between Shanghai and Nanjing and left undefended. It burned for ten days. They executed those trying to douse the fires, burned wounded Chinese soldiers alive, and raped women and girls.

---

[35] John W. Garver, *Chinese–Soviet Relations 1937–1945: The Diplomacy of Chinese Nationalism* (New York: Oxford University Press, 1988), 129–30, 142–45; 石仲泉 (Shi Zhongquan), "周恩来与新四军" (Zhou Enlai and the New Fourth Army), 近代史研究 (*Modern Chinese History Studies*) 77, no. 5 (Sept. 1993), 34–57; Gregor Benton, *New Fourth Army: Communist Resistance along the Yangtze and the Huai 1938–1941* (Berkeley: University of California Press, 1999), 511, 513, 520–21, 572, 600.

[36] Lary, *The Chinese People at War*, 78.

When forces under the command of Lieutenant General Prince Asaka Yasuhiko, Emperor Hirohito's paternal granduncle, entered Nanjing, they massacred tens of thousands, some say hundreds of thousands, over the next year. Whatever the numbers, Japanese troops committed an atrocity of horrific proportions. This became known as the Rape of Nanjing. The massacre attending the Xuzhou Campaign in 1938 also lasted for several months. Likewise, the Japanese intended their bombing campaigns to terrorize civilians into submission. As a result, between 1937 and 1945, over 95 million Chinese, or 26 percent of the population, became refugees. The economies of Taiyuan, Jinan, Changsha, Wuhan, and Nanjing required decades to recover.[37] Major epidemics ensued and continued throughout the war – cholera, malaria, and the plague. Far from laying down their arms, the Chinese fought on.

The Japanese then concluded that the Nationalist economy constituted China's center of gravity. The Chinese economy and, by extension, the tax base were concentrated, as they are today, in the coastal cities and along the Yangzi river, China's greatest internal waterway. This was the maritime world of sea-lanes connecting domestic and international markets. By the fall of 1938, Japan had taken China's five key centers of economic activity: Manchuria, the Beijing–Tianjin area, Shanghai, Wuhan, and Guangzhou.

The escalation of 1937 did indeed cause an implosion of the economy. The Nationalists tried to move their industrial base with them, bringing factories from occupied China to the two main cities of Sichuan, Chongqing and Chengde. The move inland cost them nearly 87 percent of their productive capacity. Heroic restoration efforts reached only 41 percent of the pre-escalation capacity.[38] The creeping Japanese occupation deprived the Nationalists of 90 percent of their former tax revenues from customs, salt, excise, alcohol, cigarettes, and the like.[39] Local government income plummeted by nearly one-quarter between 1936 and 1940, and the loss of China's main grain-producing areas meant that requisitioning to feed the army produced severe deprivation among farmers. In 1937, the Nationalists were already running a 37 percent government budget deficit.[40] Then, from 1937 to 1939, expenditures rose by

[37] Stephen R. MacKinnon, "Refugee Flight at the Outset of the Anti-Japanese War," in Lary and MacKinnon, *Scars of War*, 121–22.

[38] 吉沢南 (Yoshizawa Minami), "総論" (General Discussion), in 野沢豊 (Nozawa Yutaka), ed., 講座中国近現代史 (*Series of Studies in Modern and Contemporary Chinese History*), vol. 7, 中国革命の勝利 (*Victory in the Chinese Revolution*) (Tokyo: University of Tokyo Press, 1978), 11.

[39] 張瑞德 (Zhang Ruide), "抗戰時期大後方工商業者的心態與行動" (Businessmen of Nationalist China in the Great Rear during the Sino-Japanese War, 1937–1945), 台灣師範大學歷史學報 (*Taiwan Normal University Bulletin of Historical Research*) 27 (June 1999), 131.

[40] 董廷之 (Dong Tingzhi), "抗日战争时期国民党统治区的通货膨胀" (Inflation in Nationalist-Ruled Territory during the Anti-Japanese War), 中共党史研究 (*Research on the History of the Chinese Communist Party*), 2 (1989), 36–38.

one-third, while revenues fell by two-thirds.[41] From 1927 to 1937, they had relied ever more heavily on borrowing and increasing the money supply to sustain government funding.[42] The value of the Nationalist yuan plunged against the U.S. dollar from about 30 cents in 1937 to about 4 cents in 1941.[43] When the government tried to cap civil service and military salaries, the purchasing power plummeted of those vital to the survival of the regime. The government turned to the opium trade for income.

However impressive these economic effects were, they also tanked Japan's economy. In October 1937, Shanghai trade, which had totaled 31 million U.S. dollars a month before the escalation, collapsed to 6.7 million U.S. dollars, settling at a monthly average of 8.3 million for the first half of 1938. Japan sought resources and commerce in China. Instead it reaped collapsing trade and mushrooming military expenditures. Its military strategy not only undercut its economic goals, but undermined its relations with the Western powers, which protested in vain against Japan's closure of the Yangzi river to their commercial traffic and their increasing exclusion from the China market.[44]

In addition to the will, the capital, and the economy, the Japanese believed that the Nationalists' conventional forces constituted a fourth center of gravity. Destroy these forces and surely the government would have to capitulate. So Japan blockaded China, occupied its coastal cities, and moved up the Yangzi river in pursuit of Chiang Kai-shek's most loyal and proficient conventional forces. The Nationalists repeatedly lost and then rebuilt their armies: at Shanghai in 1937 when Japan decimated Chiang's German-trained troops, at Nanjing also in 1937 when Japan chased Chiang's forces up the Yangzi river and massacred those captured, at Xuzhou and Wuhan in 1938 when Nationalists built and then lost another army, in Chiang's Winter Offensive of 1939 to 1940, and, most critically, during the Ichigō Campaign of 1944.

The Nationalists did not follow the Japanese script to sue for peace, but implemented their long-standing war plans to retreat ever further inland, thus overextending Japanese lines and manpower. They also increasingly turned to a strategy often favored by the weak, guerrilla warfare. By 1938, the Nationalists had between 600,000 and 700,000 guerrillas harassing Japanese operations. Most deployed in central China, while in north China warlord troops performed

---

[41] Fenby, *Chiang Kai-shek*, 348.

[42] 金普森 (Jin Pusen) and 王国华 (Wang Guohua), "南京国民政府 1927–1931 年之内债" (The Internal Debt of the Nanjing Government, 1927–1937), 中国社会经济史研究 (*Research on Chinese Social and Economic History*), 4 (1991), 96–103.

[43] 吴景平 (Wu Jingping), "美国和抗战时期中国的平准基金" (On the U.S. Stabilization Fund for the Chinese Currency during the War of Resistance), 近代史研究 (*Modern Chinese History Studies*), 5 (1997), 94.

[44] 臼井勝美 (Usui Katsumi), 日中外交史研究 – 昭和前期 – (*Research on Sino-Japanese Diplomatic History: The Early Hirohito Period*) (Tokyo: 吉川弘文館, 1998), 317, 328, 332.

equivalent functions.[45] The combination of guerrilla and conventional forces proved lethal. The new strategy impeded the Japanese ability to launch major new offensives. Japan's conventional army needed to concentrate to fight Nationalist armies but to disperse to fight the insurgency. Yet it could not do both simultaneously. When Japanese troops dispersed, Nationalist main forces concentrated to eliminate these isolated elements. The insurgency undermined security in Japan's rear, blurred the front lines as the boundary between hostile and safe territory, and stymied economic development in Japanese-occupied China, the rationale for the invasion. As the Japanese pushed ever further from the sea and strayed from China's limited railway network, they extended their logistical lines and expanded the territory to garrison. While the Chinese could not defeat Japan, they could deny Japan victory. Their prevent-defeat strategy, which regardless of their losses still allowed them to fight another day, negated the Japanese strategy for a quick decisive victory.

The insurgency forced Japan into a point–line strategy of defending cities and the railway lines connecting them. But this left the countryside to the guerrillas and to the Communists, who remained to organize the peasantry with promises of land ownership. Japan simply lacked the forces to garrison China's vastness. Chiang Kai-shek believed that Japan would eventually choke on its conquests, when overextension and exhaustion would force it to withdraw. The Japanese conducted a vicious counterinsurgency that, together with the Communists, who were conducting their own anti-Nationalist counterinsurgency, eliminated most of the Nationalist base areas north of the Yellow river by 1941 and most of their guerrilla areas by 1943. Despite the Second United Front, during the Second Sino-Japanese War the Communists spent more time fighting the Nationalists than they did the Japanese. And rather than fighting at all, the Communists took advantage of the Nationalist preoccupation with Japan to organize behind Japanese and Nationalist lines, positioning themselves to win the postwar showdown phase of the long Chinese Civil War.

Japanese officers missed the nationalism that their strategy fed, not in Japan where they encouraged and leveraged it, but in China, where nationalism undermined their military strategy in a malignant synergy. When the Manchus had ruled during the Qing dynasty, they had done their utmost to keep their Han subjects divided, correctly guessing that Han nationalism would be fatal to Manchu minority rule. As the Chinese fought their long Civil War and soldiers deployed outside their home province, as more Chinese became literate, and as a mass media developed and was written more often in the accessible

---

[45] 莫岳云 (Mo Yueyun), "略论国民党敌后抗日游击战之兴衰" (A Brief Discussion of the Rise and Fall of Nationalist Party's Anti-Japanese Guerrilla War behind Enemy Lines), 史学集刊 (Collected Papers of Historical Studies) 69, no. 4 (1997), 38; 防衛庁防衛研修所戦史部 (Japan, Defense Agency, National Defense College, Military History Department), ed., 北支の治安戦 (The North China Insurgency), vol. 1 (Tokyo: 朝雲新聞社, 1968), 132–34, 143.

vernacular instead of the arcane classical language, as China's railway system spread to interconnect communities, and as the Japanese committed ever widening acts of violence, the Chinese acquired a deepening sense of nationalism. Every Japanese coercive act against a Chinese, now reported in the media and retold by travelers on the trains, heightened that sense of nationalism.

The Japanese decision to have their armies live off the land – in their words, "providing for the war by war"[46] – reflected an imperative to economize without consideration of the effects on Chinese public opinion. In the First Sino-Japanese War and the Russo-Japanese War, Japan had very carefully provided for its troops, paid Chinese producers for what it took, and so did not alienate the local population. Living off the land apparently worked in Manchuria, which Japan rapidly pacified, developed, and transformed into a supplier of war materiel. Pacification proved much more problematic in China south of the Great Wall. The Japanese soon turned to drug trafficking to raise funds. The Rehe Campaign in 1933 brought one of China's main opium-producing areas under Japanese administration. Japan then spread opium cultivation from Mongolia to Hainan Island in the far south.

The Japanese also turned to poison gas and germ warfare to economize. To develop these weapons, they experimented on prisoners of war and civilians at their notorious Unit 731 in Manchukuo. They equipped units with biological and chemical weapons and used them throughout China. They tried to spread anthrax, the plague, typhoid, and cholera, sickening their own and the enemy alike. As the belligerents in World War I had discovered, poison gas was not particularly effective because it often killed its deployers instead of its intended victims. So Japan used gas less frequently after 1938, but by then the damage had been done. Its use appalled Chinese and Western public opinion.

Whatever savings Japan generated from cheap provisions, narcotics sales, and exotic weapons, the savings did not offset the hatred these actions instilled. The hatred then swelled recruitment for the Nationalists and the Communists and heightened Japan's diplomatic isolation. Whereas the Han had been unwilling to fight in support of Manchu minority rule in the First Sino-Japanese War, they became determined to defend their homeland in the Second Sino-Japanese War. This change in public attitude meant the war would not be short. Yet the longer it lasted, the stronger Chinese nationalism became.

The Japanese began to perceive a fifth possible center of gravity – China's trade and aid from the outside. Initially Russia, and eventually Britain and the United States, responded to Japanese advances by increasing military and financial aid. After the fall of Shanghai, half of unoccupied China's trade

---

[46] 单冠初 (Shan Guanchu), "日本侵华的'以战养战'政策" (The Japanese Policy of "Providing for the War with War" during the Invasion of China), 历史研究 (*Historical Research*) 4 (1991), 77–91.

traveled along the Guangdong–Wuhan Railway. Therefore, in May 1938, Japan launched amphibious expeditions to take the treaty ports of Xiamen (Amoy), Fuzhou (Foochow), and Shantou (Swatow), followed in October by the Guangdong Campaign. On 21 October the great port of Guangzhou fell and on 10 February 1939 the navy took Hainan, indicating ambitions even further south. Together these victories put Japan in possession of the main ports from Guangdong north and allowed it to tighten the naval blockade. Britain responded to the Guangdong Campaign of October 1938 by helping to build the Burma Road to supply the Nationalists. The Burma Road connected Kunming, Yunnan to the railhead in Lashio, Burma, then part of the British Empire. It provided key but very limited military supplies to the Nationalists from December 1938 until July 1940 and again from October 1940 until March 1942, when the Japanese closed it for good. Beginning in February 1939, the U.S. government began extending loans to China.

The Interplay of Policy and Strategy

Over the course of the Second Sino-Japanese War, Japanese actions moved steadily along a spectrum from the limited objective of the transfer of Manchuria to Japanese sovereignty to creeping Japanese control over territories ever further south. As time went on, Japan's goals expanded to the unlimited objective of regime change in Chongqing. Economists speak of sunk costs. Such costs cannot be justified unless the investment pans out. The more resources the Japanese poured into their military efforts, the more they demanded from China to justify their sunk costs, but such escalating demands precluded the negotiated settlement they required. The military strategy of unrelenting expansion unwittingly herded Chinese of all political persuasions toward an inescapable conclusion: either co-operate with each other to fight Japan or become a servile population in their own land. As much as the many factions of China disagreed with each other about the form future Chinese institutions should take, they agreed that Japan had no place at the table to resolve the matter. Japan's escalation of its policy objective transformed a country wracked by civil war into a lethal adversary.

Both civil and military leaders in Japan made the decision to pursue an unlimited objective. On 16 January 1938, Prime Minister Konoe Fumimaro announced that his government no longer would deal with Chiang Kai-shek beyond trying to kill him; the objective had become regime change. Konoe was an aristocrat, very popular among voters, but enamored with empire. He believed the West had excluded Japan from the riches of the world so it should take its share come what may. In 1940 Konoe would head the new Imperial Rule Assistance Association, an unsuccessful attempt to create a Japanese institution to play the unifying and mobilizing role of a Fascist party.

Japanese actions confirmed the expanding policy objective. Wherever Japanese troops took territory, they set up new puppet governments. On 3 November 1938, Konoe announced the formation of a New Asian Order encompassing Japan, Korea, Manchuria, and China. His new order put the old order in Asia on death ground, attracting the attention of all the colonial powers as well as the United States, which had strong vested interests in the international legal and institutional status quo. As a result, Chiang's pleas for their aid no longer fell on deaf ears.

It remains unclear whether Japan's civil and military leaders fully examined the implications of their decision to transform a limited war into an unlimited war. One suspects not. As Japan's military costs escalated in China, so did the ultimatums that constituted their diplomacy. Japanese peace demands became a function of their sunk costs. The more the military spent, the more it required from China to justify the sacrifice to the Japanese public. Back in October 1935, Japan had demanded that the Chinese government cease seeking Western aid and slandering Japan, start co-operating on both north China economic development and the eradication of Communism, and tacitly accept Manchukuo's independence. Yet as the war dragged on, the Imperial Japanese Army leadership became increasingly intent upon detaching north China as the required compensation for its military sacrifices. By January 1938, Japanese demands were too much even for the Nazis, who also had a fondness for ultimatums. The Germans threw up their hands, abandoned their mediation efforts, and finally decided to back Japan over China.

When diplomacy by ultimatum failed, Japan consolidated its many puppet governments into a super-puppet state. In March of 1940, it set up the consolidated puppet government in Nanjing called the National Government of the Chinese Republic, under the Nationalist turncoat Wang Jingwei. The Japanese government then made it official by recognizing it as the government of China on 30 November 1940. Chiang enlisted German help one last time when he proposed trading Japanese recognition of his government and a troop withdrawal for Chinese recognition of Manchukuo, protection of Japanese privileges in north China, and Japanese naval basing rights in Shanghai, Qingdao, Fuzhou, Hong Kong, and Shantou. At that time, the Japanese were not thinking in terms of de-escalation of the conflict, but of escalation. With the outbreak of the War in the Pacific in 1941, Japan abandoned the diplomatic track.

Japan had invaded China in pursuit of national security through autarky. Yet its military strategy made its economic goals unattainable by causing the collapse of the Chinese economy. Given all that happened from 1937 to 1941, it is amazing that the Nationalists survived at all. Within a year of the 1937 escalation, Japan took all or pieces of twenty-one out of twenty-nine provinces.[47] By

[47] Stephen R. MacKinnon, "Refugee Flight at the Outset of the Anti-Japanese War," in Lary and MacKinnon, *Scars of War*, 121.

1939 it occupied one-third of China, comprising 40 percent of its agriculture, 92 percent of its modern industry, and 66 percent of its salt fields (the latter a major tax source). Together this cost the Nationalists over 80 percent of their tax revenues.[48]

Sadly for Japan, not only did its military strategy destroy the Chinese economy, but it also undermined its own home economy. Whereas from 1931 to 1936 Japanese economic statistics show flourishing growth both on the home islands and in the greater empire, from 1937 onward key economic statistics plateaued. Territorial expansion no longer benefited the economy. On the contrary, it constituted an increasing burden so that by 1940 the Japanese home islands faced food shortages.

From 1936 to 1945, the Japanese government implemented a wide variety of measures to take control of production, which instead strangled the economy just as the assassinated finance minister, Takahashi Korekiyo, had predicted.[49] Before long, central planning in Tokyo mimicked the reviled Soviet system. In September 1937 Japan jettisoned the market economy in favor of central planning with the Diet's passage of the Temporary Capital Adjustment Law and the Law Relating to Temporary Export and Import Commodities, and with the enactmant of the 1918 Law for the Application of the Armament Industry Mobilization Law. The first took over capital allocation, the second took over commodity allocation, and the third allowed the military to commandeer factories. In October 1937 the government set up the Planning Board and soon regulated prices. In 1939, it responded to inflation with price and wage freezes and in 1940, even before Pearl Harbor, it imposed rationing.

The percentage of the government budget devoted to military expenditures rose from 30.8 percent in 1931, to 69.2 percent in 1937, to 75.6 percent in 1941, to an economy-busting 85.3 percent in 1944.[50] The structure of the Japanese economy changed in tandem with these expenditures. In 1930 the division between heavy and light industry was 38.2 percent devoted to heavy

---

[48] 王磊 (Wang Lei), "抗战时期国民政府内债研究" (Research on the Internal Debt of the Nationalist Government during the War of Resistance), 中国经济史研究 (*Research in Chinese Economic History*) 4 (1993), 75.

[49] Barnhart, *Japan Prepares for Total War*, 94–95; Takafusa Nakamura, "The Age of Turbulence, 1937–54," in Takafusa Nakamura and Kônosuke Odaka, eds., *Economic History of Japan 1914–1955: A Dual Structure*, trans. Noah S. Brannen (Oxford: Oxford University Press, 1999), 63–66.

[50] 江口圭一 (Eguchi Kei-ichi), 十一年戦小史 (*A Short History of the Fifteen-Year War*) (Tokyo: 青木書店, 1996), 225–26; Boris Grigor'evich Sapozhnikov, *Японо-китайская война и колониальная политика Японии в Китае (1937–1941)* (*The Sino-Japanese War and Japan's Colonial Policy in China (1937–1941)*) (Moscow: Издательсво «наука» Главная редакция восточной литературы, 1970), 144; 荒川憲一 (Arakawa Ken-ichi), 戦時経済体制の構想と展開 ： 日本陸海軍の経済史的分析 (*Plans for and Development of the Wartime Economic System: An Economic Historical Analysis of the Japanese Army and Navy*) (Tokyo: 岩波書店, 2011), 285.

industry. This rose to 57.8 percent in 1937 and to a standard-of-living-killing 72.7 percent in 1942.[51] No light industry meant no consumer goods. Real wages in Japan plummeted. Wages indexed to buying power and set at 100 for the 1934–36 period fell to 79.1 in 1941 before shriveling to 41.2 in 1945.[52]

The strategy of escalation made Japan more, not less, reliant on imports. Whereas Japan had imported 67 percent of its oil in 1935, this grew to 74 percent in 1937 and to 90 percent in 1939.[53] Thus Japan's means to produce autarky (i.e. war) precluded the ends by making the Japanese military's consumption of imported resources skyrocket and Japan more, not less, dependent on trade. Japan was becoming less capable of executing its military strategy as well. By 1940, it was running out of troops to conduct endless campaigns in China. As it reached the limits of the Chinese railway system, it also reached the logistical limits of the Japanese way of war.

Japan's insatiable appetite for Chinese territory was bad strategy because it guaranteed a war, which, given the size of China, promised a protracted conflict that Japan, given its resource and manpower constraints, could ill-afford to wage but that the Chinese could ill-afford not to. The Japanese mistook Chiang's reluctance to fight over Manchuria for a defeatism that they assumed would extend to the rest of China as well.

Japanese leaders focused on the operational level of war – winning the battles. They did not adequately consider the strategic effects of these military operations. Chiang did not want to fight Japan at all, but Japanese military strategy left him no other choice. Victory at the strategic level required trade with the West, stability in China, Sino-Japanese economic integration, the elimination in China of Communism and Soviet influence, and the end to foreign interference with Japan's plans. Japanese military operations did not further these strategic goals, but quite remarkably precluded their achievement. The survival of the Communists, the rallying of the Nationalist coalition in order to fight Japan, and the outbreak of a virulently anti-Japanese Chinese nationalism were outcomes antithetical to these goals.

Japanese leaders of the 1930s lacked the brilliance of their Meiji generation predecessors, who had understood that a quick decisive victory in war required a generous peace so that the enemy would lay down its arms instead

---

[51] 真保潤一郎 (Shinpo Junichirō), "戦時経済の遺産と経済再建" (The Wartime Economic Legacy and Economic Reconstruction), in 奥村房夫 (Okumura Fusao) and 近藤新治 (Kondō Shinji), eds., 近代日本戦争史 (Modern Japanese Military History), vol. 4 大東亜戦争 (The Great East Asian War) (Tokyo: 同台経済懇話会, 1995), 944; 森武麿 (Mori Takemaro), "恐慌と戦争 -- １９３０-１９４５年 --" (The Great Depression and the War, 1930–1945), in 森武麿 (Mori Takemaro) et al., eds., 現代日本経済史 (Modern Japanese Economic History) (Tokyo: 有斐閣Sシリーズ, 1993), 16.

[52] Eguchi, A Short History of the Fifteen-Year War, 227.

[53] 安部彦太 (Abe Hikota), "大東亜戦争の計数的分析" (A Statistical Analysis of the Great East Asian War), in Okumura and Kondō, Modern Japanese Military History, vol. 4, 825.

of fighting for better terms. In the 1930s, the Japanese military consistently demanded far more military gains than any Chinese government could ever grant and hope to remain in power. Yet China was much too large a theater to be garrisoned in the absence of Chinese co-operation. So the costs of war escalated for all sides.

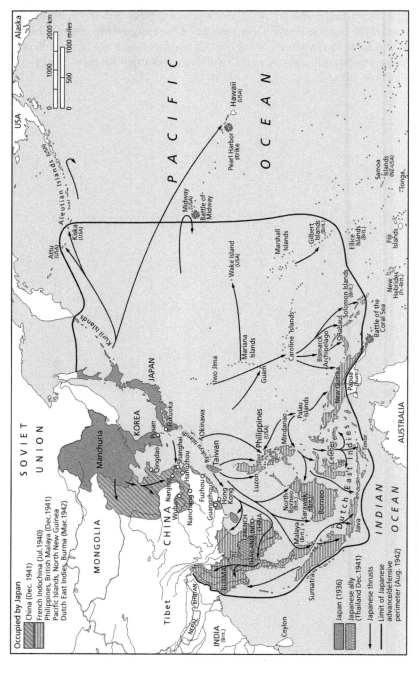

Map 5 World War II

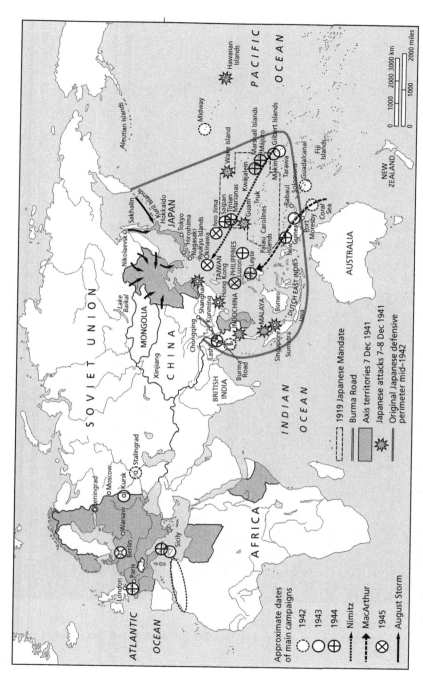

Map 5 (*cont.*)

Photo 5 Tōjō Hideki (1884–1948)
http://www.ndl.go.jp/portrait/e/datas/142_1.html (National Diet Library, Japan)

6   The General Asian War (1941–1945)

> Those who excite the public by claims of victory, just because the army has captured some out-of-the-way little area, do so only to conceal their own incompetence as they squander the nation's power in an unjustifiable war.[1]
>
> Lieutenant General Ishiwara Kanji, architect of the invasion of Manchuria in 1931

Botched war termination in regional wars usually produces one of two outcomes: either the war protracts when the weaker belligerent launches an insurgency with economy-killing and budget-busting consequences for the counterinsurgent or the war escalates when an interested third party intervenes on the opposing side. The most common way to avoid such unpleasant eventualities is to offer peace terms generous relative to the military disposition of forces. The need to offer a generous peace is particularly important for the invading power because the value of victory is usually considerably higher for those living in theater than for those intervening from afar. This means a greater likelihood for those in theater to endure high costs and protraction. As a testament to Japan's strategy, it produced both a nationwide insurgency and multiple great-power allies for Chiang Kai-shek.

Prior to Pearl Harbor, Japan had suffered 600,000 casualties in China, a sunk cost of stupendous proportions that its leaders found difficult to justify to the Japanese people.[2] Japan's situation was reminiscent of great powers in World War I that were equally incapable of reassessing the flawed military strategies that consumed the lives of a generation of young men. So the old men kept applying greater doses of the same tried and trashed remedies, rather than own up to their enormous failures.

The outbreak of war in Europe in 1939 offered Japan hope in the form of a perceived window of opportunity, akin to the ones the Meiji generation had

---

[1] Cited in Mark R. Peattie, *Ishiwara Kanji and Japan's Confrontation with the West* (Princeton: Princeton University Press, 1975), 307, 340.

[2] Edward J. Drea, *In the Service of the Emperor: Essays on the Imperial Japanese Army* (Lincoln: University of Nebraska Press, 1998), 30; David P. Barrett, "Introduction: Occupied China and the Limits of Accommodation," in David P. Barrett and Larry N. Shyu, eds., *Chinese Collaboration with Japan, 1932–1945: The Limits of Accommodation* (Stanford: Stanford University Press, 2001), 3–4.

so successfully seized in the First Sino-Japanese War and the Russo-Japanese War. With the fall of France in June 1940, Japan pressured Britain to close the Burma Road in July, putting Chiang Kai-shek in his worst situation since the outbreak of the Second Sino-Japanese War. German control of continental Europe promised open season in Asia for Japan to liberate by conquest the colonies that others could no longer defend. An Asia-wide empire, the Imperial Japanese Army hoped, would justify the sunk costs in China.

When Japan chose to attack the primary maritime powers, it reaped the consequences of misidentifying itself as a continental power. It lacked the energy and food self-sufficiency, the indigenous productive base, and by extension the capacity to maintain a dominant navy in wartime to defeat a maritime power in possession of all these strengths. A small minority understood this. In the third quarter of 1941, Admiral Inoue Shigeyoshi submitted a memo to Navy Minister Admiral Oikawa Koshirō, entitled "The New Defense Plan." Both men opposed war with the United States and both would be sidelined as a result. Inoue argued that such a war was unwinnable because Japan lacked the capacity to occupy the U.S. capital let alone its territory, or to blockade its long coastlines, while the United States could do all of these things to Japan.[3]

Back in 1936, soon-to-be-assassinated Finance Minister Takahashi Korekiyo's comments on Italy's invasion of Ethiopia contained economic advice for the Imperial Japanese Army: "If a country increases its empire and pours money into it, how big a profit is it going to have? Until the profits come in, the home country has to carry [the colony.]"[4] Government estimates indicated that it would take a minimum of two years to build the infrastructure to utilize conquered resources. In 1941 there was no analysis explaining how to get through the two lean years when extra resources would be required to conquer and access the future resources – rather Japanese leaders made a leap of faith and a vault of logic. This sin of omission allowed fond hopes to substitute for hardheaded strategy. Japan set for itself coveted but infeasible goals that threatened the vital interests of many others, who then combined to eliminate Japan as a player of global chess.

More Proximate and Underlying Causes

The best-known proximate cause of any modern war is the Japanese bombing of Pearl Harbor. That day the Japanese flagship carrier *Akagi* flew the flag flown by *Mikasa*, the Japanese flagship during the surprise attack on Lüshun. In the Russo-Japanese War, the surprise attack had been an operational failure although Japan eventually won the war. This time around the reverse proved

[3] Tadokoro, "Why Did Japan Fail to Become the 'Britain' of Asia?" 222.
[4] Cited in Smethurst, *From Foot Soldier to Finance Minister*, 294.

true. Japan laid waste to the U.S. Pacific Fleet, but the surprise attack instantly transformed the United States, a self-absorbed, isolationist nation, into a war machine bent on the destruction of Japan. Pearl Harbor is an American over-simplification. On 7–8 December 1941, Japan attacked not only Hawaii but also British and Dutch interests across the Pacific in the most operationally successful simultaneous attacks in human history. Victory, however, is always assessed at the strategic, not the operational, level.

It turns out that there was a great deal of tinder to ignite. The key underlying cause for the outbreak of World War II in 1939 in Europe and 1941 in Asia was the Axis bid to replace the global maritime order with a continental world order, based not on the global maritime commons, international law, and international institutions, but on a world divided into spheres of influence achieved by killing or imprisoning any who resisted. Germany, Italy, and Japan planned to divide much of the world among an ethnically cleansed Nazi *Lebensraum*, a Roman Empire revisited, and a jackbooted Pax Japonica. For a long time, Western leaders refused to apprehend the impending war over the practice of international relations. Such global conflicts are the most costly type of war. They sweep aside all other government tasks. So Western leaders tested Germany and Japan time and again to confirm that the two countries really meant what their propaganda said – German plans for a Eurasian Aryan wonderland with mass graves in store for the displaced and Japanese plans for a Japanese-only-need-apply Greater East Asia Co-prosperity Sphere. German and Japanese surprise attacks then confirmed their fidelity to the propaganda.

Western leaders and voters were well acquainted with world war. These leaders, the conscripts of World War I, could not believe that anyone could desire a repeat performance. So they did their best to avoid war. But no country can assume the luxury that it will determine when war starts. If attacked, it must decide whether to capitulate – avoiding war – or to resist – entering war, but it cannot choose when others will attack. It can choose only whether or not to resist and to try to prepare and deter in the meantime. Eventually Western leaders realized, like the Chinese before them, that they would have to fight to keep what they had. Capitulation and peace meant the end of a world order, however flawed in practice, based on law, diplomacy, and democratic institutions. The proximate causes leading to this conclusion were numerous and compounding.

The U.S. strategy to deter Japanese aggression in China developed slowly. In retaliation for Japan's 1931 occupation of Manchuria, in 1932 President Franklin D. Roosevelt had the Scouting Fleet remain in California after its annual exercises. On 1 January 1932, U.S. Secretary of State Henry L. Stimson circulated what became known as the Stimson Note and later as the Stimson Doctrine, which paired a U.S. refusal to recognize Manchukuo and a U.S. demand for international adherence to the Open Door Policy in China. The Open Door Policy prohibited any country from carving out exclusive spheres of influence;

rather, the door should remain open for all to trade on an equal footing. While others are wont to ignore self-important U.S. pronouncements on financial and territorial matters, often they fail to grasp that the United States, like an elephant as it lumbers along, rarely forgets, but puts up with nearly endless annoyances until, after much bluster and warning and threatening, it charges and, force being mass times acceleration, the mass counts.

For years the United States did very little. A year after Japan and Germany withdrew from the League of Nations, signaling their rejection of the global order, the 27 March 1934 Vinson–Trammell Act authorized but did not fund the building of additional navy ships. German and Japanese withdrawal from the League should have been seen as a red flag for bad things to come. When Japan expanded the Second-Sino-Japanese War in July 1937 to encompass south and central China, the United States had immediately "promised" China a loan, but did not deliver until February 1939. It also restricted arms shipments to both sides in order to remain neutral. Since Japan had a much larger industrial base than China, the embargo hurt China more than it did Japan, which could produce much of its conventional military equipment internally.

As Japanese forces swept up the Yangzi river, on 12 December 1937 they sank USS *Panay* while en route to Nanjing, which they took the following day and where they committed atrocities for months thereafter. As a sop for U.S. outrage over the sunken ship, the Japanese made a Christmas Eve apology and promise to pay an indemnity. During the two-week crisis Roosevelt had secret plans drawn up for a blockade of Japan from the Aleutian Islands to Hong Kong and began pushing for naval expansion that would culminate in the series of Vinson Acts. On 17 May 1938, a Second Vinson–Trammell Act finally funded the naval expansion promised in the first Vinson–Trammell Act passed four years earlier. Meanwhile, incidents in China involving the foreign powers kept accumulating. Japan blockaded the British Settlement in Tianjin until Britain caved in to its demands on 22 July 1939, in what Chiang Kai-shek coined "the Far Eastern Munich." Britain allowed Japan to take over the Tianjin foreign concession area, where the presumed Chinese murderer of an assassinated Japanese customs official was said to be hiding.[5] It turns out that this little thing then triggered the big thing.

On 26 July 1939, the United States retaliated by renouncing its 1911 commercial treaty with Japan, effective six months later in January 1940. This opened the way for spiraling embargoes. Unbeknownst to U.S. strategists, the Japanese had a large hidden slush fund sustaining the flow of imports and negating the embargo.[6] In April 1940, the United States made a second loan to

[5] Usui, *Research on Sino-Japanese Diplomatic History*, 332, 343; Yu, *The Dragon's War*, 48.
[6] Edward S. Miller, *Bankrupting the Enemy: The U.S. Financial Siege of Japan before Pearl Harbor* (Annapolis: Naval Institute Press, 2007), xiii, 73, 103–4.

China. In May President Roosevelt ordered the U.S. Navy to remain forward-deployed at Pearl Harbor instead of returning to California. Although some in Japan construed this as an in-your-face deployment, Hawaii was still a long way from Japan. On 22 June 1940 the unthinkable happened. France fell to Germany and Germany or its allies soon occupied virtually all of continental Europe. This put the maritime global order on the line and made the need for a large navy obvious to Americans.

As the United States prepared for war, its retaliation against Japan no longer followed its prior desultory pace. Passage of the Third Vinson Act on 28 June expanded the navy, while passage of the Export Control Act on 2 July conserved war materiel at home by embargoing Japan. On 19 July 1940 passage of the Two-Ocean Navy Act (the Fourth Vinson Act) funded a 70 percent expansion of the U.S. Navy to create separate Atlantic and Pacific Fleets – one for Germany and one for Japan. On 26 July, the first anniversary of treaty abrogation, the United States embargoed aviation gasoline and various categories of iron and steel scrap – two of the most essential categories of war materiel. Hitherto, U.S. fuel had kept Japanese bombers and fighters airborne. As long as Japan owned the skies over China, the Nationalists could not win the conventional ground fighting. The casualty rates were enormous and debilitating for those on the receiving end of the strafing and bombing. On 14 September, the United States introduced the first peacetime conscription in its history.

When Japan occupied northern Indochina on 22 September 1940, the United States embargoed iron and steel scrap on 26 September. Japan had invaded Indochina in order to cut off Chiang Kai-shek's foreign aid, the last presumed center of gravity necessary to eliminate in order to produce Chinese capitulation. After the fall of Guangdong at the end of 1938, Indochina had become the Nationalists' main supply route. In June of 1940, the Japanese military estimated that the Nationalists received 1,000 tons of aid per month from Russia via Xinjiang, 9,000 tons per month via south China, 3,000 to 4,000 tons per month via Burma, and 25,000 to 30,000 tons per month via French Indochina.[7]

Japan transformed itself from a regional irritant into a key player in the Italo-German and Japanese pincer attack on the global maritime order. On 27 September 1940, Japan's accession to the Tripartite Pact made the twosome a threesome. Japanese foreign minister Matsuoka Yōsuke apparently thought that big friends would deter further Western intervention in Asia. Again, the

[7] 戸部良一 (Tobe Ryūichi) "米英独ソ等の中国援助" (U.S., British, German, Soviet, etc. Assistance to China), in 奥村房夫 (Okumura Fusao) and 河野収 (Kōno Shū), eds., 近代日本戦争史 (*Modern Japanese Military History*), vol. 3, 満州事変・支那事変 (*The Manchurian Incident and the China Incident*) (Tokyo: 同台経済懇話会, 1995), 335, 345–48; 刘卫东 (Liu Weidong), "印支通道的战时功能述论" (A Narrative of the Wartime Function of the Indochina Passageway), 近代史研究 (*Modern Chinese History Studies*) 2 (May 1999), 173, 185; Eguchi, *A Short History of the Fifteen-Year War*, 151.

Japanese mistook an accelerant for a flame retardant. In October the United States offered China another loan and Britain reopened the Burma Road supply route for the Nationalists. On 11 March 1941, soon after his re-election, President Roosevelt made good the promise from his arsenal-for-democracy speech by signing into law the Lend–Lease Act and immediately made available ships and funds for Britain. In November, after the German invasion of Russia in June, he promised Russia the astronomical sum of one billion dollars in aid. Thus, even before entering the war, the United States was providing billions of dollars in aid to its allies – a sum that got the attention of Germany and Japan.

Then the *pièce de résistance*, the United States imposed a total oil embargo in response to Japan's invasion of southern French Indochina and occupation of the entire colony on 24–27 July 1941. By then, the United States had already embargoed virtually everything else useful in war. Great Britain and the Netherlands joined the United States to freeze Japanese assets, a fate already suffered by Germany and Italy in June. The Western powers reasoned that if Japan had no oil, it could not continue the fight in China and would have to back down. No oil meant the equipment would not run and no equipment meant that Chinese manpower superiority would carry the day. At the time Japan had oil reserves of 9.4 million kilotons and consumed 450,000 kilotons per month, giving it about a one-and-a-half-year supply at stable consumption rates.[8] Like the Japanese, Americans also mistook an accelerant for a flame retardant. Japanese leaders construed the oil embargo as a deadline for making alternative arrangements for fuel. Within the week, the Imperial Japanese Army favored war in the Pacific and concluded that the Greater East Asia Co-prosperity Sphere had to be expanded to include the oil fields of the Dutch East Indies. Japanese planners grasped for an escape hatch from their converging problems in Asia and they mistook Axis operational success in Europe as a window of opportunity to do so.

In September the Cabinet and then an Imperial Conference confirmed the Imperial Japanese Army and Navy's recommendation for the Southern Advance war plan to take advantage of the war in Europe to take over Europe's colonies in Asia. The navy, not the army, then added Hawaii to the list of targets. The window actually had four parts: Hitler's defeat of the colonial powers in Europe opening the window, the rapidly shifting naval balance, the U.S. military buildup in the Philippines, and Japan's inelastic resource supplies in the face of Western sanctions potentially closing the window. The Two-Ocean Navy Act passed in July 1940 promised a U.S. Navy with four times the

---

[8] Eguchi, *A Short History of the Fifteen-Year War*, 162; 近藤新治 (Kondō Shinji), " 「物的国力判断」 " ("An Evaluation of National Material Strength"), in Okumura and Kondō, *Modern Japanese Military History*, vol. 4, 212–18.

tonnage and four times the air power of Japan's. This meant Japan's relative naval strength would peak in late 1941 at near parity with the U.S. Navy before rapidly declining. Over the summer of 1941 the United States had begun reinforcing the Philippines, which stood between Japan and the oil it coveted in the Dutch East Indies. The blanket oil embargo imposed on 1 August 1941 by the United States, soon in co-operation with Great Britain and the Netherlands, threatened to shut down all Japanese military operations.

On 26 November 1941, the United States had delivered to the Japanese ambassador in Washington, Nomura Kichisaburō, the Hull Note, authored by U.S. Secretary of State Cordell Hull. It required Japan to evacuate Indochina and China including Manchuria, and to repudiate its consolidated puppet government under Wang Jingwei as well as its alliance with Germany and Italy. The Japanese interpreted the Hull Note not as an ultimatum that required compliance, but as the end to diplomacy and the countdown to war. This triggered the final proximate cause in the series when Japan brought multiple adversaries into a war that was not going well. On 7–8 December 1941, it conducted roughly simultaneous attacks against Hawaii, Thailand, Malaya, the Philippines, Wake Island, Guam, Hong Kong, and the international settlement at Shanghai, eliciting declarations of war by the United States, Britain, Australia, New Zealand, and the Netherlands. Germany then interpreted its alliance with Japan broadly to declare war against the United States on 11 December. The treaty required German aid should Japan become the victim, not the perpetrator, of an attack. And the United States set about enforcing the Open Door Policy and the global maritime order it represented. After 7 December, the elephant finally charged. The equation of mass times acceleration produced a force that overwhelmed Japan's problems in China.

The Great Gamble: Alliance with Germany and War with the United States

On 27 September 1940 Foreign Minister Matsuoka Yōsuke signed the Tripartite Pact with Germany and Italy in the mistaken belief that this would deter the United States from risking war with Japan and in the false hope that Russia would soon join the Axis, cutting off aid across China's northern border. Evidently he had not bothered to read with care Adolf Hitler's main literary effort, *Mein Kampf*. The Japanese publishers had tactfully edited out its racist sections in their translation and, therefore, readers did not grasp that Hitler had also classified the Japanese as subhumans, so they maintained cordial relations with Germany. Even so, they should not have missed Hitler's vision, clearly laid out in the book, of genocide for the Slavs in the East to open up *Lebensraum*, or living space, for the master race (the Aryans of Germany). Hitler had slated Russia and the Russians for death so any negotiations with

Russia were but a temporary expedient en route to Hitler's ultimate destination, which was Moscow. Hitler's plans also made Matsuoka's vision for a German–Russian–Japanese Eurasian heartland a nonstarter. Navy Minister Yoshida Zengō was the sole strong opponent of the alliance, arguing that it would produce a war with the United States for which Japan was not prepared. In early September 1940 he had a nervous breakdown and stepped down. The army had argued relentlessly that the alliance would protect Japan from its primary enemy, Russia. While this was the theory, in practice Japan's primary enemy remained China but soon would become the United States, as Admiral Yoshida had accurately warned. State Shintō absolved the army of the need to solve such problems of logic with logic.

Japan's diplomacy with Germany had long been troubled. The Germans had attempted to maintain amicable relations with both China and Japan through 1937, providing the former with extensive military aid and advice that increased Japanese casualty rates. On 21 May 1939, Japan had declined Germany's original invitation to ally. The following day Germany and Italy had allied without Japan in their "Pact of Steel." Then, as Japan lost to Russia at Nomonhan, Germany paid Japan back, by signing a non-aggression pact with Russia on 23 August in preparation for its invasion of Poland nine days later. This breach of Article 2 of the secret protocol to the Anti-Comintern Pact rendered the Japanese–German alliance against Russia under the pact useless, outraged Japan, and caused the immediate fall of the Cabinet. A week and a half later, on 3 September, World War II broke out in Europe when France and Britain declared war on Germany for its invasion of Poland two days earlier. On 17 September Russia joined the German attack on Poland and Russia and Germany soon divided up Eastern Europe between them. This was when a Eurasian alliance seemed promising to Matsuoka.

But in early 1941, the Germans warned Japan of their impending invasion of Russia and had initially hoped that the Japanese would attack Western interests in Asia. On 16 April Lieutenant General Ōshima Hiroshi, Japan's ambassador to Germany, a fluent German-speaker and good friend of numerous high-ranking Nazis, wired Foreign Minister Matsuoka that Hitler intended to attack Russia. He sent repeated reconfirmations thereafter. These all became known to the United States, which had broken the Japanese diplomatic code in September 1940, in the decryption effort known as MAGIC. When the Russians later reconstructed events, they believed that by February or March the Japanese were aware of German plans to invade Russia. The decryptions transformed Ambassador Ōshima into the most reliable Allied informant of German battle plans for the duration of the war. This information included the details of the German defenses at Normandy, essential for the success of the Allied invasion of France in 1944. The United States also broke parts of the Japanese navy and army codes, in a decryption effort known as ULTRA.

Japan, despite having signed the Axis alliance, chose not to co-operate with Germany. On 13 April 1941, a month and a half prior to Germany's invasion of Russia, Japan concluded a neutrality pact with Russia to the horror of Germany, which expected Japan to maintain military pressure on Russia's Siberian frontier. Perhaps Foreign Minister Matsuoka, the negotiator of the pact, believed he was paying Germany back for its nonaggression pact with Russia concluded during the Battle of Nomonhan. More likely, he hoped to cut Soviet aid to Chiang Kai-shek – he saw the regional war, not the developing global war. The pact also outraged both the Chinese Nationalists and the Chinese Communists because, as Matsuoka had anticipated, Russian neutrality entailed halting aid to China.

The pact served a long-standing Russian ambition to set up the United States and Japan to fight each other, thereby eliminating two enemies. In a speech in 1920, Vladimir Lenin, the founding father of the Soviet Union, had recommended leveraging the differences among the capitalist powers. "We would be even safer if the imperialist powers were to start a war among themselves ... The capitalist thieves sharpen their knives for use against us; it is our duty to see that their knives are directed against one another." He anticipated a war between Japan and the United States over China.[9] In 1935, U.S. ambassador to Russia William C. Bullitt had warned of Russia's ambition to promote a U.S.–Japanese war in which Russia would "avoid becoming an ally until Japan had been thoroughly defeated and would then merely use the opportunity to acquire Manchuria and Sovietize China."[10] The 1941 neutrality pact fit this scenario by allowing Japan to focus its forces on the United States.

The Japanese failed to consider the world from a Russian perspective. Apparently Matsuoka also missed the crosscutting logic of his 1940 alliance with Germany and his 1941 neutrality pact with Russia. Rather than working with a consistent list of allies, he concluded the neutrality pact with the main enemy (Russia) of his own main ally (Germany), making him an ally to both soon-to-be-warring parties. The diplomacy was tenable only as long as Germany and Russia remained at peace with each other, a situation that Matsuoka knew was about to end. When Germany invaded Russia on 22 June 1941, Russia immediately allied with Japan's potentially most dangerous enemies (Britain and the United States). Afterward, some Japanese leaders belatedly wondered whether the neutrality pact was compatible with their Tripartite Pact with Germany and Italy. Matsuoka's solution was a diplomatic about-face to implement the long-standing Northern Advance Plan to invade

---

[9] David J. Dallin, *The Rise of Russia in Asia* (Hamden, CT: Archon Books, 1971, reprint, first published 1949), 164–65.

[10] Cited in Bruce A. Elleman, *International Competition in China, 1899–1991: The Rise, Fall, and Restoration of the Open Door Policy* (London: Routledge, 2015), 132.

Russia in support of Germany, but by this time the army and navy were wedded to the Southern Advance Plan for empire in the Pacific. Within a month of the German invasion of Russia, another Cabinet reshuffle left Matsuoka out of a job, and the Cabinet fell again in October because Prime Minister Konoe wanted to avoid responsibility for war with the United States, while the army was set on a fight to the finish with all comers. Japan was stuck with the combined handiwork of Matsuoka's diplomacy and the army's military strategy that had required his diplomatic acrobatics. The army got the fight but not the finish that it sought.

Hitler launched Operation Barbarossa with lethal efficiency on 22 June 1941. Russian defenses fell before him. Within three months the Germans had taken nearly 1.5 million prisoners, including nearly 665,000 in the Ukraine in the largest mass surrender in history. By December the Germans arrived within twenty-five miles of Moscow.[11] Over the summer, they urged the Japanese to join the attack but Japan declined. The Imperial Japanese Navy remained adamant not to take advantage of the German invasion. Although from 1941 to 1942 the army increased its troop strength in Manchuria from 300,000 to a million men, it did not plan to cross the border until a German victory at Stalingrad and a removal of Soviet border forces that never occurred. Japan anticipated the role of a jackal state, ready to jump in for the choice pickings of a kill made by others. In doing so, the Japanese made a fatal error of strategy. Russia barely won the Battle of Stalingrad. Had Japan put aside thoughts of a Southern Advance to attack in Siberia in the fall of 1941, it might have tipped the balance.[12] Instead, from the summer of 1941 until early 1945, Japan made repeated attempts to broker a peace between Germany and Russia so that Japan and Germany could focus on fighting Britain and the United States. Just as Japan did not want Germany to fight Russia, Germany did not want Japan to fight China. Each wished the other had a different primary enemy.

Finance and economics were not strong suits for the Imperial Japanese Army. Of the thirty-two commodities deemed indispensable for belligerency, Japan produced adequate quantities of only two: graphite and sulfur. Missing almost entirely were the two big-ticket items in modern warfare: oil and iron.[13]

---

[11] Michael Clodfelter, *Warfare and Armed Conflicts: A Statistical Reference to Casualty and Other Figures 1618–1991*, vol. 2 (Jefferson, NC: McFarland, 1992), 817–19.

[12] Wang Zhen, "The Nature of the Soviet Policy to Assist China Early in the Anti-Japanese War," 50–51; Japan, Defense Agency, Defense Research Archives, 満洲全般 223 満洲に関する用兵的観察, vol. 1, part 1, 満洲に於ける日本軍の対ソ作戦計画 (Soviet War Plans against the Japanese Army in Manchuria), May 1952, 復員局資料整理課元陸軍大佐股部四郎 (Demobilization Bureau, Documents Section), p. 77; and 満洲全般 225 満洲に関する用兵的観察, vol. 13, part 5, 極東ソ軍の戦略的特性に関する調査 (Survey of the Strategy of the Far Eastern Soviet Military), March 1953, 復員局資料整理課元陸軍大佐林三郎 (Demobilization Bureau, Documents Section, Former Army Colonel Hayashi Saburō?), p. 62.

[13] S.C.M. Paine, "The Allied Embargo of Japan, 1939–1941: From Rollback to Deterrence to Boomerang" in Bruce A. Elleman and S.C.M. Paine, eds., *Navies and Soft Power: Historical*

Ninety-five percent of its oil and 88 percent of iron ore came from overseas.[14] In 1941 the United States had a GNP twelve times that of Japan. In 1931 it had been Japan's most important trading partner, several orders of magnitude greater than the second- and third-most-important markets, China and British India. Prior to hostilities, the United States had bought 40 percent of Japanese exports, and had provided 34.4 percent of Japan's total imports, 49.1 percent of its iron imports, 53.6 percent of its machine tool imports, and 75.2 percent of its oil.[15] Japan had built an empire to overcome its resource shortages, but the longer the fighting continued, the more resources Japan consumed. The more of China it occupied, the larger the theater of military operations, and the longer the duration of hostilities, the greater the resource requirements in an ever-expanding reverse Ponzi scheme.

By 1939 the Second Sino-Japanese War had stalemated with Ponzi problems looming large. In mid-1941 a critical moment arrived in Japan's gambit to strangle the Nationalist economy (by cutting off the Indochina supply line) before the strangulation of Japan's own economy (from escalating U.S. embargoes). What to do while enough oil remained to think big? According to a popular American aphorism, insanity is doing the same thing over and over again and expecting different results. The Imperial Japanese Army's universal solution to plans gone awry was escalation. It applied it on a stupendous scale on 7–8 December 1941 in an attempt to halt Western aid to China and expropriate the entirety of East Indies oil production.

Admiral Yamamoto Isoroku, the commander of the Combined Fleet, developed the operational plan to eliminate the U.S. Pacific Fleet based at Pearl Harbor. Yamamoto was one of Japan's leaders most knowledgeable about the United States, where he had spent over five years in the 1920s, two at Harvard University and three as a naval attaché in Washington. He opposed war with the West. He, like former navy minister Yoshida Zengō and Admiral Yonai Mitsumasa, who had served as navy minister and then prime minister, opposed Japan's formal membership in the Axis alliance because they correctly predicted that the United States and Britain would respond by ratcheting up their aid to Chiang Kai-shek. They accurately understood Japan's vulnerability as an island state to attack by the dominant naval powers. Meanwhile, the army, through Japan's ambassador to Berlin, Lieutenant General Ōshima Horoshi,

Case Studies of Naval Power and the Nonuse of Military Force (Newport, RI: Naval War College Press, 2015), 69–90.

[14] Shan Guanchu, "The Japanese Policy of 'Providing for the War with War'," 90.

[15] Thomas W. Burkman, *Japan and the League of Nations: Empire and World Order, 1914–1938* (Honolulu: University of Hawaii Press, 2008), 107; Akira Iriye, *The Cambridge History of American Foreign Relations*, vol. 3, *The Globalizing of America, 1913–1945* (Cambridge: Cambridge University Press, 1993), 162–64, 166, 180; Eguchi, *A Short History of the Fifteen-Year War*, 140; Barnhart, *Japan Prepares for Total War*, 144.

worked to strengthen ties with the Axis. In the end, the navy traded in its acquiescence to the alliance in return for a larger proportion of the military budget.

Great powers routinely maintain war plans against the other great powers in order to prepare for all eventualities, no matter how remote. From September 1939 on, Admiral Yamamoto had been working on navy war plans targeting the United States. In the fall of 1940, he warned Prime Minister Konoe,

If you order us to do so, we will show you how ferocious we can be for six months to a year of battle. The Tripartite Alliance has been agreed and it can't be altered now, but I beg you to do everything within your power to avoid war with the United States, whatever else may happen.[16]

After the U.S. oil embargo a year later, Admiral Yamamoto apparently assumed that Japan could not take Dutch East Indian oil fields without provoking war with the United States, whose role as imperial overlord of the Philippines put it astride the sea lanes between Japan and the oil. This assumption, which was probably correct, had enormous consequences because it led to attacking rather than bypassing U.S. territories. Yamamoto understood that Japan could not win a protracted war against the United States, so his hopes lay in a short war like the First Sino-Japanese War and the Russo-Japanese War. Apparently he did not inquire into what had made those wars short.

Yamamoto's war plan scripted the destruction of the U.S. fleet at its base in Pearl Harbor, Hawaii. With the U.S. fleet out of action, Japan would rapidly occupy the minimally defended colonies of the Western powers and build an impregnable defensive perimeter of airbases on the islands at the far edges of the empire. The plan then scripted a showdown with the remnants of the U.S. fleet to take place from these fortified positions while the United States scrambled to supply itself over lengthy logistical lines. The United States would quickly recognize the great cost and futility of its military efforts in comparison to its minor national interests in Asia and would finally abandon China.

U.S. policymakers believed that Germany and not Japan posed the greatest threat to long-term U.S. interests and therefore agreed with Britain and Russia to pursue a Germany-first strategy. The German economy was a multiple of that of Japan. Germany had just taken over most of the industrialized world; it could cut off key U.S. markets, which were in Europe, not Asia; and it could threaten U.S. merchant shipping in U.S. waters, as it had done to such great effect in World War I. Japan, on the other hand, could not strike the United States in force, except in remote outposts such as Hawaii or the Aleutian Islands, and was already bogged down in an endless war in China.

---

[16] Cited in Takafusa Nakamura, *A History of Shōwa Japan 1926–1989*, trans. Edwin Whenmouth (Tokyo: University of Tokyo Press, 1998), 200.

Japanese leaders understood these differences clearly and so could not fathom why the United States would ever engage in an unlimited war in Asia – U.S. stakes were simply not high enough to warrant a protracted war. American voters remained hopelessly isolationist as they floundered in the aftereffects of the Great Depression. The Japanese carefully struck only military targets in Hawaii, then a U.S. territory and not a state until 1959. But Japan's quest for a sphere of influence eventually extending to the Middle East negated two cardinal principles of U.S. foreign policy: free trade and self-determination. American leaders correctly interpreted Japanese actions as an attack on the global order, which meant the stakes were actually very high. The foundational principle of that order was the territorial integrity of all states, no matter how small or inconsequential. Otherwise the strong few could do what they liked to the numerous weak. Whereas continental orders empower the strong and expropriate from the weak, maritime orders protect the weak and foster economic development.

Within the week of the total oil embargo, the Imperial Japanese Army favored going to war in the Pacific. Both Admiral Yamamoto and General Tōjō Hideki, soon to become the all-in-one prime minister, war minister, and home affairs minister, concluded that Japan would be better off acting pre-emptively to engage the U.S. fleet. At an Imperial Conference in September of 1941, General Tōjō, who would become prime minister as negotiations with the United States went from bad to worse, argued that together the U.S. oil embargo, its Lend–Lease aid to Russia, and its increasing military aid to Chiang Kai-shek constituted an attempt to encircle and threaten the existence of Japan. General Tōjō and Japan's other leaders – civil, army, and navy – who rarely agreed on much, concluded that peace on American terms, entailing a withdrawal from China, would lead to the gradual impoverishment of Japan and would undo the efforts of the Meiji generation to transform their country into a modern power. War with the United States, on the other hand, offered a fifty–fifty chance of success. Finance Minister Kaya Okinori alone repeatedly raised economic concerns indicating the infeasibility of Tōjō's plans. The others ignored him. At least, unlike his predecessor, Takahashi Korekiyo, no one murdered him. On 5 November, Prime Minister Tōjō had predicted, "America may be enraged for a while, but later she will come to understand [why we did what we did]."[17] He argued that risking war with the United States was better than "being ground down without doing anything."[18]

---

[17] Ike Nobutaka, trans. and ed., *Japan's Decision for War: Records of the 1941 Policy Conferences* (Stanford: Stanford University Press, 1967), 239.

[18] Cited in Alvin D. Coox, "The Pacific War," in John W. Hall, Marius B. Jansen, Madoka Kanai, and Denis Twitchett, eds., *The Cambridge History of Japan*, vol. 6 (Cambridge: Cambridge University Press, 1988), 329.

As it turns out, Japanese leaders did not perceive the U.S. strategy as one designed to deter. They concluded that U.S. demands put at stake the existence not only of their country, but of themselves personally as those responsible for Japan's China policy, leaving them a stark choice of fight or perish. Dictatorships do not offer failed leaders the soft landing of electoral defeat, but rather predispose entire populations to go down in flames with their dictators. Japan's leaders perceived an overarching Russian threat, which the United States overlooked at this juncture. For two generations after the war, however, U.S. leaders would frame foreign policy in similar terms – the Russian threat that had so consumed the Japanese in the 1930s. Unimaginative strategy from both the United States and especially Japan brought a U.S.–Japanese war that benefited neither and left postwar Asia in shambles and vulnerable to Soviet plans.

Japan and Germany gave Roosevelt the provocation he needed to galvanize Americans to intervene massively in both the European and Asian wars, which after Pearl Harbor became linked. The logic of the European theater would extend to the Asian theater: the Allies would demand unconditional surrender in both, a turn of events unsuspected by Japanese leaders, who never thought that they could win a protracted war against the United States. Like all their past modern wars, they planned a quick decisive victory with a cost-efficient negotiated settlement to wrap it up. Like the Germans, the Japanese dismissed the fighting ability and will power of others. Both also grossly underestimated U.S. productive capacity and the implications for a protracted war. They had forgotten the lessons from their own histories: short wars against peer competitors require a generous peace. The Germans failed to appreciate this legacy of Otto von Bismarck just as the Japanese failed to appreciate the same legacy from the Meiji generation. Both demanded a punitive peace and got a punitive war instead.

Peripheral Operations

Japan and the United States fought their war against each other in a series of peripheral operations; that is, in theaters peripheral to the main theater, which until the very end was China for Japan and always was Japan for the United States. Japanese military planners conceived of Pearl Harbor as one of a series of simultaneous peripheral operations to secure victory in China. The Japanese execution of their war plan was impressive: on 7 December 1941 (Hawaii time), their forces landed in Thailand and half an hour later on the Malay peninsula. An hour later, the Imperial Japanese Navy began the attack on Pearl Harbor. Two hours later the Japanese bombed Singapore. One hour later, the Japanese landed on Guam and began bombing Wake Island. Six hours later they attacked Clark Air Base in the Philippines. Japanese forces also bombed Hong Kong and overran the international settlements in Shanghai and elsewhere in China. Emperor Hirohito's naval aide, Lieutenant Commander Jō Eiichirō, confided in his diary, "Throughout the day the emperor wore his naval uniform and seemed to be in a splendid mood."[19]

Operationally, Japan achieved stunning success. The Imperial Japanese Navy took the United States by surprise, sinking four out of eight battleships at anchor in harbor, destroying 180 aircraft and damaging 128 others, much of it parked in close rows on the tarmac. Japan, in contrast, lost just twenty-nine planes and five midget submarines.[20] The Thai government folded within two days. On 15 December the Japanese began bombing Burma. On 16 December Japan occupied the vital Dutch oil field in Borneo. On 25 December Hong Kong fell, followed by Manila on 2–3 January 1942, the Australian military bases at Rabaul on 22–23 January, Malaya on 31 January, Singapore and the Palembang oil fields on Sumatra on 15 February, Lashio on 8 March closing the Burma Road, and Corregidor on 6 May, marking the surrender of U.S. forces in the Philippines. In the first five months of 1942, Japan took more territory over a greater area than any country in history and did not lose a single major ship.

Given the size of the many theaters, the Japanese deployed minimal forces with minimal equipment, but they succeeded by calling the Western bluff. The colonial powers had stationed inadequately equipped and marginally trained troops to protect their far-flung interests in Asia. Japan's battle-hardened veterans from China made short work of them. General Terauchi Hisaichi, commander of the Southern Expeditionary Army Group, was credited with the success and promoted to field marshal. The statistics overwhelm. Japan took 250,000 Allied prisoners of war, sank 105 Allied ships, and seriously damaged ninety-one others, while it lost only 7,000 dead, 14,000 wounded, 562 planes, and twenty-seven ships, but no cruiser, battleship, or carrier.[21]

This series of conquests had followed two prongs, one through the Southeast Asian mainland to take Thailand, Burma, Malaya, and Singapore, and the other through the Pacific to take the Philippines, Guam, Borneo, Java, and Sumatra. Thereafter the army wished to consolidate the winnings, while Admiral Yamamoto insisted that success depended on maintaining the military pressure in the hopes of breaking American will. The army and navy compromised to take Fiji and Samoa in the hopes of cutting U.S. links to Australia.

---

[19] Cited in Herbert P. Bix, *Hirohito and the Making of Modern Japan* (New York: HarperCollins, 2000), 437.

[20] Evans and Peattie, *Kaigun*, 488; Ronald H. Spector, *The Eagle against the Sun* (New York: Free Press, 1985), 6; Ken Kotani, "Pearl Harbor: Japanese Planning and Command Structure," in Daniel Marston, ed., *The Pacific War Companion: From Pearl Harbor to Hiroshima* (Oxford: Osprey, 2005), 41.

[21] Nakamura, *A History of Shōwa Japan*, 204.

Some quibble that Admiral Nagumo Chūichi, the operational commander of the attack at Pearl Harbor, should have sent in a third wave of bombers to take out the refitting facilities, submarine base, and especially the oil tanks, which contained more oil than the entire Japanese strategic reserves at the time. Like Yamamoto, who was no fan of attacking the United States, Nagumo was no fan of Yamamoto's plan to attack Hawaii. Others noted that Japan sank none of the U.S. aircraft carriers that just happened to be out of port. But at the time battleships were considered the core capital ships of navies. Carriers acquired their cachet only as a result of the war for the Pacific. Nagumo may have believed he could not afford to risk losing capital ships in another bombing run that might have roused a posse of carriers in close pursuit. His country lacked the capacity to build a replacement fleet in any militarily useful timeframe – another limitation of its strategy. So Nagumo ruled out a third wave of bomber attacks. It remains unclear how many months the loss of the oil storage facilities on Hawaii would have delayed the U.S. counterattack and thereby extended Japan's breathing space to reinforce its defensive perimeter and to access the key resources within. In any case, stunning operational successes did not produce the desired strategic outcome of a negotiated peace.

On the strategic level Pearl Harbor was a disaster because it metastasized a malignant quagmire in China into a terminal disease for Japan with little likelihood of remission. The Japanese misjudged the intangibles of warfare – what motivated the Chinese and what motivated the Americans. As in China, Japanese military strategy against the United States produced a mortal enemy. Whatever the problems in the China theater, the Chinese lacked the capacity to threaten the Japanese home islands. The United States, of course could and did. In military strategy, it is sometimes wise to open a new theater in order to attack an enemy from an additional and unexpected direction. Opening a theater that introduces a new adversary is particularly unwise in a war that has already caused overextension. Japan opened multiple theaters, introducing multiple enemies.

The United States would also fight its entire Pacific Ocean war against Japan through a succession of peripheral operations. Other than some aviation aid, it never fought on Japan's main front, which remained China. The most important peripheral operations were the Battle of the Coral Sea (4–8 May 1942) to impede Japanese progress toward Australia; the Battle of Midway (3–7 June 1942) to degrade the Japanese fleet; the Guadalcanal Campaign (7 August 1942 to 9 February 1943) to wall off Japan from Australia; the Battles of Makin and Tarawa in the Gilbert Islands (20–23 November 1943) to acquire stepping stones on the way to the Japanese home islands; the Battles of Kwajalein and Majuro Atolls of the Marshall Islands (31 January–7 February 1944) to extend the stepping stones toward Japan; the Mariana and Palau Islands Campaign (June–November 1944) to acquire airfields on the stepping stones of Saipan and Tinian to bomb the Japanese home islands; and the Battles of Iwo Jima (19 February–26 March 1945) and Okinawa (1 April–22 June 1945) to acquire airfields even closer to the Japanese home island necessary for their invasion. Other large campaigns in New Guinea and the Philippines served to protect Australia and attrite Japanese forces, but the main event was the closing noose around the Japanese home islands, where, most amazingly of all, the United States never fought. It sidestepped the main front, the home islands of Japan, by securing unconditional surrender before this became necessary.

It took months before the United States could muster the forces for a major battle. In the meantime, on 18 April 1942 it improvised to conduct a one-way aircraft carrier bombing raid over the Japanese home islands, the so-called Doolittle Raid, under the command of Lieutenant Colonel James H. Doolittle. The heavy bombers were too large and lacked the fuel capacity to return to their ships and so had to ditch in China. The raid was not meant to do real damage but to bolster American morale at home. But the Doolittle Raid, by mortifying the Imperial Japanese Army for its inability to protect the home skies, induced a major, although unanticipated, Japanese blunder. The Imperial Japanese Navy had been pushing for an attack on Midway in the expectation that it would sink the rest of the U.S. fleet, which would surely defend the U.S. base there. Yamamoto, the planner of both the Pearl Harbor and Midway attacks, threatened to resign if the army did not go along, but the army would not budge until the Doolittle Raid, when army leaders reversed themselves to support revenge forthwith at Midway.

Unknown to the Japanese, the United States had broken their diplomatic and naval codes and so knew the courses of the ships converging on Midway, where it sank four, or one-third of Japan's twelve, difficult-to-replace aircraft carriers. In doing so, it overturned vague German and Japanese plans to meet up in India and also precluded further Japanese expansion in the Pacific. Midway was Japan's first major defeat since the beginning of the Second Sino-Japanese War. Henceforth it would have to defend what it had. For many months the Imperial Japanese Navy concealed its aircraft carrier losses from both the army and the civilian leadership. It did inform Emperor Hirohito, who had no idea what to do and so apparently kept the bad news to himself. So no one examined how the United States, with inferior naval assets, had miraculously managed to converge them at just the right spot in the vast Pacific theater to sink one Japanese carrier after another. The army continued with its war plans on the assumption that Japan still had twelve carriers.

Simultaneous with the infamous day in Hawaii, the Imperial Japanese Army launched the first in a sequence of battles from December 1941 through December 1942 intended to take over the central China railway system south of the Yangzi river and to culminate in the war-winning Gogō Campaign in Sichuan, flushing the Nationalists from their capital in Chongqing. The battles leading up to the Gogō Campaign included the Third Battle of Changsha, Hunan from December 1941 to January 1942, which failed, and the Battle of Zhejiang and Jiangxi from May to September 1942, taking the Zhejiang–Jiangxi Railway connecting Shanghai and Nanchang. By then the Nationalists had some Lend–Lease arms to fight conventionally, and the Imperial Japanese Navy, which had conducted most of the bombing of central China, had redeployed its planes to the Pacific theater, reducing the bombing of Chinese cities by more than half in 1942. So Japan no longer owned the skies over China. Before long Japan began transferring troops from the China theater to the Pacific. During bitter fighting, cities repeatedly changed hands.

As U.S. military capacity grew but still remained insufficient to engage the main armies of Germany on the main front in continental Europe or to conduct sustained military operations against the Japanese home islands, the United States turned to peripheral theaters. It took what assets it had to engage elements of the German and Japanese armed forces in locations comparatively more inconvenient for its enemies than for itself. This allowed the United States to leverage its naval assets to bear down on theaters which neither enemy would naturally have chosen. In Asia, America's peripheral strategy initially centered on Guadalcanal, a tropical nightmare, which was bad for all sides, but worse for the Japanese, because of an inferior ability to protect their logistical lines by sea to supply their men on land. President Roosevelt believed that U.S. resource superiority should yield victory in the end, so he chose resource-intensive theaters.

Japan's Southern Advance strategy required a heavily defended outer perimeter of airfields on far-flung islands to parry the expected Allied counterattack. The Imperial Japanese Navy had failed to inform the Imperial Japanese Army that, as attractive as its strategy was, it had not yet built the required Maginot Line of airfields. One of the airfields under construction was at Guadalcanal, which the United States discovered and then attacked on 7 August 1942. The Imperial Japanese Navy desperately called on the Imperial Japanese Army for help. From August 1942 to February 1943, Japan tried in vain to defend Guadalcanal, where U.S. forces pierced the defensive perimeter, halted the advance toward Australia, and forced the Japanese remnants to withdraw. Japan also lost its vital elite cadre of naval aviators, on whom its defense rested. From the second half of 1942 to the first half of 1943, Japanese pilots from land-based aircraft suffered an 87 percent casualty rate and carrier-based aircraft had an astounding 98 percent casualty rate. Although these numbers dropped in the second half of 1943 to 60 and 80 percent respectively, Japan could never replace its lost elite pilots.

Guadalcanal drained so many Japanese resources that, mid-campaign in December 1942, Japan called off the Gogō Campaign aimed at Chongqing. If these losses had not forced deployment of forces from the China theater to the

Pacific, Chiang Kai-shek might have lost his last foothold in China to end up at the headwater of the Yangzi river in Tibet or Burma, neither a promising location for a comeback. The Nationalists had fled from Shanghai in 1937 all the way upriver to Chongqing and verged on re-embarking for destinations further west in 1942 until Guadalcanal saved them.

The Kinetics of War Termination

In 1942 the tide of battle turned in both the European and Asian wars. In Europe, Russia won the Battle of Stalingrad that raged from 13 September 1942 until 2 February 1943. Stalingrad was the largest and bloodiest battle of World War II and Germany's greatest defeat. Combined casualties for both sides exceeded 750,000.[22] Henceforth, Russian troops moved westward. Again Germany unsuccessfully pressured Japan to open a second front on Russia. Britain and the United States defeated Italy in September. After calling off the Gogō Campaign, Japan fought the Battle of Western Hubei from May to June 1943 and the Battle of Changde, Hunan from November through December 1943. Throughout 1943 the Japanese conducted offensives along broad fronts, taking territory, but only temporarily for a lack of manpower to garrison the vastness of China. In 1943, the United States began its two-pronged offensive, one led by General Douglas MacArthur to reclaim the Philippines, which he had lost in May 1942, and another led by Admiral Chester Nimitz to follow the island chains to establish bomber bases within range of Japan. Japanese forces scrambled to maintain their defensive perimeter in the campaigns for the Solomons and New Guinea.

The Japanese assumed that the United States would take each position on the way to Tokyo. They planned to fight to the death at each one, understanding that more men are required to storm a well-fortified position than to hold it. They believed that the United States would not have the stomach to continue but would come to a negotiated settlement long before reaching Tokyo. Instead the United States bypassed many, taking only those necessary for naval logistics, and, more importantly, for bomber bases to bring the air war to the Japanese home islands. Simultaneously, the United States used its submarine service to eliminate the Japanese merchant marine, an unexpected primary mission from both the Japanese and the U.S. submariners' perspective, given the illegality of unrestricted submarine warfare. Pearl Harbor, however, produced an instant change of heart concerning what had been the *casus belli* of World War I – Germany's unrestricted submarine campaign sinking the passenger ship *Lusitania*. The U.S. unrestricted submarine warfare against Japan made German submariners seem like amateurs.

---

[22] Clodfelter, *Warfare and Armed Conflicts*, vol. 2, 823–25.

The Imperial Japanese Navy fixated on the heroic task of fighting the U.S. Navy, not picking off sitting-duck merchantmen that posed no match for naval vessels. It fought the symmetric fight, conventional force on conventional force, while the United States also fought the asymmetric fight of naval ship on merchant vessel, imposing unsustainable losses on Japan. Code breaking allowed the United States to predict the location of Japanese supply ships and troop transports, which submarines destroyed with great regularity. During the Pacific Ocean war, U.S. submarines sank 201 warships out of 686 and 1,314 of the 2,117 Japanese merchantmen lost in the war.[23] By war's end Japan's merchant marine had been reduced to one-ninth its pre-Pearl Harbor capacity. Only half the men and supplies sent from Japan and Manchuria reached the Pacific theater.[24] The Japanese empire depended on resources and their transport home and its expeditionary forces scattered throughout the Pacific required supplies brought by sea. U.S. submariners starved both the home islands and the expeditionary forces.

Back in January 1942, in order to support Britain, a key ally in the European theater, the United States had supplied and pressured China to counter Japan's Burma Campaign. Japanese leaders had hoped that their operations in Burma would lead to an invasion of India and an Indian uprising against British rule. The Allies lost the Burma Campaign in 1942. Japan cultivated Subhas Chandra Bose, the charismatic orator, and the Provisional Government of Free India, who supported a violent campaign for independence. The British deeply felt the Japanese threat to India. The 1944 Burma Campaign then poisoned Sino-American relations. Chiang Kai-shek saw some of his best remaining troops deployed in a theater that had become irrelevant to his survival. He had warned that Japan would take advantage of the Allied preoccupation with the impending invasion of France. As predicted, in March 1944 the Japanese launched against India the Ugō Campaign (known in the West as the Battles of Imphal and Kohima), and in April the Ichigō Campaign against China.

The Ichigō Campaign, under the command of General Okamura Yasuji, the instigator of the Three Alls Campaign, was the final and the largest campaign

[23] George W. Baer, *One Hundred Years of Sea Power: The U.S. Navy, 1890–1990* (Stanford: Stanford University Press, 1993), 233–34; Williamson Murray and Allan R. Millet, *A War to Be Won: Fighting the Second World War* (Cambridge, MA: Harvard University Press 2000), 225; Clodfelter, *Warfare and Armed Conflicts*, vol. 2, 948; Richard B. Frank, *Downfall: The End of the Imperial Japanese Empire* (New York: Random House, 1999), 78; S. Woodburn Kirby, *The War against Japan*, 5 vols. (London: Her Majesty's Stationery Office, 1957–69), vol. 5, 476.

[24] Coox, "The Pacific War," 378; Nakamura Takafusa, "Depression, Recovery, and War, 1920–1945" in Stephen S. Large, ed., *Shōwa Japan: Political, Economic and Social History 1926–1989*, vol. 1 (London: Routledge, 1998), 76; 藤原 彰 (Fujiwara Akira), 日本軍事史 (*Japanese Military History*), vol. 1 (Tokyo: 日本評論社, 1987), 262–63; Kirby, *The War against Japan*, vol. 3, 475–76; Tohmatsu Haruo, "The Strategic Correlation between the Sino-Japanese and Pacific Wars" in Peattie, Drea, and Van de Ven, *The Battle for China*, 434.

in the history of the Imperial Japanese Army. It ran from mid-April 1944 to early February 1945 and followed the Beijing–Wuhan, Guangdong–Wuhan, and Guangxi–Hunan railway lines. The campaign had multiple objectives: it attempted to carve a passage through central south China to create an inland (and submarine-proof) transportation route between Pusan, Korea and Indochina; to take the airfields in Sichuan and Guangxi to preclude U.S. bombing of Taiwan and Japan; and to target elite Nationalist units to cause the Nationalist government to collapse. Japan deployed twenty divisions composed of 510,000 men against 700,000 Nationalist soldiers. From April to December 1944, the Nationalists lost most of Henan, Hunan, Guangxi, Guangdong, and Fujian, and a large part of Guizhou.[25] Key battles included the Battle of Central Henan from April to June, the Battles of Changsha and Hengyang from May through August, and the Battle of Guilin–Liuzhou from September to December. By the time the Nationalists realized that they faced not another Japanese "cut-short" operation, intended to attrite Chinese forces and hold territory temporarily, but the largest Japanese campaign of the war, it was too late.

In the first phase of the campaign, lasting until late May 1944, Japan launched a north–south pincer to take Luoyang, Henan and to clear the southern Beijing–Wuhan Railway all the way to Wuhan. Luoyang fell on 25 May. In the second phase, from May to December 1944, Japanese forces cleared the Guangdong–Wuhan Railway, the Guangxi–Hunan Railway, and their junction at Hengyang, the location of the largest airbase in Hunan. On 18 June Changsha finally fell in the Fourth Battle of Changsha, followed on 8 August by Hengyang, on 10 November by both Guilin (the capital of Guangxi) and Liuzhou, and on 24 November by Nanning. In early 1945, Japanese forces broke through to Indochina, opening a continuous land route and eliminating many, but not all, U.S. airbases.

The Nationalists lost over 130,000 killed in action, ten major air bases, and thirty-six airports, as well as their key remaining source for food and recruits with the occupation of Henan, Hunan, and Guangxi.[26] Japanese killed from twenty to forty Chinese soldiers for each one of theirs – a kill ratio attributable to superior conventional equipment. Given the rapid approach of the U.S. Navy to the Japanese home islands – the Marshall Islands in January, the Caroline Islands in February, and the Marianas ongoing – a win in the regional war in

---

[25] Ishijima, *A History of China's Anti-Japanese War*, 181–83; 加藤公一 (Katō Kōichi), "中国共産党の対米認識とソ連の対日参戦問題、１９４４–１９４５年"("The Chinese Communist Party's Recognition of the United States and the Soviet Entry into the War against Japan, 1944–1945"), 歴史学研究 (*Journal of Historical Studies*) 751 (July 2001), 36; Drea, *Japan's Imperial Army*, 244–45.

[26] Galina Fominichna Zakharova, *Политика Японии в Маньчжурии 1932–1945* (*The Policy of Japan in Manchuria 1932–1945*) (Moscow: «Наука» Главная редакция восточной литературы, 1990), 193; Hara Takeshi, "The Ichigō Offensive" in Peattie, Drea, and Van de Ven, *The Battle for China*, 394.

China at this late date contributed nothing to the defense of the home islands in the global war.[27]

In the midst of the campaign, in September of 1944 Japan again attempted to make peace with the Nationalists. Japan agreed to withdraw all of its troops from China in return for a withdrawal of the U.S. air forces, whose planes, based in Chengdu, Sichuan, on 15 June for the first time since the Doolittle Raid, had started bombing Kyūshū, the southernmost of Japan's main home islands. Japan would let Chiang Kai-shek determine his relations with the United States, Britain, and the Wang Jingwei puppet government. Chiang continued to negotiate, but agreed to nothing.

Meanwhile Admiral Chester Nimitz's Central Pacific Campaign, not General Douglas MacArthur's high-casualty campaign in the direction of the Philippines, delivered airfields in the Marianas, much closer to Japan than the bases in Sichuan. From 16 June 1944 to 9 January 1945, the United States had been able to launch one bombing raid per month from Chengdu with an average of fifty-three planes. Beginning on 24 November 1944, it began bombing raids from the Marianas, running an average of four raids of sixty-eight planes each per month. From March through August 1945, the bombing raids intensified, with daily raids of over 100 planes.[28] As a result, the China theater became irrelevant to the outcome of the U.S. war against Japan. Likewise, Ichigō lost its rationale as the Japanese home islands became the main theater, under air attack not from China, but from the inaccessible Marianas. At the end of 1944, the Japanese called off the Ichigō Campaign in order to redeploy as many troops as possible to defend Japan. Ichigō had a greater impact on the long Chinese Civil War than on the global war by making the Nationalists look militarily incompetent, wiping out Nationalist formations vital to defeat the Communists, and leaving central China wide open to Communist infiltration.

When U.S. precision bombing of Japan proved imprecise and ineffective, the new U.S. commander of the air war over Japan, "bombs-away" General Curtis E. LeMay, who took over on 19 January 1944, realized that Japan's cities filled with wooden housing and narrow streets made excellent tinder. Despite the shameless false advertising from air-power buffs, precision bombing did not become technologically feasible for nearly three decades until late in the Vietnam War. In the meantime, civilian populations bore the brunt of bombing. The U.S. firebombing of Japan deliberately targeted civilians, who were the overwhelming majority of its victims. It proved brutally successful.

---

[27] Hsi-sheng Ch'i, *Nationalist China at War: Military Defeats and Political Collapse, 1937–45* (Ann Arbor: University of Michigan Press, 1982), 76.

[28] 辻秀雄 (Tsuji Hideo), "本地防空と本土決戦準備" (Preparations for the Aerial Defenses and the Decisive Battle for Japan), in Okumura and Kondō, *Modern Japanese Military History*, vol. 4, 630, 632, 636; Tohmatsu Haruo, "The Strategic Correlation between the Sino-Japanese and Pacific Wars," 437; Richard B. Frank, *Downfall*, 363.

During the night of 9–10 March 1945, firebombing destroyed sixteen square miles of central Tokyo, where the high temperatures made the canals boil. More people died that night – an estimated 84,000 – than were killed during the atomic bombing of Nagasaki. Over the following ten days, firebombing destroyed the four next-largest cities: Kobe, Nagoya, Osaka, and Yokohama. By the end of the war sixty-six Japanese cities lay in ruins, leaving 9.2 million homeless. Only Kyoto, Nara, and Kanazawa survived unscathed.[29]

By this time, American military planners understood that Japanese soldiers fought to the death, treated prisoners of war with appalling and also pointless cruelty, and meted out cut-throat treatment to occupied civilian populations. So they focused on minimizing Allied casualties and putting the maximum pressure on Japan in order to end the war as soon as possible. Firebombing met these criteria, but it gave no quarter to the young or old, the innocent or the guilty, the powerful or the powerless.

The Politics of War Termination

Emperor Hirohito made one decision of consequence during the war – the decision to throw in the towel. Above all he sought to preserve the imperial line. The imperial Japanese system of government in which emperors legitimized power exercised by others has been called variously "government by acquiescence"[30] or a "system of irresponsibility."[31] If everyone is responsible for policy then policy formation becomes anonymous so that no one is actually accountable. The primary value emphasized in decision-making was consensus reached through informal procedures.

General Tōjō Hideki, who became prime minister just in time to give his support to the strategy to attack Western interests across the Pacific, and who remained in office until U.S. bombs began raining down on the home islands in mid-1944, was powerful not because of himself personally but because he combined at least three offices: prime minister, war minister, and munitions minister, as well as short stints as foreign minister, home affairs minister, and education minister. He demonstrated no profound powers of perception.

As the war in China went badly and the military needed to spread the blame, the Imperial Conference was resurrected on 11 January of 1938 after a more than thirty-year hiatus. Select civil and military leaders of the Cabinet met

---

[29] Clodfelter, *Warfare and Armed Conflicts*, vol. 2, 951–52; Nakamura, *History of Shōwa Japan*, 219, 245; Frank, *Downfall*, 77; Kirby, *The War against Japan*, vol. 5, 102–5, 162, 484–86.

[30] Oka Yoshitake cited in Nish, *Japanese Foreign Policy 1869–1942*, 222.

[31] Term from Masao Maruyama. Tsuyoshi Hasegawa, *Racing the Enemy: Stalin, Truman, and the Surrender of Japan* (Cambridge, MA: Harvard University Press, 2005), 4; Sadako N. Ogata, *Defiance in Manchuria: The Making of Japanese Foreign Policy, 1931–1932* (Berkeley: University of California Press, 1964), 192; Bix, *Hirohito*, 329, 436.

together to present unanimous recommendations to the emperor. As the war went from bad to worse, Imperial Conferences met more frequently so that the emperor could personally approve major policy and strategy shifts. Some post-war historians have excoriated Emperor Hirohito for not stopping the military escalation. This argument rests on the assumption that the emperor had the power to force his generals to do what they did not wish to do. In major matters of state, Emperor Hirohito rubber-stamped the advice provided, just as he did after the war when he rubber-stamped General Douglas MacArthur's fiats concerning the terms of the occupation and, more importantly, the nature of the postwar Constitution, written by U.S. military lawyers in one week, that has remained the unamended fundamental law of Japan.

Only when the dynasty faced extinction did events force Emperor Hirohito to take a more active role in governance regardless of any fears of army reprisals. The loss of Okinawa on 22 June 1945 made the invasion of the home islands imminent. The bombing of the Imperial Palace must have made the threat concrete to Emperor Hirohito. The United States rained down seven million leaflets on Japan containing the peace terms, and dangled the prospects of survival for the dynasty with the tantalizing line, "Even the powerful military groups cannot stop the mighty march for peace of the Emperor and the people."[32] Emperor Hirohito apparently read one that landed in the palace grounds. It outlined both the Potsdam Declaration and Japan's official response to it. The day Okinawa fell, Hirohito informed the Supreme War Leadership Council that it was time to take the necessary diplomatic actions to end the war.

On 26 July, on the sixth anniversary of the U.S. abrogation of its commercial treaty with Japan, the United States, Britain, and China, but not Russia, had issued the Potsdam Declaration. It called for the unconditional surrender, demilitarization, democratization, and occupation of Japan; the prosecution of war criminals; and the payment of reparations. Former ambassador to Japan from 1931 to 1941 Joseph C. Grew unsuccessfully urged senior U.S. policy-makers to guarantee the survival of the Japanese monarchy as a useful tool for the anticipated U.S. postwar occupation. U.S. policymakers left the fate of the dynasty ambiguous until after the capitulation, when they ultimately followed Grew's advice. Because Russia had not signed the declaration, the Japanese hoped for a separate peace or Russian mediation of the end of the war. Since at least August 1944 and continuing into June of 1945, the Japanese secretly but ineffectively negotiated with Russia.

For a short but critical period between 7 April and 17 August 1945, the seventy-eight-year-old baron and vice admiral, Suzuki Kantarō, who had been seriously wounded in the Young Officers' Revolt back in 1936, served as prime minister. As a former grand chamberlain he had close ties to Emperor Hirohito.

---

[32] Cited in Bix, *Hirohito*, 494–95.

On 28 July, he held a press conference in which he said he intended to "ignore" the Potsdam Declaration. The United States interpreted this as rejection. So atomic bombs followed. On 6 August, 100,000 to 140,000 Japanese perished at Hiroshima, followed by another 100,000 over the following five years from radiation sickness. On 9 August, 35,000 to 40,000 died at Nagasaki.[33]

Starting in February 1945 Russia began transferring troops and equipment from European Russia to Siberia. On 5 April, Stalin declined to extend his neutrality pact with Japan, which legally remained in force for one year after the renunciation. Regardless, in the opening minutes of 9 August battlefield time, Russia attacked Manchuria just ten minutes after it informed Japan's ambassador, on 8 August at 5:00 p.m. Moscow time, of its declaration of war effective 9 August. One and a half million troops crossed the border. Russia's invasion, known as Operation August Storm, broke two treaties: its neutrality pact with Japan, by failing to wait the stipulated full year, and the Yalta Agreement requiring a prior treaty with China. At the Yalta Conference from 4 to 11 February 1945, Joseph Stalin, Franklin D. Roosevelt, and Winston Churchill had agreed on strategy for the final campaigns of the global war. This included Stalin's promise to declare war on Japan after the defeat of Germany.

Operation August Storm was the Russian Army's most ambitious campaign of World War II over extraordinarily difficult terrain. From 9 to 18 August, Russian troops drove from 310 to 590 miles (500 to 950 kilometers) into Manchuria and put to flight Japan's army.[34] When Japan formally capitulated on 15 August, all military operations should have ceased. At 7 p.m. that evening, President Harry S. Truman ordered a cease-fire for U.S. military operations. Japan dithered for two days before ordering its own cease-fire, giving Russia an excuse to press on, but by 17 August Russia still had yet to take the major cities. Meanwhile, on 16 August, Lieutenant General Hata Hikosaburō, the Kantō Army chief of staff, despite having received no official instructions from Tokyo, ordered an end to hostilities and concluded a cease-fire agreement with the Russians on 19 August. Nevertheless, Russian forces pressed on from 18 to 20 August, occupying Harbin, Qiqihar, Changchun, Shenyang, Chengde, Lüshun, and Dalian. Meanwhile the battle to take Sakhalin Island continued from 11 to 25 August. Wherever the Russians went, they raped, looted, and murdered civilians, angering even their allies, the Chinese Communists.

Until 22 August, Stalin remained intent upon occupying the northern half of Hokkaido, before bowing to strong U.S. opposition. The Yalta Agreement stipulated that the American zone of occupation included all the Kurils save the

---

[33] Bix, *Hirohito*, 500–2; Richard Fuller, *Shōkan Hirohito's Samurai: Leaders of the Japanese Armed Forces, 1926–1945* (London: Arms and Armour, 1992), 289–90; Nakamura, *History of Shōwa Japan*, 221.

[34] David M. Glantz, *The Soviet Strategic Offensive in Manchuria, 1945 "August Storm"* (London: Frank Cass, 2003), xviii, xxv–xxvi.

northernmost four, but once Stalin confirmed that the United States would not intervene over the southern Kurils, he ordered their occupation on 19 August, taking Etorofu on 28 August, and Kunashiri and Shikotan both on 1 September. The southern Kurils had never been tsarist or Soviet territory. (Japan had negotiated sovereignty over the northern Kurils in the 1875 St. Petersburg Treaty in exchange for southern Sakhalin Island.) On 2 September, Japan formally surrendered by signing the capitulation documents in a grand ceremony in Tokyo Bay aboard USS *Missouri*, a ship named after the home state of President Truman. USS *Missouri* flew the flag that Commodore Perry had flown when he had forced the unequal treaty system on Japan in 1854 and 1855. This was the official ending of the four-year War in the Pacific and also the fifteen-year Second Sino-Japanese War in China. Three days later, Russia completed its occupation of the Habomai Islands. The Russian occupation of territories after the surrender left an enduring territorial dispute and the absence of a peace treaty between Japan and Russia.

The Japanese Cabinet had remained split on the subject of capitulation even with the Russian declaration of war on 8 August and the two atomic bombs dropped three days apart on 6 and 9 August, and the bluff that the U.S. would rain down more atomic bombs (when it could not finish a third until 22 August and could produce only seven by the end of October). War Minister Anami Korechika, the loser of the Second and Third Battles of Changsha, believed the bluff, thinking the United States might possess over 100 atomic weapons, yet he remained adamant on rejecting the Potsdam Declaration. General George C. Marshall thought Japan would not capitulate before both U.S. and Russian troops had landed on the home islands.[35]

A decision to surrender required unanimity among the so-called Big Six: the prime minister, the foreign minister, the war minister, the navy minister, the naval chief of staff, and the army chief of staff. In other words, the military had four votes to the civilian side of government's two. And when the prime minister was a military officer – which was often – then the military had five votes to one. No one with economic expertise, such as the finance minister, participated. The requirement for unanimity gave each of the Big Six veto power. In the terrible four days when atomic bombs fell and the Russians invaded, the Big Six fixated on four peace conditions: an independent military, Japanese (not foreign) prosecution of any war criminals, no foreign occupation of Japan, and the retention of the imperial system. When the Big Six deadlocked, Prime Minister

---

[35] Barton J. Bernstein, "Conclusion," in Tsuyoshi Hasegawa, ed., *The End of the Pacific War: Reappraisals* (Stanford: Stanford University Press, 2007), 228; Japan, Foreign Ministry, Diplomatic Records Office, A.7.0.0-9-55, 大東亜戦争関係一件戦争終結ニ関スル日蘇交渉関係 (Concerning the War of the Pacific and Soviet–Japanese War Termination Diplomacy), vol. 2, Tōjō address to the Privy Council, 15 August 1945; Drea, *In the Service of the Emperor*, 213–15; Hasegawa, *Racing the Enemy*, 104, 208, 235.

Suzuki Kantarō requested Emperor Hirohito to cast the tiebreaking vote. On 10 August, Emperor Hirohito supported acceptance of the Potsdam Declaration and left the army out to dry by dropping the first three conditions protecting the military and concentrating on the fourth to save the emperor system and, by extension, his own skin. War Minister Anami Korechika, Army Chief of Staff Umezu Yoshijirō, and Navy Chief of Staff Toyoda Soemu remained opposed. Yet from the beginning Admiral Toyoda had considered war against the United States to be unwinnable. He had developed the plans for the two most disastrous battles in Japanese naval history, the Battle of the Philippine Sea (19–20 June 1944), known to Americans as the Great Marianas Turkey Shoot for the ease with which U.S. pilots shot down Japanese aircraft, and the Battle of Leyte Gulf (23–26 October 1944), which eliminated the Imperial Japanese Navy. On 12 August, the imperial clan gathered in an unprecedented meeting. On the night of 14 August, the emperor recorded a speech to be broadcast to the Japanese people the following day to announce Japan's surrender.

Emperor Hirohito's intervention would have been meaningless unless the military agreed to comply. With the Russian invasion of Manchuria, there were discussions at the Army General Staff Headquarters about making itself the government. A coup attempt brewed, with the brother-in-law of War Minister Anami, Lieutenant Colonel Takeshita Masahiko, a key instigator. On the night of 14–15 August, the coup leaders murdered General Mori Takeshi, the officer in charge of defending the Imperial Palace, and forged orders in his name, but could not find the emperor's taped speech. General Mori's successor, General Tanaka Shizuichi, put an end to the coup. If the rebels had kidnapped the emperor as planned, the war would have continued. While army officers intrigued and Emperor Hirohito and the Big Six dithered, the United States firebombed seven more Japanese cities.

Immediately before the Imperial Conference on 14 August, War Minister Anami had three marshals petition Emperor Hirohito to reject the Potsdam Declaration. Instead, the emperor rejected their petition. At the ensuing Imperial Conference a tearful emperor implored Anami to honor the Potsdam Declaration. Afterward, Anami no longer supported the coup attempt. That same day Emperor Hirohito dispatched members of the imperial family to communicate the surrender to Japan's armies in the field: Lieutenant Colonel Prince Takeda Tsuneyoshi went to Korea and Manchuria to inform the Chōsen and Kantō Armies; General Prince Asaka Yasuhiko went to China to inform the China Expeditionary Army Group; Major General Prince Kanin Haruhito went to China, Indochina, and Singapore to inform the Southern Expeditionary Army Group; and Emperor Hirohito's younger brother, Prince Takamatsu Nobuhito, who had served as a navy captain, ordered the Special Attack Corps not to resist the U.S. landing in Japan. Still the Southern Expeditionary Army Group, under the command of General Terauchi Hisaichi whose 1942 offensive throughout the Pacific had been so successful, stalled on surrender until 23 August after it learned all other commands had complied.

In the early hours of 15 August, War Minister Anami committed ritual suicide. Emperor Hirohito's speech accepting the Potsdam Declaration, the so-called Jade Voice Broadcast, was aired at noon, and two coup leaders, Major Hatanaka Kenji and Lieutenant Colonel Shiizaki Jirō, committed suicide. The Cabinet resigned and Emperor Hirohito made his paternal uncle, Major General and Prince Higashikuni Naruhiko, prime minister. The Jade Voice Broadcast obliquely referred to the atomic bombs, but made no mention of the Russian invasion. On 17 August, the emperor issued a rescript to the armed forces ordering them to lay down their arms. The rescript emphasized the Russian invasion but made no reference to the atomic bombs. In this way, he left ambiguous which factor, the atomic bombs or the Russian invasion, had decisively influenced his own thinking.

Russia's deployment of 1.5 million men in Manchuria delivered the Imperial Japanese Army a morale-breaking nightmare scenario of Communist forces sweeping toward Japan. Stalin proposed to the United States a divided Japan with his country in possession of the northern half of Hokkaido, Japan's northernmost main island.[36] Prime Minister Suzuki Kantarō concluded, "If we don't act now, the Russians will penetrate not only Manchuria and Korea but northern Japan as well … We must act now, while our chief adversary is still only the United States."[37] The Japanese had a choice: capitulate immediately to the Americans or capitulate later to the Russians with their well-known appetite for other people's territory. Americans lived far away and could be expected to leave, but Russians had no history of willingly returning their conquests. Soon Russian atrocities in Manchuria gave a taste of things to come should their troops reach the home islands. Thus Russia entry into the war in Asia created a powerful incentive to capitulate immediately.

Navy Minister Yonai Mitsumasa and former prime minister Prince Konoe Fumimaro favored acceptance of the Potsdam Declaration. Both considered the atomic bombs in combination with Russian entry into the war in Asia as a "gift from heaven," in Yonai's words, to force the army to comply with war termination. They and others feared a social revolution from below if the war continued and an army rebellion if Japan surrendered. Thus the atomic bombings and Russian entry affected each group differently. The imperial court feared for

[36] Hasegawa, *Racing the Enemy*, 271; David Holloway, "Jockeying for Position in the Postwar World: Soviet Entry into the War with Japan in August 1945," in Hasegawa, *The End of the Pacific War*, 180; Glantz, *The Soviet Strategic Offensive in Manchuria*, 141, 305.

[37] Yukiko Koshiro, *Imperial Eclipse: Japan's Strategic Thinking about Continental Asia before August 1945* (Ithaca: Cornell University Press, 2013), 243.

the survival of the royal house, while Russian entry particularly affected the army.[38] Without ships or fuel to fight, the navy could do nothing.

The Costs

Postwar, analysts debated the ethics of dropping atomic weapons on Japan. More people actually died in the firebombings. Not only the Japanese and Germans targeted civilians, but so did the Allies. They did so because alternative strategies would have caused far more deaths of their own armed forces and would have prolonged the war, causing further civilian deaths from starvation in the occupied areas and, in the case of Japan, would have yielded a divided Japan with Russia in possession of at least the northern half of Hokkaido. Such alternative strategies might have produced an enemy capitulation, but not unconditional surrender with the utter destruction of both the Japanese Empire and the regime that went with it. The Japanese government barely capitulated after two atomic bombings. During the war, Americans did not feel angst over the enemy civilian death toll from the air war or even from the atomic bombs. They had lost too many of their own children and wanted a victory that minimized their own children's deaths. Only from the security of a postwar world, no longer under threat of imperial Japanese or Nazi German aggression, have subsequent generations criticized the air war.

By war's end, the Japanese had earned a legendary reputation for atrocities. It turns out that they were not particularly good even at taking care of their own. Japanese veterans and witnesses described the common practice of executing their own men who could not keep up and encouraging, if not requiring, Japanese civilians to kill their families and themselves rather than surrender.

The Imperial Japanese Army leadership did not look kindly on those who failed in combat – either enemy prisoners of war or their own soldiers. According to the 1908 Army Criminal Code,

A commander who allows his unit to surrender a strategic area to the enemy shall be punishable by death ... If a commander is leading troops in combat and they are captured by the enemy, even if the commander has performed his duty to the utmost, he shall be punishable by up to six months confinement.[39]

It was illegal for Japanese forces to withdraw or surrender. This meant that officers who were careful of their men's lives were considered cowardly. So

---

[38] Richard B. Frank, "Ketsu Gō: Japanese Political and Military Strategy in 1945," in Hasegawa, *The End of the Pacific War*, 111–12; John Toland, *The Rising Sun: The Decline and Fall of the Japanese Empire, 1936–1945* (New York: Modern Library, 1970), 807, 826; Leon V. Sigal, *Fighting to a Finish: The Politics of War Termination in the United States and Japan, 1945* (Ithaca: Cornell University Press, 1988), 278–79.

[39] Cited in Ienaga Saburō, *The Pacific War 1931–1945*, trans. Frank Baldwin (New York: Pantheon Books, 1978), 49.

the profligate were promoted instead. The 1941 Field Service Code ordered Japanese soldiers, "Do not be taken prisoner alive."[40] So often they did not take others alive either and their enemies responded in kind. Such rules and the attitudes embedded in them made for a brutal war and a historical legacy that still haunts the Japanese, despite all their numerous achievements in other areas. As the Second Sino-Japanese War protracted and then metastasized into a world war, the Imperial Japanese Army became increasingly brutal with the blockade, massacres, germ warfare, the 1940 Three Alls strategy (kill all, burn all, and pillage all), depopulated zones, death marches, internment camps, and biological experiments on prisoners. When the tables turned, others felt little compunction about raining down firebombs and atomic weapons on them.

Japan's brutality proved singularly counterproductive. If the goal was empire and autarky, making the colonies ungovernable by leaving the colonial population no alternative but resistance indicated a stunning lack of perception. Everywhere the Japanese went, they alienated those whom they encountered. They conducted serial disingenuous diplomacy with the United States, Germany, China, and Russia, alienating each in turn. Despite great expertise in the technical aspects of economic development demonstrated in Manchukuo, Japan's gratuitous brutality transformed potential sympathizers into bitter enemies, particularly in China, where their cruelty transformed a fractured people into a deadly foe, and also in Korea. For a short time Asians living in the Pacific theater looked upon Japan as their liberator from the colonial powers, but Japanese actions rapidly made clear their own colonial ambitions. Their oppressive rule soon outdid all powers save Russia, Germany, and China, the record-setters for mass murders in the twentieth century.

Japan's quest for national security via war destroyed 66 percent of its national wealth,[41] 25 percent of its fixed assets, 25 percent of its building stock, 34 percent of its industrial machinery, 82 percent of its merchant marine, 21 percent of its household property, 11 percent of its energy infrastructure, and 24 percent of its production.[42] Between 3 and 3.5 percent of Japan's population died in the Pacific War, which, including all sides, took 20 million lives.[43] From 1937 to 1945, 410,000 Japanese soldiers died in China – 230,000 after December 1941. Nine hundred thousand were wounded. They killed at least 10 million Chinese soldiers and civilians – a conservative estimate. Some triple this number. Whatever the toll, China suffered far more casualties than any other part of the Pacific theater of World War II where Japan's military

[40] Ienaga, The Pacific War, 1931–1945, 49.
[41] Nakamura, History of Shōwa Japan, 255.
[42] Shinpo, "The Wartime Economic Legacy and Economic Reconstruction," 933.
[43] Eguchi, A Short History of the Fifteen-Year War, 172, 226; Nakamura, History of Shōwa Japan, 253–54.

operations threatened or occupied lands with nearly twice the population of those so abused by Germany.[44]

The costs for Japan did not end with the war. Russia took 639,635 Japanese prisoners, including 148 generals, and kept most of them for four years of forced labor in violation of Article 9 of the Potsdam Declaration. The last prisoners did not return home until the 1990s and 62,068 died in captivity.[45] Although Japan released thousands of Western prisoners held in its internment camps, which were known for their brutality and high mortality rates, it held virtually no Chinese prisoners of war. Apparently, those captured alive and not summarily executed became forced laborers often sent to Manchukuo. Despite fifteen years of war in China, the Japanese allegedly held only fifty-six Chinese prisoners of war at the end of World War II – a death rate outdoing even the extermination camps of the Germans, a hard record to beat. Apparently, the Chinese did not take prisoners of war either.[46]

Not only were the costs high, but Japan's strategy was incapable of delivering the desired strategic outcome. As a trade-dependent island state without a rich internal endowment of oil or iron, Japan lacked the capacity to win a global war against the major naval powers. The strategy for security through resource control made Japan more, not less, dependent on imported raw materials. Although its blockade of China succeeded at the operational level, its complementary strategy to secure resources in the global war consumed more resources in gluttonous military operations than it provided and brought defeat in both the global and regional wars. Japan's oil consumption in the southern theater exploded in tandem with military operations from 15.4 million barrels in 1942 to 35.1 million barrels in 1943. As Japan ramped up merchantman and tanker construction, the United States ramped up submarine warfare. Japanese merchant marine losses followed the pattern of naval ship losses. Sinkings increased in the second half of 1942 and then snowballed once the United States fixed its defective torpedoes in October 1943. Japanese oil imports peaked in 1943 and then plunged in 1944 when inability to

---

[44] Edward J. Drea and Hans van de Ven, "An Overview of Major Military Campaigns during the Sino-Japanese War, 1937–1945," in Peattie, Drea, and Van de Ven, *The Battle for China*, 46; R.J. Rummel, *China's Bloody Century: Genocide and Mass Murder since 1900* (New Brunswick, NJ: Transaction Publishers, 1991), 24–25; Werner Gruhl, *Imperial Japan's World War Two 1931–1945* (New Brunswick, NJ: Transaction Publishers, 2007), 19–20, 59.

[45] Eguchi, *A Short History of the Fifteen-Year War*, 250–51; 幕内光雄 (Maku'uchi Mitsuo), 満州国警察外史 (*An Unofficial History of the Manchukuo Police*) (Tokyo: 三一書房, 1996), 287; Max Beloff, *Soviet Policy in the Far East 1944–1951* (London: Oxford University Press, 1953), 38; 徐焰 (Xu Yan), 一九四五年　満州進軍　：日ソ戦と毛沢東の戦略 (*The Manchurian Invasion of 1945: The Japanese–Soviet War and Mao Zedong's Strategy*), trans. 朱建榮 (Zhu Jinrong) (Tokyo: 三五館, 1993), 191, 193; Lary, *The Chinese People at War*, 189–90; S.I. Kuznetsov, "The Situation of Japanese Prisoners of War in Soviet Camps (1945–1956)" *Journal of Slavic Military Studies* 8, no. 3 (Sept. 1995), 620.

[46] Bix, *Hirohito*, 360; Dreyer, *China at War*, 215; Ju Zhifen, "Labor Conscription in North China: 1941–1945" in MacKinnon, Lary, and Vogel, *China at War*, 218, 222.

access supplies reduced consumption to 32.0 million barrels. Most of the oil came from the Dutch East Indies, which provided Japan with 8.1 million barrels in 1942, 9.8 million barrels 1943, but only 1.6 million barrels in 1944 due to losses from U.S. submarine attacks.[47] In the largest naval battle of World War II at Leyte Gulf in the Philippines from 23 to 26 October 1944, the United States sank forty Japanese ships and damaged forty-six, and destroyed 405 planes, crippling the Imperial Japanese Navy.[48] After May 1944, the shipping routes for oil from the Dutch East Indies were cut. In 1945 all Japan's sea lines of communication were under assault so that even transportation to Korea became dangerous.[49]

Although war materiel production continued to rise until 1944, output of food and daily basic necessities peaked in 1937.[50] The loss of transport for oil and metals undermined steel and aluminum output after 1943. Plane production got first priority on resources and increased until 1944, but then imploded in 1945. The United States still outproduced Japan by a margin of over three-to-one for airplanes.[51]

The Japanese leadership also set the stage for a very unpromising postwar regional balance of power. Japan had occupied thirteen provinces plus parts of eight others and taken 90 percent of Chinese industry, resulting in huge war-time economic and agricultural losses.[52] This included the destruction of 55 percent of Nationalist China's industry and mining, 72 percent of its shipping, and 96 percent of its railways.[53] In January 1940, the Chinese Communists estimated that of China's one million-plus military casualties from 1937 to August 1938, only 31,000 were Communists. By December 1944, the total number of Communists killed in action remained shy of 110,000.[54] In contrast,

---

[47] The rough conversion of tons to barrels of oil is six to eight barrels per ton depending on the fuel grade. Shinpo, "The Wartime Economic Legacy and Economic Reconstruction," 947; Arakawa Ken-ichi, "The Shipping of Southeast Asian Resources Back to Japan: National Logistics and War Strategy," Tokyo: National Institute for Defense Studies, Military History Department, unpublished paper, c.2002; Abe, "A Statistical Analysis of the Great East Asian War," 830, 832.

[48] Peter Teed, *Dictionary of 20th-Century History 1914–1990* (Oxford: Oxford University Press, 1992), 269; William H. Harris and Judith S. Levey, *The New Columbia Encyclopedia*, 4th edn. (New York: Columbia University Press, 1975), 269; Duncan Townson, *The New Penguin Dictionary of Modern History 1789–1945* (London: Penguin Books, 1994), 467–68.

[49] Nakamura, *History of Shōwa Japan*, 236–39.

[50] Nakamura, "The Age of Turbulence," 70–71.

[51] Abe, "A Statistical Analysis of the Great East Asian War," 830, 835.

[52] 朱玉湘 (Zhu Yuxiang), "抗日战争与中国经济" (The Anti-Japanese War and the Chinese Economy), 文史哲 (*Journal of Literature, History, and Philosophy*) 230, no. 5 (1995), 3–9; 居之芬 (Ju Zhifen), "抗战时期日本对华北沦陷区劳工的劫掠和催残" (Japanese Humiliation and of Workers in Occupied Areas of North China during the Anti-Japanese War), 中共党史研究 (*Research on the History of the Chinese Communist Party*) 4 (1994), 325–28.

[53] William C. Kirby, "The Chinese War Economy," in James C. Hsiung and Steven I. Levine, eds., *China's Bitter Victory: The War with Japan 1937–1945* (Armonk, NY: M.E. Sharpe, 1992), 185.

[54] Jay Taylor, *The Generalissimo: Chiang Kai-shek and the Struggle for Modern China* (Cambridge, MA: Harvard University Press, 2009), 169, 298.

unrelenting conventional warfare diminished Chiang's armies so that after 1941 additional recruitments required extreme coercion and undermined the already beleaguered civilian economy.

Thus Japan's intervention in China tipped the balance in the long Chinese Civil War in favor of the Communists. In 1934, Chiang Kai-shek had the Communists on the run in the Long March to one of the most inhospitable parts of China. Japan's long war against the Nationalists gutted Chiang Kai-shek's conventional forces while giving the Communists a respite from Nationalist persecution to organize the ungoverned countryside in preparation for the final phase of the Civil War. Japan would have been much better off with Chiang Kai-shek than with Mao Zedong at the helm in China. The grandchildren and great-grandchildren of Japan's wartime leaders continue to pay the price for an ill-conceived military strategy that yielded a viscerally anti-Japanese China still bent on settling old scores. In the end, the Japanese did achieve a major war aim: they booted the European colonial powers from Asia, but at extraordinary cost to the civilians caught in the war zone. Although the Netherlands, Britain, and France would attempt to retrieve their colonies, they all failed. Japan did indeed create a new regional order in Asia, although not the one its leaders had in mind.

Japan's leaders, unlike their predecessors, failed to balance ends and means, and, when their chosen strategies threatened disaster, they refused to downgrade their policy objective to the attainable. These failures prevented timely war termination and caused the pointless deaths of millions of Japanese. Japan suffered 28,000 military deaths in 1941, 66,000 in 1942, 100,000 in 1943, 146,000 in 1944, and a stunning 1,127,000 in 1945.[55] If it had surrendered in 1944 it would have avoided the vast majority of these fatalities. But the grand-strategy capabilities necessary for conducting timely war termination had been lost when the army demanded and the navy allowed the reduction of strategy to a single instrument of national power: theirs.

Had Japan failed to capitulate when it did, U.S. planners envisioned a full-scale invasion of the home islands, where they had grossly underestimated the number of Japanese troops awaiting their arrival. By 15 August 1945, unbeknownst to the United States, Japan had redeployed over one million men out of the China theater to the home islands.[56] On 18 June, when Truman approved Operation Olympic for the invasion of the home islands, General Marshall estimated that Kyūshū had no more than 350,000 men to face an onslaught of 766,700 Americans. In fact, by mid-August, the Japanese had 625,000 soldiers

---

[55] Eguchi, *A Short History of the Fifteen-Year War*, 172, 226; Nakamura, *History of Shōwa Japan*, 253–54.

[56] 藤原彰 (Fujiwara Akira), 太平洋战争爆发后的日中战争" ("The Sino-Japanese War after the Outbreak of the Pacific War"), trans. 解莉莉 (Xie Lili), 中共党史研究 (*Research on the History of the Chinese Communist Party*) 1 (1989), 85.

on Kyūshū, or nearly double Marshall's estimate, as part of their Decisive Operation (Ketsu-Gō).[57]

Given what Americans had endured to take Okinawa, a mere 454-square-mile island compared to Japan's 142,811 square miles, the invasion of the home islands would have yielded an American and Japanese bloodbath, and perhaps a permanent blockade of Japan instead of the unconditional surrender. Okinawa, one of the greatest battles of the Pacific Campaign, in which 182,821 Americans fought 100,000 Japanese, was a mere fraction of the Shanghai or Ichigō Campaigns that China had endured, let alone what the United States would have faced invading the home islands.[58] On Okinawa, 12,520 U.S. soldiers died along with 65,908 Japanese soldiers and 122,228 Okinawan soldiers and civilians.[59]

Victory did not come easily to the United States. It did defeat the Imperial Japanese Navy without Chinese assistance, but it never fought more than a fraction of the Imperial Japanese Army. At the end of the war, Japan still had nearly one-third of its total armed forces deployed in Manchuria and China, or 1.8 million men, while another 2 million men defended Japan, Korea, and Taiwan, the nucleus of the prewar Japanese Empire. This left about one million men facing the United States in the Pacific theater. Thus China played a crucial role in keeping nearly 1.8 million Japanese soldiers fully occupied and far away from U.S. forces. The theaters where U.S. fighting concentrated had comparatively small numbers of Japanese troops, 100,000 in the Philippines and 186,100 in the central Pacific. Japan remained fundamentally a land power with its armies concentrated at home or on the Asian mainland.[60]

For most of the Pacific Ocean war, China pinned down more Japanese land forces than did any other theater. From 1941 to 1942, Japan deployed about 60 percent of its army to China. This fell to 44 percent in 1943, and to 31 percent for the final two years when Japan redeployed its forces initially to the South Pacific and then to the home islands. Deployments in the South Pacific rose from 21 percent of the army in 1942, to 32 percent in 1943, and to 40 percent in 1944. When the home islands came under attack, Japanese forces in the Pacific could no longer alter the course of the war because so much of the navy and merchant marine lay at the bottom that Japan could not easily resupply or

[57] Hasegawa, *Racing the Enemy*, 263; Frank, "Ketsu Gō," 65–67, 71; Frank, *Downfall*, 85.

[58] Clodfelter, *Warfare and Armed Conflicts*, vol. 2, 929.

[59] 吉田裕 (Yoshida Yutaka) and 纐纈厚 (Kōketsu Atsushi), "日本軍の作戦・戦闘・補給" (Military Operations, Combat, and the Supply of the Japanese Military), in 藤原彰 (Fujiwara Akira) and 今井清一 (Imai Seiichi), eds., 十五年戦争史 (*A History of the Fifteen-Year War*), vol. 3 (Tokyo: 青木書店, 1989), 222.

[60] 防衛庁防衛研修所戦史部 (Japan, Defense Agency, National Defense College, Military History Department), edn. 関東軍 (*The Kantō Army*), vol. 2 (Tokyo: 朝雲新聞社, 1974), 296.

redeploy the army. Likewise most of Japan's army expenditures focused on China and Manchuria – 77 percent in 1941, falling to 68 percent in 1945.[61]

China as an enormous continental power became a sinkhole for Japanese manpower, much in the same way that Russia's vast and inhospitable theater became a sinkhole for German manpower. Without either continental power's participation in the war and the gross overextension this caused for Germany and Japan, it is hard to imagine unconditional surrender by either. The maritime powers, Britain and the United States, ate away at the periphery, but the continental powers fought on the main front at great cost from the beginning to the end.

As in their previous wars, Japanese leaders saw the world in terms of fleeting windows of opportunity and undertook high-reward but high-risk operational strategies to utilize the perishable opportunities. In the past, the roll of the dice had favored the Japanese. This time, their luck ran out. Without co-operative adversaries or grand strategy, their operational strategy brought strategic disaster. Unlike the previous wars, their adversaries were resilient and no longer shattered with operational disaster. By focusing on the battlefield, Japan's leaders failed to give adequate attention to the social, diplomatic, and economic repercussions. Atrocities fed animosities and conjured countervailing alliances. Inadequate attention to diplomacy, rather than isolating the adversary, isolated Japan by creating enemies everywhere. Unrelenting warfare undermined first the Chinese and then the Japanese economy. Japan went to war to secure resources, first in Manchuria, then in China south of the Great Wall, and finally throughout the Pacific theater. It sought resources to insure prosperity at home. Yet each phase of the escalation made Japan more, not less, resource-dependent; burdened rather than strengthened the home economy; and expanded rather than decreased Japan's list of foreign enemies. Japanese leaders proved singularly incapable of cutting their losses so in the end they bet all and lost all. A maritime power, because of its moat and attention to grand strategy, normally can avoid unconditional surrender. Imperial Japan died a continental death because of a self-inflicted misidentification of Japan as a continental power.

[61] Yoshida and Kōketsu, "Military Operations, Combat, and the Supply of the Japanese Military," 106.

7   Japan betwixt Maritime and Continental World Orders

[Japan] prospers when she allies with such naval powers as the Anglo-Saxon Britain and the United States, but must trudge a road of hardship when she allies with continental powers.[1]

Hirama Yōichi, historian, *Anglo-Japanese Alliance: Alliance Choice and the Fate of a Nation*, 2000

Imperial Japan fought two pairs of wars. In the first pair, Japan co-operated with maritime powers to work in concert with their preferred maritime global order based on the maritime commons, international law, and international commerce – all common, not exclusive, places, rules, and activities. In the second set of wars, Japan allied with the continental powers, bent on imposing a continental order based on exclusive spheres of influence, each operating under different rules. Imperial Japan flourished under the former and perished under the latter.

The maritime world order is positive-sum. For all its many flaws, it is the only world order that benefits all who join because its laws and institutions are designed to promote economic growth in order to create wealth. The common rules protect the weak from the strong and thus incentivize the weak to join. The aggregate power of the many then dwarfs the strength of even the greatest continental power. Continental world orders – the world of traditional empires that flourished prior to the Industrial Revolution – are zero-sum at best and more typically negative-sum, given all the fighting over the spheres of influence. The motivating goals are the confiscation of territory and wealth, but the wars entail damage to both, producing a negative sum. The continental paradigm characterized the preindustrial world when land was indeed the source of wealth because agriculture was the primary economic sector. After the Industrial Revolution, trade, industry, and service became the primary economic sectors, so land was no longer the ultimate source of power, money was.

---

[1] Cited in Frederick R. Dickinson, "Japan Debates the Anglo-Japanese Alliance: The Second Revision of 1911," in O'Brien, *The Anglo-Japanese Alliance, 1902–1922*, 100. Original source was 平間洋一 (Hirama Yōichi), 日英同盟 ： 同盟の選択と国家の盛衰 (*The Anglo-Japanese Alliance: Alliance Choice and the Fate of the Nation,* (Tokyo: PHP, 2000), 4.

Money bought armies. And money came mainly from industry, commerce, and service.

Japan was not geographically situated to become a great land power. Seas separated it from military theaters so under all circumstances, except an invasion of the home islands, it operated on extended lines. It lacked the natural resource endowment necessary to conduct war: iron and energy. There are two rules for continental empire and Japan broke both. Taking on more than one adversary at once violates the first cardinal rule: no two-front wars. Great-power neighbors violated the second rule: no great-power neighbors. Japan potentially had two – China and Russia. Both two-front wars and powerful neighbors are dangerous. Today's friend may become tomorrow's foe. Successful continental powers whittle away at large neighbors and sequentially ingest and gradually digest their fragmenting parts as well as any small neighbors. The two immediate neighbors Japan proposed to fight dwarfed it in size and resources, and so exceeded its digestive capacity.

By the time it had finished, Japan had also violated all the rules of the maritime global order: it had walked out of the League of Nations – the primary rule-making body – ignored its treaty obligations, and attacked its trading partners, one of which was the dominant naval power. Once Japan lost its navy – a likely consequence of attacking the dominant naval power – it could not survive in either a continental or a maritime world. Without a navy it could not protect the home islands from blockade or attack and it soon lost its merchant marine, so it could not deliver troops and supplies to the theater or bring resources home. Yet it depended on trade.

Too many of Japan's leaders, even in the Meiji generation, failed to appreciate their great gift of geography. By geography they were a sea power. They did not have to play the land-power game of sequential conquest. No neighboring country could reach them by land to force a negative-sum war upon them. Maritime powers need not fight on the main front because the sea protects them from invasion. They do best to leverage their economic productivity to provide economic and military aid to enable continental allies to do the fighting that threatens the maritime power only indirectly. Had Japanese leaders followed a maritime strategy, they would have supported the Nationalist struggle to eliminate the Communists in China and then supported a unified Nationalist China to form a bulwark against further Soviet expansion into Asia. Fighting toe-to-toe on the main front at great cost is the land power's unenviable game forced on it by geography. Japanese leaders embroiled themselves in great land wars on the Asian mainland that geography allowed them to avoid.

This failure to understand both Japan's critical strength – its moat – and its critical vulnerability – its dependence on overseas trade – led to military strategies antithetical to Japanese interests. The chosen strategies, rather than promoting either national security or economic prosperity, devastated both. Japan's arrested institutional development then amplified this failure in vision.

Arrested Institutional Development

Ironically, success in the first pair of wars predisposed disaster in the second. Japanese of all walks of life attributed their victories in the First Sino-Japanese War and the Russo-Japanese War to the achievements of their military. They believed that their diplomats had squandered these achievements to bring home inadequate winnings. They did not see the benefits from a generous peace: the enemy quits, the war ends, and victory comes at an affordable cost. As a result of these misperceptions, over the course of the first two conflicts and then more rapidly during the interwar period, the balance of power between civil and military institutions reverted to the traditional shogunate system of military rule. This meant that Japan's leadership would increasingly measure victory in the operational terms of battlefield winnings, not in the strategic terms of the achievement of the policy objective, which remained retaining great-power status for Japan. Military overextension and diplomatic isolation, however, jeopardized the policy objective.

The oligarchs had predisposed this reversion to army rule by their failure to stipulate civil and military authority in written law and by the comparatively long survival until 1922 of the pre-eminent military leader, Yamagata Aritomo, versus the premature death of the pre-eminent civil leader, Itō Hirobumi, assassinated in 1908. Yamagata had an additional decade and a half to assure army dominance of the government. His success ended grand strategy because strategy reduced to one element, the military, and really just one service, the army, is not grand but crippled.

Japan would increasingly rely on just one element of national power: the coercive powers of its military. Over the course of the 1920s and 1930s, it lost its ability to implement grand strategy, to cultivate useful allies, or even to conduct joint military operations. The Meiji generation had excelled in all these areas; however, they had carefully avoided institutionalizing their authority through written law because they preferred to operate with maximum flexibility and power while they lived. But they could not transfer their prestige, their wisdom, or their cross-institutional contacts with each other. These strengths died with them. As a result, the Japanese government became stovepiped into competing fiefdoms, which the army closed off in succession. In doing so, it sequentially blinded Japan to the utility and limitations of one instrument of national power after another, until only military power remained and grand strategy was no more.

Modern governments operate through cabinets precisely because effective strategy, whether for domestic or foreign policy, requires multiple instruments of national power. The diverse portfolios of cabinet ministers constitute the elements not only of national power but also of grand strategy. Japan's Cabinet became the political equivalent of student government, a form divested of content. Finance was no longer taken into serious consideration. Career diplomats were sidelined. Although Japan lined up allies, it picked the wrong ones. Or if it insisted on Fascist friends, then it picked the wrong strategy to go with them – the pointless invasion ever deeper into China instead of a combined German–Japanese attack on Russia to eliminate Communism. Worse still was the decision to solve overextension in China by attacking the United States, a much more powerful adversary, delivering great-power allies to Chiang Kai-shek. Prior to 1931, Chiang Kai-shek might well have bandwagoned with the Fascists. Ideologically, he would have fit right in. Germany, China, and Japan all could have shared the spoils from vivisecting the Soviet empire. But Japan's leaders did not think in terms of win–win strategies, but insisted on beggaring their neighbors continental-style.

Although the leaders of the Meiji generation were brilliant, the institutions they built were incomplete. They were the virtuoso performers of their age, who failed to leave a completed score to guide others after their deaths. An encompassing set of enduring institutions is the great innovation of the West and hallmark of Western civilization. Institutions create durability beyond the horizons of human mortality. The political and economic brilliance of the West comes from its institutions, which its citizens take for granted and often assume that others either have or can spontaneously create. Neither Japan's leaders nor its institutions were up to the increasingly difficult international circumstances they faced.

Changed Circumstances

Simultaneous with Japan's reversion to a continental power and the passing of its great leaders, the international environment changed from benevolent to threatening and the wars no longer turned out well for Japan. The continuities between the two periods of warfare are surprisingly limited given that the conflicts began in the same theater, Northeast Asia. Chinese instability was the fundamental underlying cause. From the mid-nineteenth-century internal rebellions to the fall of the Qing dynasty in 1911, China was a failing state. Thereafter, until the Communist victory in the long Civil War in 1949, it was a failed state, whose implosion had enormous security implications for its neighbors. Russia and Japan became interested in filling the emerging power vacuum. This instability threatened Japan's substantial overseas investments and produced escalating Japanese intervention, particularly after the Russian Revolution with the admixture of Communism to the original problem of Russian imperial expansion. The great continuity was China the failed state.

In other areas continuities intertwined with discontinuities. In all four wars, Japanese leaders dismissed risks to focus on rewards. This was the second great continuity. But the discontinuities were numerous: in the first two wars, the Japanese government's objectives were limited (it did not seek regime change), it made comprehensive preparations marshalling all elements of national power, the peace terms were not punitive, and the adversaries were co-operative – so the Japanese dodged the risks without fully grasping their magnitude or the nearness of disaster. Competent military strategy by Romanov Russia or Qing China could easily have resulted in Japan's defeat. Given its wealth and manpower constraints, and its extended lines of operation, Japan should have lost both wars, but co-operative adversaries made its high-risk, high-reward approach successful.

Jubilation upon victory then blinded the Japanese to the reality that their country had not so much won the First Sino-Japanese War and the Russo-Japanese War as their adversaries had lost them. If either adversary studied the lessons of these conflicts – as defeated countries commonly do – then Japan could expect much more competent enemy strategists in the future. In the third conflict, China was no longer a co-operative adversary and Japanese leaders sought the infeasible objective of ruling its vastness in the age of rising nationalism. In the fourth war, the United States was a lethal adversary.

In all four wars, Japanese leaders perceived a window of opportunity that must be used before it slammed shut. A window of opportunity, as enticing as the term sounds, means that circumstances actually are not favorable because time is on the side of the enemy. In the second pair of wars, Japanese leaders failed to keep firmly in mind that by definition a window of opportunity is brief. Therefore the war must not only begin within the window but, equally importantly, also end within the window. An unlimited objective puts the enemy on death ground by forcing a choice to fight or perish. So unless the enemy is completely overmatched, the policy objective must be limited, lest the enemy on death ground continue to fight beyond the required time frame.

In all four wars, when the Japanese got into trouble on the battlefield, they upped the military ante – notably in General Nogi's repeated costly storms of Lüshun in the Russo-Japanese War and in his successors' constant escalation of the second pair of wars. In the first pair, the Japanese applied the increasing military dosages mainly to combatants; in the second pair they gave no quarter to noncombatants either. In doing so, their cruelty to civilians became a powerful recruitment tool for their enemies. The tenacity of both sides then produced war on such a scale that generations later it continues to set Chinese and Japanese at odds.

Although modernization continued in Japan during both sets of wars, westernization did not. Instead, with the passing of the Meiji generation, there was a reversion to the traditional dominance of military institutions over civil institutions. In all four conflicts, the Japanese government used foreign policy to secure fickle public loyalties, but the international environment became increasingly treacherous. The political objective to maintain Japan as a great power was a constant. But the impediments grew. The original problem of the containment of Russia amplified to the containment of Communism. The requirement for commerce in China expanded to the exclusion of others. The stabilization of China through commercial development amplified to stabilization through conquest and occupation.

The discontinuities between the two periods are more numerous and more significant than the continuities. Many lay outside Japanese control. Others were self-inflicted. In the first period, Japan faced a collapsing regional order, in which its relative strength grew dramatically, better positioning it to achieve its aims. Korea and China were imploding in the face of unprecedented internal rebellions. Russia lacked the transportation infrastructure to interfere effectively and tsarism was increasingly under siege at home. In the second period, Japan faced a collapsing international order brought on by incompetent military strategy in World War I that overturned the continental order in Europe followed by incompetent economic strategy in the Great Depression that greatly magnified its effects. The ensuing international economic collapse undermined Japanese prosperity and put Communism and Fascism on the march not only in Europe but also in Asia. The Chinese soon discovered the destructive power of a counterstrategy of boycott in combination with a controlled military retreat, which together deprived Japan of income while producing continent-wide overextension. Japan, however, did not have the luxury of not acting. Passivity guaranteed poverty. Japan tried to swim lest it drown.

The timing of these events was particularly bad. In the period between the two sets of wars, nationalism had become a global phenomenon. During the wars of the French Revolution, France had first cultivated nationalism, which had imbued its armies with the will power to overrun continental Europe. Nationalism broke through the divisions of native place to transform divided peoples into armies in pursuit of a common cause. Nationalism came late to Asia. The First Sino-Japanese War brought its first bloom in Japan. The Second Sino-Japanese War then made it powerful in China. The development of nationalism in Japan and China impeded the de-escalation of conflicts. Each country vilified the other, which predisposed incidents, which predisposed escalation and further jingoism, which predisposed more incidents in an escalatory spiral. The development of nationalism ultimately meant that the day of empires was done. Empires were no longer profitable because nationalism fueled local resistance so that the garrisoning costs exceeded the value of any extracted resources. Those that retained their empires bought poverty, not prosperity. It is no coincidence that decolonization occurred within a generation of World War II.

Nationalism in Japan and China had a strong undercurrent of racism disguised to outsiders by the limited and ambiguous vocabulary available in Asian and Western languages. The terms "China" and "Japan" and "Chinese" and "Japanese" conflate race and citizenship. The vocabulary to describe Western nations is much richer and clearly distinguishes between race and citizenship: Caucasian, Slav, and the like denote race; French, German, and the like denote citizenship; the West and Western denote civilization; and Europe denotes the core area of Western civilization. In contrast, the word "China" encompasses the race, the country, the region, and the civilization. The limited Asian vocabulary does not allow the topic of race to be removed from the discussion of nation. And racism is a powerful accelerant in international conflicts.

As a result of the Russian Revolution and the development of nationalism in China, Japan's enemies became lethal. Japan no longer faced declining royal houses, the Qing dynasty in the case of the First Sino-Japanese War or the Romanov dynasty in the case of the Russo-Japanese War. Instead it faced a Chinese people increasingly unified by a viscerally anti-Japanese nationalism and Russians spreading a messianic export version of Communism. A quick decisive victory is highly unlikely without a co-operative adversary. It is also highly unlikely without generous peace terms. In the first two wars, Japan had offered terms generous relative to its military achievements. In the second two, it offered punitive terms that no Chinese government could accept and hope to survive the ensuing domestic backlash. These changed circumstances and Japanese leaders' reaction to them greatly magnified the effects of their misidentification of their country as a continental power and their incomplete institution–building. The misidentification, the arrested institutions, and the inclement circumstances all became impediments to war termination.

War Termination

Peace terms were a matter of choice. In the first pair of wars, Japanese civil and military leaders had outlined clear military objectives as well as a set of fallback positions should events take a turn for the worse. They had an exit strategy. In the case of the Russo-Japanese War, this entailed U.S. mediation of war termination. In the second set of wars, Japanese leaders had no clear idea when to stop and so kept on going. In the first set, they had carefully considered the interests of others to avoid trampling upon them. In the second set, they put on their cleats and stomped on enemies and neutrals alike. As a result, whereas they avoided third-party intervention during the hostilities (if not during the peace negotiations) in the first set, they brought on intervention from multiple directions in the second set. And one of those intervening parties was the dominant naval power with the capacity to launch a sustained attack on the Japanese home islands. When the United States joined the war, the quagmire in China escalated into the annihilation of imperial Japan.

War termination on desired and desirable terms has three intertwined components: the level of operational success, the nature of the political demands, and the mechanisms to enforce the peace.[2] In the first pair of wars, Japan went far enough militarily to put enormous political pressure on the Qing and Romanov dynasties to end hostilities. The simultaneous threat of internal rebellion in both countries heightened this pressure. Japan then offered peace terms that were generous relative to the territories its armies occupied so its enemies settled on Japanese terms. Japan acquired Taiwan and the Pescadores, then backwaters of the Qing empire, in the first war, and the southern halves of Manchuria and Sakhalin, then backwaters of the Russian empire, in the second war. In neither case did Japan seek regime change, which promises a fight to the finish by the regime put on death ground. After the Russo-Japanese War, it signed a series of spheres-of-influence agreements with Russia to maintain the peace, which worked well enough until World War I swept away the Romanov dynasty and the Russian Revolution brought Communists to power.

In the second pair of wars, Japanese leaders never decided in advance how far to go militarily. As long as the Chinese would not settle, the Japanese went further. Their universal answer to the question of what to demand politically was "more." Even before World War II, the Japanese government had put the Nationalist government on death ground by demanding regime change, leaving nothing to negotiate and no choice for the Nationalists but to fight to survive.

Apparently Japanese army and navy leaders suffered from the same lack of imagination paralyzing the civilian leadership. Like the major belligerents in World War I, which responded to the terrible costs of a nonperforming military strategy with increasing doses of the same, Japan responded to Chinese intransigence with escalation. Japanese conquests became a function of both operational success and strategic failure. They took territories because they could and in anger they did, but the more they took and the harder they fought, the more militarily and financially overextended they became. Japanese leaders never seemed to ask the question, how much territory could Japan take before the garrisoning costs exceeded the value of the resources that could be extracted? The answer was probably Manchuria. Had the Japanese frozen their conquests in 1933, in all likelihood they would have kept them and avoided the world war. Or if the world war seemed too promising to pass up, had they actively co-ordinated with Germany, they probably could have defeated Russia, which had fallen to a one-front war in World War I even with great-power allies. This

---

[2] This framework is based on three questions that must be answered for war termination: How far to go militarily? What to demand politically? And how to enforce the peace? The first two questions come from Bradford A. Lee and the third from Karl F. Walling, both former members of the Strategy & Policy Department of the U.S. Naval War College.

time around Russia began the war diplomatically isolated and was still rebuilding from the last world war and its own civil war. Had Japanese leaders made others choices, the world we live in today would be completely different.

Avoiding third-party intervention requires competent strategists. In the first set of wars, Japan's diplomats worked hard to prevent third-party intervention by isolating the adversary and eschewing actions that might provoke others to intervene. They did so by protecting third-party investments, adhering to international law, treating Chinese civilians equitably, and, in the Russo-Japanese War, negotiating prewar diplomatic agreements with the other great powers, most notably the Anglo-Japanese alliance. Even so, Japan suffered the postwar Triple Intervention in the settlement of the First Sino-Japanese War. Japanese leaders did none of the above during the Second Sino-Japanese War. Their Pearl Harbor strategy then guaranteed third-party intervention on an unprecedented scale. Responding to overextension in one theater by bringing in a host of new adversaries in a host of new theaters was a singularly bad strategy.

The United States, not Japan, integrated its military and political strategies. It demanded unconditional surrender. This put Japan on death ground. But the long war in China had already severely weakened Japan and the U.S. air campaign undermined its ability to conduct offensive operations. The dropping of two atomic bombs in rapid succession implied many more to follow. The United States also had a great-power ally about to enter the fray with the largest army in the world. The Russian invasion of Manchuria, threatening a Communist Russian occupation of at least part of Japan, then put enormous pressure on the Japanese government to surrender to the United States immediately before it had to surrender to Russia later. The result: the United States never had to invade the home islands – an incredible feat in war termination, particularly against such an implacable foe.

There are two ways to make an enduring peace: eliminate either the enemy's means or will to resist, and, better yet, eliminate both.[3] In the first set of wars, Japan adopted a combination of both sufficient for war termination and for peace in the short term. In the medium term, revolutions in Russia and China brought into being new political forces intent upon overturning the balance of power in Asia so that the will grew to overturn the peace settlement.

In the second set of wars, Japan proved unable to eliminate the enemy's means to resist and its own chosen military means fueled the enemy will to resist. This yielded a protracted war, great-power intervention, and Japanese economic and military exhaustion. In contrast, the United States devised a formula that eliminated both the Japanese means to conduct offensive operations

---

[3] This observation is an old chestnut from the Strategy & Policy Department of the U.S. Naval War College that is based on Clausewitz, although the master does not put it so succinctly. See Clausewitz, *On War*, 90.

and, more importantly, the will to overturn the postwar maritime global order. U.S. generosity after the surrender helped transform Japan into a stalwart of the maritime order it had fought so hard to overturn.

Underlying and proximate causes account for the outbreak of all four wars. Likewise, underlying and proximate causes explain the transformation of Japan from a westernizing, modernizing country, content to work within the maritime global order, into a country with an army-dominated government bent on combining with the Axis powers to overturn the global order. The underlying causes behind the transformation were definitional (Japan the continental rather than the maritime power) and institutional (government by the army rather than by the full Cabinet and the Diet), while the proximate causes were circumstantial (the change to an inclement international environment). Japan and its neighbors have yet to overcome the consequences.

Select Bibliography

1. THE MEIJI GENERATION

Beasley, W.G. *Japanese Imperialism 1894–1945*. Oxford: Clarendon Press, 1987.
——. "Meiji Political Institutions." In Marius B. Jansen, ed., *The Cambridge History of Japan*, vol. 5. Cambridge: University of Cambridge Press, 1989, 618–73.
——. *The Meiji Restoration*. Stanford: Stanford University Press, 1972.
——. *The Rise of Modern Japan*. 2nd edn. New York: St. Martin's Press, 1995.
Chu, Samuel C. "China's Attitudes toward Japan at the Time of the Sino-Japanese War." In Akira Iriye, ed., *The Chinese and Japanese: Essays in Cultural and Political Interactions*. Princeton: Princeton University Press, 1980, 74–95.
Conroy, Hilary. *The Japanese Seizure of Korea, 1868–1910: A Study of Realism and Idealism in International Relations*. Philadelphia: University of Pennsylvania Press, 1960.
Dorwart, Jeffery M. *The Pigtail War: American Involvement in the Sino-Japanese War of 1894–1895*. Amherst: University of Massachusetts Press, 1975.
Duus, Peter. *The Abacus and the Sword: The Japanese Penetration of Korea, 1895–1910*. Berkeley: University of California Press, 1995.
Eastlake, Warrington and Yamada Yoshi-aki. *Heroic Japan: A History of the War between China & Japan*. 1897. Reprint, Washington, DC: University Publications of America, 1979.
Eckert, Carter J., Ki-baik Lee, Young Ick Lew, Michael Robinson, and Edward W. Wagner, *Korea Old and New: A History*. Seoul: Ilchokak Publishers, 1990.
Iriye, Akira. *Japan & the Wider World*. London: Longman, 1997.
——. "Japan's Drive to Great Power Status." In Marius B. Jansen, ed., *The Cambridge History of Japan*, vol. 5. Cambridge: University of Cambridge Press, 1989, 721–82.
Jansen, Marius B. *The Making of Modern Japan*. Cambridge, MA: Harvard University Press, 2000.
Keene, Donald. *Emperor of Japan: Meiji and His World, 1852–1912*. New York: Columbia University Press, 2002.
Paine, S.C.M. *Imperial Rivals: China, Russia, and Their Disputed Frontier*. Armonk, NY: M.E. Sharpe, 1996.
——. *The Sino-Japanese War of 1894–1895: Perceptions, Power, and Primacy*. Cambridge: Cambridge University Press, 2003.
Schencking, J. Charles. *Making Waves: Politics, Propaganda, and the Emergence of the Imperial Japanese Navy 1868–1922*. Stanford: Stanford University Press, 2005.

2. THE FIRST SINO-JAPANESE WAR (1894–1895)

Ballard, G.A. *The Influence of the Sea on the Political History of Japan.* New York: E.P. Dutton, 1921.

Chen, Edward I-te. "Japan's Decision to Annex Taiwan: A Study of Itō-Mutsu Diplomacy, 1894–95." *Journal of Asian Studies* 37, no. 1 (Nov. 1977): 61–72.

Chu, Samuel C. and Kwang-ching Liu, eds. *Li Hung-chang and China's Early Modernization.* Armonk, NY: M.E. Sharpe, 1994.

Conroy, Hilary. *The Japanese Seizure of Korea, 1868–1910: A Study of Realism and Idealism in International Relations.* Philadelphia: University of Pennsylvania Press, 1960.

Elleman, Bruce A. *Modern Chinese Warfare, 1795–1989.* London: Routledge, 2001.

Elleman, Bruce A. and S.C.M. Paine. *Modern China: Continuity and Change 1644 to the Present.* Boston: Prentice Hall, 2010.

Iklé, Frank W. "The Triple Intervention: Japan's Lesson in the Diplomacy of Imperialism." *Monumenta Nipponica* 22, nos. 1–2 (1967): 122–30.

Inouye, Jukichi. *The Japan–China War: On the Regent's Sword: Kinchow, Port Arthur, and Talienwan.* Yokohama: Kelly & Walsh, 1895.

——. *The Japan–China War: The Naval Battle of Haiyang.* Yokohama: Kelly & Walsh, 1895.

Kajima, Morinosuke. *The Diplomacy of Japan 1894–1922.* 3 vols. Tokyo: Kajima Institute of International Peace, 1976.

Keene, Donald. "The Sino-Japanese War of 1894–95 and Its Cultural Effects in Japan." In Donald H. Shively, ed., *Tradition and Modernization in Japanese Culture.* Princeton: Princeton University Press, 1971, 121–80.

Lee, Yur-bok. *West Goes East: Paul George von Möllendorff and Great Power Imperialism in Late Yi Korea.* Honolulu: University of Hawaii Press, 1988.

Lensen, George Alexander. *Balance of Intrigue: International Rivalry in Korea & Manchuria, 1884–1899.* 2 vols. Tallahassee: University Presses of Florida, 1982.

Lone, Stewart. *Japan's First Modern War: Army and Society in the Conflict with China, 1894–95.* London: St. Martin's Press, 1994.

McGiffin, Lee. *Yankee of the Yalu: Philo Norton McGiffin, American Captain in the Chinese Navy (1885–1895).* New York: E.P. Dutton, 1968.

Mancall, Mark. *China at the Center: 300 Years of Foreign Policy.* New York: Free Press, 1984.

Mutsu, Munemitsu. *Kenkenroku: A Diplomatic Record of the Sino-Japanese War, 1894–95.* Translated by Gordon Mark Berger. Princeton: Princeton University Press, 1982.

Ono, Giichi. *Expenditures of the Sino-Japanese War.* New York: Oxford University Press, 1922.

Paine, S.C.M. "The First Sino-Japanese War: Japanese Destruction of the Beiyang Fleet, 1894–95." In Bruce A. Elleman and S.C.M. Paine, eds., *Naval Blockades and Seapower: Strategies and Counter-strategies, 1805–2005.* London: Routledge, 2006, 71–80.

——. "Missed Opportunities in the First Sino-Japanese War, 1894–1895." In Bruce A. Elleman and S.C.M. Paine, eds., *Commerce Raiding: Historical Case Studies, 1755–2009.* Newport, RI: Naval War College Press, 2013, 105–20.

——. *The Sino-Japanese War of 1894–1895: Perceptions, Power, and Primacy.* Cambridge: Cambridge University Press, 2003.

——. "The Triple Intervention and the Termination of the First Sino-Japanese War." In Bruce A. Elleman and S.C.M. Paine, eds., *Naval Coalition Warfare: From the Napoleonic War to Operation Iraqi Freedom.* London: Routledge, 2008, 75–85.

Palais, James B. *Politics and Policy in Traditional Korea.* Cambridge, MA: Harvard University Press, 1975.

Rawlinson, John L. *China's Struggle for Naval Development 1839–1895.* Cambridge, MA: Harvard University Press, 1967.

Spector, Stanley. *Li Hong-chang and the Huai Army: A Study in Nineteenth-Century Chinese Regionalism.* Seattle: University of Washington Press, 1964.

Tyler, William Ferdinand. *Pulling Strings in China.* London: Constable, 1929.

Vladimir [Zenone Volpicelli]. *The China–Japan War Compiled from Japanese, Chinese, and Foreign Sources.* Kansas City, MO: Franklin Hudson Publishing, 1905.

3. THE RUSSO-JAPANESE WAR (1904–1905)

Ashmead-Bartlett, Ellis. *Port Arthur: The Siege and Capitulation,* vol. 6 of Ian Nish, comp., *The Russo-Japanese War, 1904–5.* Folkestone: Global Oriental, 2003.

Connaughton, R.M. *The War of the Rising Sun and the Tumbling Bear: A Military History of the Russo-Japanese War 1904–5.* London: Routledge, 1988.

Cordonnier, Col. E.L.V. *The Japanese in Manchuria 1904.* Translated by Capt. C.F. Atkinson, 3 vols. London: Hugh Rees, 1912.

Elleman, Bruce A. "Chinese Neutrality and Russian Commerce Raiding during the Russo-Japanese War, 1904–1905." In Bruce A. Elleman and S.C.M. Paine, eds., *Commerce Raiding: Historical Case Studies, 1755–2005.* Newport, RI: Naval War College Press, 2013, 121–34.

Esthus, Raymond A. *Double Eagle and Rising Sun: The Russians and Japanese at Portsmouth in 1905.* Durham, NC: Duke University Press, 1988.

Evans, David C. and Mark R. Peattie. *Kaigun: Strategy, Tactics, and Technology in the Imperial Japanese Navy 1887–1941.* Annapolis, MD: Naval Institute Press, 1997.

Hackett, Roger F. *Yamagata Aritomo in the Rise of Modern Japan, 1838–1922.* Cambridge, MA: Harvard University Press, 1971.

Keene, Donald. *Emperor of Japan: Meiji and His World, 1852–1912.* New York: Columbia University Press, 2002.

Malozemoff, Andrew. *Russian Far Eastern Policy 1881–1904 with Special Emphasis on the Causes of the Russo-Japanese War.* Berkeley: University of California Press, 1958.

Matsusaka, Y. Tak. "Human Bullets, General Nogi, and the Myth of Port Arthur." In John W. Steinberg, Bruce W. Menning, David Schimmelpenninck Van Der Oye, David Wolff, and Shinji Yokote, eds., *The Russo-Japanese War in Global Perspective: World War Zero,* vol. 1. Leiden: Brill, 2005, 179–202.

Menning, Bruce W. *Bayonets before Bullets: The Imperial Russian Army, 1861–1914.* Bloomington: University of Indiana Press, 1992.

Nish, Ian. *The Anglo-Japanese Alliance: The Diplomacy of Two Island Empires 1894–1907.* London: University of London Athlone Press, 1966.

——. *The Origins of the Russo-Japanese War.* London: Longman, 1985.

———. *The Russo-Japanese War, 1904–5: A Collection of Eight Volumes*, 8 vols. Folkestone: Global Oriental, 2003.

O'Brien, Phillips Payson, ed., *The Anglo-Japanese Alliance, 1902–1922*. London: RoutledgeCurzon, 2004.

Okamoto, Shumpei. *The Japanese Oligarchy and the Russo-Japanese War*. New York: Columbia University Press, 1970.

Ono, Keishi. "Japan's Monetary Mobilization for War." In John W. Steinberg, Bruce W. Menning, David Schimmelpenninck Van Der Oye, David Wolff, and Shinji Yokote, eds., *The Russo-Japanese War in Global Perspective: World War Zero*, vol. 2. Leiden: Brill, 2005, 251–70.

Paine, S.C.M. *Imperial Rivals: China, Russia, and Their Disputed Frontier*. Armonk, NY: M.E. Sharpe, 1996.

Papastratigakis, Nicholas. *Russian Imperialism and Naval Power: Military Strategy and the Build-up to the Russo-Japanese War*. London: I.B.Tauris, 2011.

Patrikeeff, Felix and Harold Shukman. *Railways and the Russo-Japanese War: Transporting War*. London: Routledge, 2007.

Pleshakov, Constantine. *The Tsar's Last Armada: The Epic Journey to the Battle of Tsushima*. New York: Basic Books, 2002.

Quested, Rosemary K.I. *"Matey" Imperialists? The Tsarist Russians in Manchuria 1895–1917*. Hong Kong: University of Hong Kong Press, 1982.

Romanov, B.A. *Russia in Manchuria (1892–1906)*. Translated by Susan Wilbur Jones. Ann Arbor: American Council of Learned Societies, 1952.

Steinberg, John W. *All the Tsar's Men: Russia's General Staff and the Fate of the Empire, 1898–1914*. Baltimore: Johns Hopkins University Press, 2010.

Steinberg, John W., Bruce W. Menning, David Schimmelpenninck Van Der Oye, David Wolff, and Shinji Yokote, eds. *The Russo-Japanese War in Global Perspective: World War Zero*, 2 vols., Leiden: Brill, 2005–7.

Warner, Denis and Peggy Warner. *The Tide at Sunrise: A History of the Russo-Japanese War, 1904–1905*. London: Angus and Robertson, 1974.

Westwood, J.N. *Russia against Japan, 1904–1905: A New Look at the Russo-Japanese War*. London: Macmillan, 1986.

White, John Albert. *The Diplomacy of the Russo-Japanese War*. Princeton: Princeton University Press, 1964.

4. THE TRANSITION FROM A MARITIME TO A CONTINENTAL SECURITY PARADIGM

Asada, Sadao. *From Mahan to Pearl Harbor: The Imperial Japanese Navy and the United States*. Annapolis, MD: Naval Institute Press, 2006.

Berger, Gordon Mark. *Parties out of Power in Japan 1931–1941*. Princeton: Princeton University Press, 1977.

Conroy, Hilary. *The Japanese Seizure of Korea, 1868–1910: A Study of Realism and Idealism in International Relations*. Philadelphia: University of Pennsylvania Press, 1960.

Cook, Theodore Failor, Jr. "The Japanese Officer Corps: The Making of a Military Elite, 1872–1945." Ph.D. diss., Princeton University, 1987.

Drea, Edward J. "Kurihara Yasuhide and the Tokyo Young Officers Movement 1918–1936." Ph.D. diss., University of Kansas, 1972.

Dunscomb, Paul E. *Japan's Siberian Intervention 1918–1922: "A Great Disobedience against the People."* Lanham, MD: Rowman & Littlefield, 2011.

Duus, Peter. *Party Rivalry and Political Change in Taishō Japan.* Cambridge, MA: Harvard University Press, 1968.

Elleman, Bruce A. *Wilson and China: A Revised History of the Shandong Question.* Armonk, NY: M.E. Sharpe, 2002.

Elleman, Bruce A. and S.C.M. Paine, *Modern China: Continuity and Change 1644 to the Present.* Boston: Prentice Hall, 2010.

Hackett, Roger F. *Yamagata Aritomo in the Rise of Modern Japan, 1838–1922.* Cambridge, MA: Harvard University Press, 1971.

Humphreys, Leonard A. *The Way of the Heavenly Sword: The Japanese Army of the 1920's.* Stanford: Stanford University Press, 1995.

Jansen, Marius B. *The Making of Modern Japan.* Cambridge, MA: Harvard University Press, 2000.

Lensen, George Alexander. *Japanese Recognition of the U.S.S.R.: Sino-Japanese Relations 1921–1930.* Tallahassee, FL: Diplomatic Press, 1970.

Lone, Stewart. *Army, Empire and Politics in Meiji Japan: The Three Careers of General Katsura Tarō.* New York: St. Martin's Press, 2000.

Morton, William Fitch. *Tanaka Giichi and Japan's China Policy.* New York: St. Martin's Press, 1980.

Nakamura, Takafusa. *History of Shōwa Japan.* Translated by Edwin Whenmouth. Tokyo: University of Tokyo Press, 1998.

Nish, Ian. *Japanese Foreign Policy 1869–1942: Kasumigaseki to Miyakezaka.* London: Routledge & Kegan Paul, 1977.

Nitobe, Inazo. *Bushido the Soul of Japan: An Exposition of Japanese Thought.* Revd. edn. 1905. Reprint, Boston: Tuttle Publishing, 1969.

O'Brien, Phillips Payson. "Britain and the End of the Anglo-Japanese Alliance." In Phillips Payson O'Brien, ed., *The Anglo–Japanese Alliance, 1902–1922.* London: RoutledgeCurzon, 2004, 264–84.

Oka, Yoshitake. *Five Political Leaders of Modern Japan: Ito Hirobumi, Okuma Shigenobu, Hara Takashi, Inukai Tsuyoshi, and Saionjji Kimmochi.* Translated by Andrew Fraser and Patricia Murray. Tokyo: University of Tokyo Press, 1979.

Paine, S.C.M. *Imperial Rivals: China, Russia, and Their Disputed Frontier.* Armonk, NY: M.E. Sharpe, 1996.

Peattie, Mark R. "The Japanese Colonial Empire, 1895–1945." In John W. Hall, Marius B. Jansen, Madoka Kanai, and Denis Twitchett, eds., *The Cambridge History of Japan,* vol. 6. Cambridge: Cambridge University Press, 1988, 217–70.

Ramseyer, J. Mark and Frances M. Rosenbluth. *The Politics of Oligarchy: Institutional Choice in Imperial Japan.* Cambridge: Cambridge University Press, 1995.

Schencking, J. Charles. *Making Waves: Politics, Propaganda, and the Emergence of the Imperial Japanese Navy 1868–1922.* Stanford: Stanford University Press, 2005.

Shillony, Ben-Ami. *Revolt in Japan: The Young Officers and the February 26, 1936 Incident.* Princeton: Princeton University Press, 1973.

Skya, Walter A. *Japan's Holy War: The Ideology of Radical Shintō Ultranationalism.* Durham, NC: Duke University Press, 2009.

Smethurst, Richard J. *From Foot Soldier to Finance Minister: Takahashi Korekiyo, Japan's Keynes.* Cambridge, MA: Harvard University Press, 2007.

Tadokoro, Masayuki. "Why Did Japan Fail to Become the 'Britain' of Asia?" In John W. Steinberg, Bruce W. Menning, David Schimmelpenninck Van Der Oye, David Wolff, and Shinji Yokote, eds., *The Russo-Japanese War in Global Perspective: World War Zero*, vol. 2. Leiden: Brill, 2007, 295–324.

Takenaka, Harukata. *Failed Democracy in Prewar Japan: Breakdown of a Hybrid Regime*. Stanford: Stanford University Press, 2014.

Titus, David Anson. *Palace and Politics in Prewar Japan*. New York: Columbia University Press, 1974.

Yoshihashi, Takehiko. *Conspiracy at Mukden: The Rise of the Japanese Military*. New Haven: Yale University Press, 1963.

Young, A. Morgan. *Japan under the Taisho Tenno 1912–1926*. London: George Allen & Unwin, 1928.

5. THE SECOND SINO-JAPANESE WAR (1931–1941)

Arakawa Ken-ichi. "Japanese Naval Blockade of China in the Second Sino-Japanese War, 1937–41." In Bruce A. Elleman and S.C.M. Paine, eds., *Naval Blockades and Seapower: Strategies and Counter-strategies, 1805–2005*. London: Routledge, 2006, 105–16.

Barnhart, Michael A. *Japan Prepares for Total War*. Ithaca: Cornell, 1987.

Chao, Kang. *The Economic Development of Manchuria: The Rise of a Frontier Economy*, Michigan Papers in Chinese Studies no. 43. Ann Arbor: The University of Michigan Center for Chinese Studies, 1982.

Coox, Alvin D. *The Anatomy of a Small War: The Soviet–Japanese Struggle for Changkufeng/Khasan, 1938*. Westport, CT: Greenwood Press, 1977.

———. *Nomonhan: Japan against Russia*. Stanford: Stanford University Press, 1990.

Drea, Edward J. *Japan's Imperial Army: Its Rise and Fall, 1853–1945*. Lawrence: University Press of Kansas, 2009.

Dreyer, Edward L. *China at War, 1901–1949*. London: Longman, 1995.

Dryburgh, Marjorie. *North China and Japanese Expansion 1933–1937: Regional Power and Nationalist Interest*. Richmond: Curzon, 2000.

Elleman, Bruce A. *Modern Chinese Warfare, 1795–1989*. London: Routledge, 2001.

Evans, David C. and Mark R. Peattie. *Kaigun: Strategy, Tactics, and Technology in the Imperial Japanese Navy 1887–1941*. Annapolis, MD: Naval Institute Press, 1997.

Fenby, Jonathan. *Chiang Kai-shek: China's Generalissimo and the Nation He Lost*. New York: Carroll & Graf, 2003.

Garver, John W. *Chinese–Soviet Relations 1937–1945: The Diplomacy of Chinese Nationalism*. New York: Oxford University Press, 1988.

Haslam, Jonathan. *The Soviet Union and the Threat from the East, 1933–1941*. Pittsburgh: University of Pittsburgh Press, 1992.

Hsiung, James C. and Steven I. Levine, eds. *China's Bitter Victory: The War with Japan 1937–1945*. Armonk, NY: M.E. Sharpe, 1992.

Hsu Long-hsuen and Chang Ming-kai. *History of the Sino-Japanese War (1937–1945)*. Translated by Wen Ha-hsiung, 2nd edn. Taipei: Chung Wu Publishing, 1972.

Ienaga, Saburō, *The Pacific War, 1931–1945*. Translated by Frank Baldwin. New York: Pantheon Books, 1978.

Jones, F.C. *Japan's New Order in East Asia: Its Rise and Fall 1937–1945*. London: Oxford University Press, 1954.

——, *Manchuria since 1931*. London: Royal Institute of International Affairs, 1949.

Jordan, Donald A. *Chinese Boycotts versus Japanese Bombs: The Failure of China's "Revolutionary Diplomacy," 1931–32*. Ann Arbor: University of Michigan Press, 1991.

Kikuoka, Michael T. *The Changkufeng Incident: A Study in Soviet–Japanese Conflict, 1938*. Lanham, MD: University Press of America, 1988.

Kinney, Ann Rasmussen. *Japanese Investment in Manchurian Manufacturing, Mining, Transportation, and Communications 1931–1945*. New York: Garland, 1982.

Lary, Diana. *The Chinese People at War: Human Suffering and Social Transformation, 1937–1945*. Cambridge: Cambridge University Press, 2010.

Lary, Diana and Stephen MacKinnon, eds. *Scars of War: The Impact of Warfare on Modern China*. Vancouver: UBC Press, 2001.

Liu, F.F. *A Military History of Modern China 1924–1949*. 1956. Reprint, Port Washington, NY: Kennikat Press, 1972.

MacKinnon, Stephen R. *Wuhan 1938: War, Refugees, and the Making of Modern China*. Berkeley: University of California Press, 2008.

MacKinnon, Stephen R., Diana Lary, and Ezra F. Vogel, eds. *China at War: Regions of China, 1937–1945*. Stanford: Stanford University Press, 2007.

Matsusaka, Yoshihisa Tak. *The Making of Japanese Manchuria, 1904–1932*. Cambridge, MA: Harvard University Press, 2001.

Morley, James William, ed. *Dilemmas of Growth in Prewar Japan*. Princeton: Princeton University Press, 1971.

——, ed. *Japan Erupts: The London Naval Conference and the Manchurian Incident, 1928–1932*. New York: Columbia University Press, 1984.

Nish, Ian. *Japanese Foreign Policy 1869–1942: Kasumigaseki to Miyakezaka*. London: Routledge & Kegan Paul, 1977.

Ogata, Sadako N. *Defiance in Manchuria: The Making of Japanese Foreign Policy, 1931–1932*. Berkeley: University of California Press, 1964.

Oka, Yoshitake. *Konoe Fumimaro: A Political Biography*. Translated by Shumpei Okamoto and Patricia Murray. Lanham, MD: Madison Books, 1992.

Paine, S.C.M. *Wars for Asia 1911–1949*. Cambridge: Cambridge University Press, 2012.

Peattie, Mark R. *Ishiwara Kanji and Japan's Confrontation with the West*. Princeton: Princeton University Press, 1975.

——. *Sunburst: The Rise of Japanese Naval Air Power, 1909–1941*. Annapolis, MD: Naval Institute Press, 2001.

Peattie, Mark R., Edward J. Drea, and Hans van de Ven, eds. *The Battle for China: Essays on the Military History of the Sino-Japanese War of 1937–1945*. Stanford: Stanford University Press, 2011.

Shimada Toshihiko. "Designs on North China, 1933–1937." In James William Morley, ed., *The North China Quagmire: Japan's Expansion on the Asian Continent 1933–1941*. New York: Columbia University Press, 1983, 11–231.

Smith, Kerry, *A Time of Crisis: Japan, the Great Depression, and Rural Revitalization*. Cambridge, MA: Harvard University Press, 2001.

Sun, Kungtu C. and Ralph W. Huenemann. *The Economic Development of Manchuria in the First Half of the Twentieth Century*. Cambridge, MA: Harvard University Press, 1969.

Taylor, Jay. *The Generalissimo: Chiang Kai-shek and the Struggle for Modern China*. Cambridge, MA: Harvard University Press, 2009.

Van de Ven, Hans J. *War and Nationalism in China 1925–1945*. London: Routledge, 2003.

Wilson, Sandra. *The Manchurian Crisis and Japanese Society, 1931–33*. London: Routledge, 2002.

Yoshihashi, Takehiko. *Conspiracy at Mukden: The Rise of the Japanese Military*. New Haven: Yale University Press, 1963.

Young, Louise. *Japan's Total Empire: Manchuria and the Culture of Wartime Imperialism*. Berkeley: University of California Press, 1998.

6. THE GENERAL ASIAN WAR (1941–1945)

Baer, George W. *One Hundred Years of Sea Power: The U.S. Navy, 1890–1990*. Stanford: Stanford University Press, 1993.

Bagby, Wesley M. *The Eagle–Dragon Alliance: America's Relations with China in World War II*. Newark: University of Delaware Press, 1992.

Bix, Herbert P. *Hirohito and the Making of Modern Japan*. New York: HarperCollins, 2000.

Boyd, Carl. *The Extraordinary Envoy: General Hiroshi Ōshima and Diplomacy in the Third Reich, 1934–1939*. Washington, D.C.: University Press of America, 1980.

——. *Hitler's Japanese Confidant: General Oshima Hiroshi and MAGIC Intelligence, 1941–1945*. Lawrence: University Press of Kansas, 1993.

Burkman, Thomas W. *Japan and the League of Nations: Empire and World Order, 1914–1938*. Honolulu: University of Hawaii Press, 2008.

Ch'i, Hsi-sheng. *Nationalist China at War: Military Defeats and Political Collapse, 1937–45*. Ann Arbor: University of Michigan Press, 1982.

Cook, Haruko Taya and Theodore F. Cook. *Japan at War: An Oral History*. New York: New Press, 1992.

Coox, Alvin D. "The Pacific War." In John W. Hall, Marius B. Jansen, Madoka Kanai, and Denis Twitchett, eds., *The Cambridge History of Japan: The Twentieth Century*, vol. 6, Cambridge: Cambridge University Press, 1988.

Dallin, David J. *The Rise of Russia in Asia*. 1949. Reprint, Hamden, CT: Archon Books, 1971.

Drea, Edward J. *In the Service of the Emperor: Essays on the Imperial Japanese Army*. Lincoln: University of Nebraska Press, 1998.

Edgerton, Robert B. *Warriors of the Rising Sun: A History of the Japanese Military*. New York: W.W. Norton, 1997.

Frank, Richard B. *Downfall: The End of the Imperial Japanese Empire*. New York: Random House, 1999.

Gatchel, Theodore. "The Shortest Road to Tokyo: Nimitz and the Cental Pacific War." In Daniel Marston, ed., *The Pacific War Companion: From Pearl Harbor to Hiroshima*. Oxford: Osprey, 2000, 159–78.

Glantz, David M. *The Soviet Strategic Offensive in Manchuria, 1945: "August Storm"*. London: Frank Cass, 2003.

Gruhl, Werner. *Imperial Japan's World War Two 1931–1945*. New Brunswick, NJ: Transaction Publishers, 2007.

Harries, Meirion and Susie Harries. *Soldiers of the Sun: The Rise and Fall of the Imperial Japanese Army*. New York: Random House, 1991.

Hasegawa, Tsuyoshi, ed., *The End of the Pacific War: Reappraisals*. Stanford: Stanford University Press, 2007.

——. *Racing the Enemy: Stalin, Truman, and the Surrender of Japan*. Cambridge, MA: Harvard University Press, 2005.

Hayashi, Saburo and Alvin D. Coox. *Kōgun: The Japanese Army in the Pacific*. Quantico, VA: Marine Corps Association, 1959.

Hsiung, James C. and Steven I. Levine, eds. *China's Bitter Victory: The War with Japan 1937–1945*. Armonk, NY: M.E. Sharpe, 1992.

Ienaga Saburō. *The Pacific War 1931–1945*. Translated by Frank Baldwin. New York: Pantheon Books, 1978.

Ike, Nobutaka, trans. and ed. *Japan's Decision for War: Records of the 1941 Policy Conferences*. Stanford: Stanford University Press, 1967.

Koshiro, Yukiko. *Imperial Eclipse: Japan's Strategic Thinking about Continental Asia before August 1945*. Ithaca: Cornell University Press, 2013.

Large, Stephen S. *Emperor Hirohito and Shōwa Japan: A Political Biography*. London: Routledge, 1992.

Lee, Bradford A. "A Pivotal Campaign in a Peripheral Theatre: Guadalcanal and World War II." In Bruce A. Elleman and S.C.M. Paine, eds., *Naval Expeditionary Warfare: Peripheral Campaigns and New Theaters of Naval Warfare*. Milton Park: Routledge, 2011, 84–98.

Marston, Daniel, ed. *The Pacific War Companion: From Pearl Harbor to Hiroshima*. Oxford: Osprey, 2005.

Miller, Edward S. *Bankrupting the Enemy: The U.S. Financial Siege of Japan before Pearl Harbor*. Annapolis: Naval Institute Press, 2007.

Morley, James William, ed. *Deterrent Diplomacy: Japan, Germany, and the USSR 1935–1940*. New York: Columbia University Press, 1976.

——, ed. *The Fateful Choice: Japan's Advance into Southeast Asia, 1939–1941*. New York: Columbia, 1980.

——, ed. *The North China Quagmire: Japan's Expansion on the Asian Continent 1933–1941*. New York: Columbia University Press, 1983.

Nakamura, Takafusa. *A History of Shōwa Japan 1926–1989*. Translated by Edwin Whenmouth. Tokyo: University of Tokyo Press, 1998.

Paine, S.C.M. "The Allied Embargo of Japan, 1939–1941: From Rollback to Deterrence to Boomerang." In Bruce A. Elleman and S.C.M. Paine, eds., *Navies and Soft Power: Historical Case Studies of Naval Power and the Nonuse of Military Force*. Newport, RI: Naval War College Press, 2015, 69–90.

——. *Wars for Asia 1911–1949*. Cambridge: Cambridge University Press, 2012.

Peattie, Mark R. *Sunburst: The Rise of Japanese Naval Air Power, 1909–1941*. Annapolis, MD: Naval Institute Press, 2001.

Peattie, Mark R., Edward J. Drea, and Hans van de Ven, eds. *The Battle for China: Essays on the Military History of the Sino-Japanese War of 1937–1945*. Stanford: Stanford University Press, 2011.

Sigal, Leon V. *Fighting to a Finish: The Politics of War Termination in the United States and Japan, 1945*. Ithaca: Cornell University Press, 1988.

Spector, Ronald H. *The Eagle against the Sun*. New York: Free Press, 1985.

Thorne, Christopher. *Allies of a Kind: The United States, Britain, and the War against Japan, 1941–1945*. Oxford: Oxford University Press, 1978.

Toland, John. *The Rising Sun: The Decline and Fall of the Japanese Empire, 1936–1945*. New York: Modern Library, 1970.

Index

Bold page numbers indicate maps.
Underlined page numbers indicate photographs.